CHARRED ROOT OF MEANING

INTERVENTIONS

Conor Cunningham

GENERAL EDITOR

Coming from the Centre of Theology and Philosophy at the University of Nottingham, England, Interventions is a genuinely interdisciplinary series of mediations of crucial concepts and key figures in contemporary thought.

RECENTLY PUBLISHED

Aaron Riches, *Ecce Homo: On the Divinity of Christ* (2016)

Edward T. Oakes, SJ, *A Theology of Grace in Six Controversies* (2016)

Nicholas M. Healy, *Hauerwas: A (Very) Critical Introduction* (2014)

Johannes Hoff, *The Analogical Turn:
Rethinking Modernity with Nicholas of Cusa* (2013)

Karen Kilby, *Balthasar: A (Very) Critical Introduction* (2012)

For a complete list of published volumes in this series,
see the back of the book.

CHARRED ROOT OF MEANING

*Continuity, Transgression, and the
Other in Christian Tradition*

Philipp W. Rosemann

WILLIAM B. EERDMANS PUBLISHING COMPANY

GRAND RAPIDS, MICHIGAN

Wm. B. Eerdmans Publishing Co.
2140 Oak Industrial Drive NE, Grand Rapids, Michigan 49505
www.eerdmans.com

27 26 25 24 23 22 21 20 19 18   1 2 3 4 5 6 7 8 9 10

ISBN 978-0-8028-6345-4

Library of Congress Cataloging-in-Publication Data

Names: Rosemann, Philipp W., author.
Title: Charred root of meaning : continuity, transgression, and the other in
    Christian tradition / Philipp W. Rosemann.
Description: Grand Rapids : Eerdmans Publishing Co., 2018. | Series:
    Interventions | Includes bibliographical references and index.
Identifiers: LCCN 2018006912 | ISBN 9780802863454 (hardcover : alk. paper)
Subjects: LCSH: Tradition (Theology) | Philosophical theology.
Classification: LCC BT90 .R67 2018 | DDC 231/.042—dc23
    LC record available at https://lccn.loc.gov/2018006912

Vere tu es Deus absconditus Deus Israhel salvator.

—Isaiah 45:15

Contents

Series Preface   ix

Foreword by John Milbank   xi

Preface   xix

Introduction: Break on through (to the Other Side)   1

The Other in the Christian Tradition   2

Transgression   4

Foucault's Nietzschean Roots   7

Foucault's Critique of Kant   14

Return to Transgression   23

1: The Irruption of the Divine   25

The Mount Sinai Narrative   26

Pseudo-Dionysius on the Mystical Ascent   33

The Pseudo-Peter of Poitiers Gloss   42

2: The Incarnate God as the New Moses   51

The New Moses   52

"I Am Not Come to Destroy . . ."   59

The Incident at Antioch   66

3: The Christian Tradition in the Pagan World   77

The Foolishness of the Cross   78

CONTENTS

A New Socrates   83

The Spoils of Egypt   89

A First Summary   100

4: The Unfolding of the Christian Tradition   104

Another Dionysius   105

Reading Denys the Carthusian with Alasdair MacIntyre   113

From Pillaging to Translation   119

5: Folding Back the Tradition   133

The Lord of Song   136

Tradition between Memory and Forgetting   143

The Remedy for Forgetting: Destruction   145

From *Destructio* to *Destruktion*   153

6: A Genealogy of Transgression   165

The Genesis Narrative of the Ur-Transgression   166

Kant's Transvaluation of the Ur-Transgression   174

Transgressive Images, Medieval and Contemporary   186

Conclusion   198

*Appendix: Excerpts from the Pseudo-Poitiers Gloss and from
   Denys the Carthusian's* Sentences *Commentary*   201

Bibliography   205

Index of Subjects and Names   227

Index of Scripture   235

Series Preface

It's not a question of whether one believes in God or not. Rather, it's a question of if, in the absence of God, we can have belief, any belief.

"If you live today," wrote Flannery O'Connor, "you breathe in nihilism." Whether "religious" or "secular," it is "the very gas you breathe." Both within and without the academy, there is an air common to both deconstruction and scientism—both might be described as species of *reductionism*. The dominance of these modes of knowledge in popular and professional discourse is quite incontestable, perhaps no more so where questions of theological import are often relegated to the margins of intellectual respectability. Yet it is precisely the proponents and defenders of religious belief in an age of nihilism that are often among those most—unwittingly or not—complicit in this very reduction. In these latter cases, one frequently spies an accommodationist impulse, whereby our concepts must be first submitted to a prior philosophical court of appeal in order for them to render any intellectual value. To cite one particularly salient example, debates over the origins, nature, and ends of human life are routinely partitioned off into categories of "evolutionism" and "creationism," often with little nuance. Where attempts to mediate these arguments are to be found, frequently the strategy is that of a kind of accommodation: How can we adapt our belief in creation to an already established evolutionary metaphysic, or, how can we have our evolutionary cake and eat it too? It is sadly the case that, despite the best intentions of such "intellectual ecumenism," the distinctive voice of theology is the first one to succumb to aphonia—either from impetuous overuse or from a deliberate silencing.

The books in this unique new series propose no such simple accommodation. They rather seek and perform tactical interventions in such debates in a manner that problematizes the accepted terms of such debates. They propose something altogether more demanding: through a kind of refusal of the disciplinary isolation now standard in modern universities, a genuinely interdisciplinary series of mediations of crucial concepts and key figures in contemporary thought. These volumes will attempt to discuss these topics as they are articulated within their own field, including their historical emergence, and cultural significance, which will provide a way into seemingly abstract discussions. At the same time, they aim to analyze what consequences such thinking may have for theology, both positive and negative, and, in light of these new perspectives, to develop an effective response—one that will better situate students of theology and professional theologians alike within the most vital debates informing Western society, and so increase their understanding of, participation in, and contribution to these.

To a generation brought up on a diet of deconstruction, on the one hand, and scientism, on the other, Interventions offers an alternative that is *otherwise than nihilistic*—doing so by approaching well-worn questions and topics, as well as historical and contemporary figures, from an original and interdisciplinary angle, and so avoid having to steer a course between the aforementioned Scylla and Charybdis.

This series will also seek to navigate not just through these twin dangers, but also through the dangerous "and" that joins them. That is to say, it will attempt to be genuinely interdisciplinary in avoiding the conjunctive approach to such topics that takes as paradigmatic a relationship of "theology and phenomenology" or "religion and science." Instead, the volumes in this series will, in general, attempt to treat such discourses not as discrete disciplines unto themselves, but as moments within a distended theological performance. Above all, they will hopefully contribute to a renewed atmosphere shared by theologians and philosophers (not to mention those in other disciplines)—an air that is not nothing.

Connor Cunningham

Foreword

Philipp Rosemann is a very unusual historian of theology and philosophy whose work is always informed by strongly theoretical interests, deeply explored, yet lightly borne and lucidly expounded, as the reader of his latest book will quickly discover.

As a historian he has explored both the Western metaphysical tradition from Plato to Aquinas and what one might describe as "the tradition of tradition," the emergence in the Middle Ages of reflexive accounts of the development of Christian thought from the Scriptures onwards. In either case he is strikingly concerned with two things. First, with processes of outgoing and return, marked in either case by moments of rupture. Second, with the obstinacy of particularity, difference, and alterity that intrudes in the rupturing instance.

There is a metaphysical circle which characterizes the entirety of being and every particular being whose very existence is a returning to self. In the Christian variant of the Neoplatonic scheme, the outgoing rupture that gives rise to the Creation is more benign and contingently various. But Christianity envisages a second and more catastrophic, though still more contingent, rupture that is "the fall," whose correction requires the third contingency of grace.

But there is also a historically recurrent cycling which manifests in ever more radiating circles an initial event of inspiration. From the outset this may involve also a tragic and inevitable and so, as it were, "Neoplatonic" loss, besides a more culpable "Christian" forgetting of the original fount of revelation. Repair of these catastrophes within time involves a certain drastic taking of periodic stock—a clearing away of unnecessary and dubious accretions in order to recover the spirit of the essential.

xi

These twin concerns of Rosemann are combined for him in their iso-morphism in the pivotal figure of the fifteenth-century Carthusian mys-tic and scholastic Denys the Carthusian. In his mystical thought Denys cleaved to the Christianized Neoplatonism of the first Denis, the Areopa-gite, and his fundamental story of a going out from and return to God as the Sun of the Good. In his vast written work the second Denys sought to correct what he saw as an excessive intrusion of logic and philosophy upon scripturally based theology since the time of Peter Lombard in the twelfth century.

By collating, summarizing, and commenting on all the commentar-ies on Lombard's *Sentences*, which had been adopted in the schools as their main theological textbook, Denys sought both to distance himself from nominalism and to a degree Scotism, and to accentuate the mystical and Augustinian rather than the Aristotelian element in the great thir-teenth-century realists. It is notable that this did not mean any demoting of the pivotal position that Aquinas had already started to acquire in De-nys's day, but rather the reverse. Thus in historical terms also he sought to gather from a dispersal, and to repent of deviations, in order to return to the first springs of theological inspiration: Lombard and his summary of patristic responses to the Bible.

In the current book Rosemann, as it were, generalizes and extends Denys's approach to tradition in modern and postmodern terms for our own day, with something like Denys's metaphysical vision hovering in the margins. The Carthusian is exemplary in the sense that his very conser-vatism and call for a return to purity and authenticity involved a certain "transgression" of the scholarly norms of his time and even a preparedness to "destroy" them in order to recover what had been lost.

However, Rosemann goes much further than this on his own account. His main concern is to break with accounts of Christian tradition which would see its sole defining mark as being "continuity." For this would pre-clude any sense of development and of a "handing over" of an original reality whose compelling truth lies in its inexhaustible fecundity. For this reason "tradition" and "transgression" should not be regarded as opposites. Nothing is really "handed over" unless the recipient is thereby "breaking through" to something unanticipated by her, or even by the giver, if she is merely the instrument of the Holy Spirit.

What is more, as Rosemann insists, tradition begins always with trans-gression. The norms of polytheistic religion were trampled upon by the Jews; their religious norms were in turn violated by the sect of Christians who sustained, more globally, the refusal of paganism. The ancient Hebrews broke through to a universalism of ethical law and prophetic expectation only by adopting a cult of the absolute hidden God on the inaccessible heights. In this way tradition commenced as the most drastic initiatic imaginable. And transgression was doubled when, with the Incarnation, the claim was not just that humans might step into the divine darkness on the mountain summit, but that God himself had overstepped the boundary between himself and his Creation in order to initiate a new universalism of love and eschatologically realized cultic presence.

But if tradition is sustained only through a series of ruptures and reforms, and if it begins with transgression, then it is equally true to say, if one reads Rosemann carefully, that transgression is from the outset also tradition, that stepping across is also always already handing over. For the context of the story of Moses and the giving of the law, as of the story of the new Moses, Jesus, is entirely a liturgical one—besides being one of a founding and so of a conferral. Rites do not just later celebrate the giving of the law; the law is given in the context of a rite involving fearful exclusions, uncanny music, and repeated processions forth into and back from a natural sanctuary. Within this new rite, Israel's past is commemorated as well as questioned and renewed. And the same goes for the Christian liturgical foundation proffered by the Gospels. The Jewish past of law and writing is shockingly denied, and yet it is also paradoxically sustained, both as authentic past and as figural precedent. As something that retains a regional validity for some and an equivalent universal validity for all in the shape of the continuing need everywhere for enforceable law and regular custom, even though these are now de-absolutized in a historically unprecedented fashion.

Of course there are huge tensions here, which Rosemann does not gloss over. Indeed, the very honest unease of his book lies in acknowledging that revolution often involves new modes of oppression. One might say that this is precisely a hesitation between modernism and postmodernism. For on the one hand, Rosemann insists upon the transgressive ingredient that more traditionalist or "Romantic" Catholics are wont to play down. He stresses that, to the contrary, monotheism and Christianity were drastic breaks with what had gone before and that later Christian history, far from being smooth, has been marked by a series of reforms that often seek to undo much in the immediate past, like those attempted in the fifteenth and sixteenth centuries.

On the other hand, he emphasizes equally that the refusal of old oppressions can bring new ones in their train. Herein lies Rosemann's more postmodern bent. Every vaunted universalism turns out to be somewhat illusory insofar as it rests upon a covert new act of exclusion. Pagan gods and cultic laws may be attacked as being themselves too exclusive, but then the exclusion of exclusion can turn out to be, ironically and yet patently, itself unjust. If pagan learning and Jewish practice are significant only insofar as they are fulfilled by the gospel, then their rich singularity and diverse validity have been denied. Thus monotheists have proved persecutors, and Christianity has an abominable (if importantly diversified) history with regard to its treatment of Jews.

What is more, Christianity came increasingly to sustain an exclusion of all bodily based ecstasy and festivity. Where once in the earlier Middle Ages this was half-integrated in terms of both an understanding of the divine as transfiguring of all natural energies, and a kind of performative apophasis, or allowance through the periodic sway of "misrule" that normal human order may be no order at all, now a stricter duality of sense and nonsense, prayer and laughter, awake and dreaming, elevated spirit, and vile embodiment was elaborated.

In the wake of Michel Foucault, one can see that one does not here have to do with the dialectics of suppression, but rather with the falsely positive "Victorian" construction of a far too simple opposition. Rosemann here appropriately alludes to Nietzsche's later half-mad hints that one might serve both Christ and Dionysius. But the point, presumably, is that that would be truly to serve the Incarnate God for whom no false transgressions remain possible, since every stepping over has been transmuted upwards and temptation robbed of its very temptingness.

The simplistic exclusion of Dionysius resulted then from a lapse into a still pagan sense of virtue and spirit as simply breaking, in a philosophically "transgressive" way, with the hold of the flesh deemed still to be conservatively attractive, where Augustine rather announced to the Romans the Christian possibility of removing the very instance of false desire, since its lure is truly unreal.

Yet Rosemann also finally explores the possibility of a purely Dionysian transgression that denies the higher erotic lure of spirit altogether. As he well indicates, this simply leaves us with a desperate and desperately sad secular version of the Victorian game, where boundaries must be further and further transgressed in the name of authenticity, such that they asymptotically recede, resulting, of course, in ever-increased human danger and insecurity. That in turn gives rise to new boundaries and new taboos that are alternately transgressed and drastically policed in an ever more oscillating spiral. Transgression in this context no longer, as Rosemann in the wake of Foucault argues, opens us out towards the sacred infinite, but towards a sterile nullity.

Given the historical value of "modernist" religious revolution and yet the postmodern recognition of its dangers and the apparent impossibility of a totally innocent and all-embracing universalism, does Rosemann argue for what has been dubbed a forlorn "metamodern" search for a kind of elusive balance between the two? Decidedly not. He does not seek to instill a vague cultural mood with respect to tradition but rather gestures to its genuine metaphysical grounding.

Here he implicitly breaks with the merely postmodern. As he probingly considers, Foucault was ultimately preoccupied with the "empirico-transcendental" doublet, whereby on the one hand we are supposedly doomed to see things only through an a priori anthropocentric lens, but on the other we must acknowledge, after Schelling, that humanity itself belongs to nature and is a wholly natural product. Foucault tried to resolve this dilemma by historicizing the transcendental. Yet for all his vaunted post-humanism, this merely transcribes the anthropocentric gaze into the terms of historically shifting discourses. For this reason the transcendental now becomes a formally governing inevitability of rupture and uncertainty, but it remains a transcendental. If, instead, continuity and rupture are to be musically blended, as Rosemann suggests, with neither moment hypostasized, then we must gesture towards a vision of the imperfect participation of stuttering natural and historical processes in a transcendent ground which ineffably combines process and singularity.

In terms of such a vision, it is not that we need some rupturing transgression and some balancing continuity of tradition in the right sort of mixture. It is rather that the two are always fully fused as liturgical transfiguration towards God. Thus Christianity is not a sort of weak combination of a refusal of Judaic norms with some concession towards them. Instead, it is truly constituted by a paradoxical tension towards those norms, as St. Paul expresses them. Everything Jewish has validity in its own time that can be perpetuated even to the Second Coming (though need not be) and also, by analogical extension, in its own sphere that is the sphere of all human life in time. Equally, it has another validity as secretly pointing to Christ. But this does not mean, as for Luther (as Rosemann so well points out), that really, directly, and literally the prime religious meaning of the Old Testament concerns Jesus. Rather, since this reference lies only with its second, hidden allegorical meaning, in order to understand just what it is that Christ fulfills (and so to understand Christ at all), we must look again and again at the Jewish literal sense. Allegory appears to point only forward by always having also to point back.

This might be one way to understand the "spoliation" motif which, as Rosemann says, was sometimes applied to the Christian relation to the Jews as well as to the pagans. Alien riches must now be offered to the true God or the God-Man as their true proprietor, but this does not mean that one does not have to attend to their first inherent character as once made or found in different cultural contexts. In order to be offered more truly, they must indeed be "transgressively" transmuted, and yet this true offering still requires a "traditional" continuity with their first origins and first sense.

Rosemann brilliantly shows how this was guaranteed by adding or even in effect opposing to the motif of physical plunder one of semantic literalness. Thus the decision of Jerome to translate in terms of an equivalence of word rather than sense (in order not to betray any hidden nuance of the divine meaning) was later remarkably extended not just to pagan philosophical authors, but also to Arabic Muslim ones, resulting in several neologisms in the Latin philosophical vocabulary. This surely suggests that the Islamic philosophers were held in the West to lie within an authentic Peripatetic tradition that carried a real authoritative and, as it were, "revelatory" weight. In this sense an extreme concern to be loyal to a partially alien cognitive culture and so to guarantee translation as sustained "tradition" nonetheless involved a considerable "transgression" of one's own linguistic norms.

These conclusions can suggest an unease, which Rosemann strongly indicates, concerning Luther's extreme mode of transgressive destruction in returning (somewhat like Denys the Carthusian) to the Lombard and then to Augustine and to Paul. For in taking such "literal" care for the New Testament, he scarcely sees that in terms of its own new evangelical logic, this implies an extension of such literal care also to the Jewish and pagan in their "otherwiseness."

Luther's "transgressive" going over to God alone indeed bequeaths to the West a terrible suspicion of now destroyed and abandoned human ethical culture as such, even of the human sense of "good" as such, of which his novel call for the expulsion of the Jews from the empire is surely a symptom.

It is in Luther's wake, as Rosemann expertly details, that Kant, after (the Calvin-influenced) Rousseau, can essay such a transvaluation of values that both pure individual inclination and sheerly willed cultural production on the part of the collective human species become two conflicting sides of a new "good." The two sides can be harmonized and perfected only by the operation of the "second nature" of a perfected ethical and political order based on absolute mutual respect for the possession of freedom. The same Lutheran impulse to drastic axiological revision through a return to origins takes already, as Rosemann indicates, a more postmodern, despairing form in Heidegger, for whom the recovery of Being is but the recovery of its fatedness to be occluded in every merely ontic and, thereby for him, sheerly arbitrary historical epoch.

Rosemann well sees that, by contrast, a non-duality of tradition and rupture is most of all secured by recovering an older sense of "revelation" as first disinterred in our own day by the youthful Joseph Ratzinger. For this view, patristic commentary on the Bible added itself to the original deposit, to compose one continuous "disclosure." With this understanding, one can see that revealed authority lies neither in a single pure, original instance, falsely prized away from its ritual context (whereby, as Charles Péguy saw, it is already its own first ritual repetition), nor in an unbroken chain of authoritative ecclesial command. Instead, it lies at once in the source and in the source's co-belonging emanation, its multiple flowing forth and outwards through time.

This vision can allow us both to receive a tradition that is continuously and surprisingly new, and yet freely to "transgress" without ever exiting the series of loyal following after our predecessors and exemplars. It is a matter of the true composing of a psalm, as Rosemann suggests, after Augustine. And, as he also points out, this is because Augustine can invoke God as himself a kind of completed psalm or liturgy. In this way it is only possible to think tradition as also rupture, suture as also continuity, and fall as fortunate, since bound to be redeemed by love, because the exitus and reditus in time participatively echoes that of being itself.

But the latter can show itself in temporal order, discontinuity, and recovery because it is in itself, as it has historically been revealed to be, as absolutely free and personal as it is existential, subsistent, and abiding. The remarkable unity of Rosemann's ultimate vision shines through all the careful scholarly precision and ecclesial good sense of the following work.

John Milbank

Preface

Out in far West Texas, there is a region called the "Big Bend"—after the big bend to the north that the Rio Grande takes on its way to the Gulf of Mexico. The Big Bend is a sparsely populated area of mountainous desert, where the visitor from the city is starkly reminded of the precariousness and finitude of life, but also of the beauty of nature. The plants able to survive in this environment are mostly small shrubs with tiny leaves, grasses, and succulents. Among the latter, the sotol is prominent, *Dasylirion texanum*, a plant that with age develops a palm-like trunk to which hard pointy leaves are attached. The edges of the leaves have such sharp teeth that rangers trim them along the trails in the parks, lest inexperienced hikers suffer deep cuts. Once every few years, the sotol shoots a spectacular flower toward the sky, up to fifteen feet tall.

In 2011, a devastating fire hit much of the Big Bend. The Rock House Fire, which was the largest in Texas history, burned over three hundred thousand acres of land. As it devoured everything in its path, the sotols were reduced to charred trunks. What remained was a landscape of scorched earth, black and dry as dust. Yet, when I visited the area one year after the fire, many of the seemingly dead plants were stirring with life again, growing small green leaves out of their charred roots. Life had triumphed over death, even though death is—in the form of heat, and drought, and fire—an ever-present threat in the Big Bend. Indeed, ecologists tell us that periodic wildfires, albeit devastating, are necessary to the rhythm of nature.

The intuition that I have attempted to develop into an argument in the present book is that tradition works in a similar way. The title captures the gist of my argument: the life of tradition comes out of, and periodically returns to, a charred root of meaning.[1]

There is a lot of literature on the topic of tradition, from both theological and philosophical perspectives, as well as others (literary, for example). This literature—which includes, most famously, the classic treatment in Yves Congar's *Tradition and Traditions*—is, however, one-sided in that it focuses exclusively on tradition as a vehicle of religious and, more broadly, cultural continuity. Such a focus underestimates the element of discontinuity that is essential in both the foundation and development of tradition. When God reveals himself to his people, this divine irruption overturns the existing order in a cataclysmic way. Consider most paradigmatically the crucifixion, in which the Son of God dies the horrific, abject death of a Roman slave. *That* is the price of salvation, as well as the foundation of the Christian tradition: a total revaluation of all values.

Similarly, as the tradition unfolds, there is more to its development than the tranquil handing down of the deposit of faith. The Christian church first constituted itself in a painful separation from the Jewish community—a separation whose ambiguity will never cease to haunt us, Jews and Christians alike. Furthermore, since a tradition cannot remember all that is of value in it, parts of its content are continually subject to sedimentation, in the sense that they are covered over by subsequent layers and, hence, forgotten. This forgetfulness, in turn, requires periodic retrievals. Phenomena such as reformation, *ressourcement*, and "destruction" are attempts to bring about such retrievals.

We associate the term "destruction" most commonly with Heidegger (Derrida preferred the term "deconstruction"), but its origins lie in Luther's theology of the cross. Methodologically, the most distinctive feature of this book is that it combines scriptural scholarship with postmodern philosophy, in a way that is not meant to be irreverent and "destructive" in relation to the Christian tradition, but endeavors to bring out aspects of the traditional phenomenon that have "traditionally" been neglected. Postmodern philosophy emphasizes what could, on the surface, appear to be the mere opposite of tradition—namely, otherness, disruption, marginality, transgression—but that emphasis is precisely what has been missing in theological and philosophical discussions of tradition. In this book, therefore, postmodern theory complements Christian reflection: postmodern

---

1. I first discovered the metaphor of the charred root of meaning in the preface to Foucault's *History of Madness*. For further discussion, see the Introduction, esp. p. 13.

theory brings out neglected aspects of Christian tradition, while in turn the Christian framework of the discussion enables a sympathetic reading of authors who most often stand in open rebellion vis-à-vis the Christian heritage.

*   *   *

This book is a parting gift to the University of Dallas, where I taught from 1997 to 2017. My reflection on the question of tradition was spurred both by the curriculum at UD and by several courses on the topic that I was able to teach in Texas. I am grateful for the university's support of my work over two decades, and in particular for a sabbatical that I was granted in the fall of 2016. In 2011, the university sponsored a paper that I delivered at a conference entitled "Transgression and the Sacred" held at the Humanities Institute of Ireland (University College Dublin); Chapter 1 represents a reworked version of this paper.

John Milbank has for many years been generous in his encouragement. He wanted me to write another book on Thomas Aquinas—*Deo volente*, it will come, in due course.

Conor Cunningham, the editor of the Interventions series, has been both encouraging and patient—the latter over several years, as I kept postponing this daunting project. His always cheerful support was much appreciated. I am happy that my book appears in his series.

Several colleagues in Dallas have offered advice on parts of this book. I would like to thank, in particular, Father John Bayer, OCist; Scott Crider; Andrew Glickman; Bruce Marshall; and Lance Simmons. I also wish to return thanks to Ms. Alice Puro, who until her retirement was in charge of the interlibrary loan service of the Cowan-Blakley Memorial Library of the University of Dallas, for her unfailing assistance.

I am grateful to James South, editor of *Theology and Philosophy*, who has allowed me to reuse some material from my essay "Tradition and Deconstruction," which appeared in volume 25 (2013), pages 79–107. Before it appeared in print, I delivered "Tradition and Deconstruction" at King's College (London, Ontario), at the invitation of Antonio Calcagno and Steve Lofts, and at the Simon Silverman Phenomenology Center of Duquesne University, which I was able to visit when Ryan McDermott invited me to Pittsburgh. I have changed my views on some points since then, for example, distinguishing more clearly between Heidegger's and Luther's "destruction" and Derridean "deconstruction."

The photograph of the Bacchus mosaic at the Villa Romana del Casale was taken by Dr. Michael Wilson, York, England. Monsieur Wael El Khader of the Bibliothèque municipale de Lille made available the high-resolution image of the horned Moses depicted in the fourteenth-century *Somme le Roi*. The image of the horned Jew on the title page of Martin Luther's pamphlet *On the Jews and Their Lies* has quite a different meaning; the image reproduced in this book stems from a copy that is now in possession of the Universitäts- und Landesbibliothek Sachsen-Anhalt. To the Bodleian Library of the University of Oxford, I am grateful for permission to reproduce the strikingly illuminated page from the Psalter for Louis de Nevers.

*   *   *

Finally, two notes on style. References to Scripture in this book are to the Douay-Rheims version, which defamiliarizes the scriptural text, removing it from the banality of everyday speech. Because of its proximity to the Vulgate, the Douay-Rheims text is particularly appropriate in a context where medieval texts are cited. Note that the Vulgate, and hence the Douay-Rheims version, follow the Greek numbering of the Psalms. Also, in quoting from British sources, I have adjusted the spelling to American English for consistency's sake.

Break on through (to the Other Side)

> What is it, then, which has made the souls forget their father, God, and be ignorant of themselves and him, even though they are parts which come from his higher world and altogether belong to it?
>
> —Plotinus, *Enneads*, V.1.1[1]

To be human is to forget. Unlike God, human beings depend on memory because they do not live in divine self-presence: their minds distend existence into the dimensions of past, present, and future. Distension, however, carries the risk of dispersal.[2] We therefore "get lost," forgetting who we are as we get caught up in the business of everyday life. Such forgetting can occur at the most fundamental ontological level, which Plotinus had in mind in the quotation above; but sometimes we just forget the name of an acquaintance or a friend's phone number. We can get lost in these superficial ways only because we are already lost ontologically.

The trivial types of forgetfulness are of course not what interests the philosopher and the theologian. From their fundamental perspective, we are structurally forgetful because of sin—*tolma*, Plotinus calls it—or perhaps because, when Being unconceals itself in beings, the latter prevent us from perceiving unconcealment itself. According to this Heideggerian explanation, there is no sin or fault to blame for our forgetfulness, which is due, rather, to the ineluctable manner in which Being gives itself in time.

---

1. Plotinus, *Enneads* 5.1.1, trans. A. H. Armstrong, Loeb Classical Library 444 (Cambridge, MA: Harvard University Press, 1984), 11.

2. For commentary on the term *distentio* in the *Confessions*, see Augustine, *Confessions*, ed. and comm. James J. O'Donnell, 3 vols. (Oxford: Clarendon, 1992), 3:289–90.

Memory, then, is the result and remedy of forgetfulness. Tradition, in turn, is collective memory: the handing down of ideas and teachings—and perhaps more importantly, more primally, ways of living, acting, and worshiping—from generation to generation. When such memory is exteriorized, as it has to be, it is sometimes enacted in gestures or liturgical forms; sometimes it is told in stories; sometimes it is written down, printed, or even stored in the "cloud." Yet this exteriorization will always be partial. Traditions forget aspects of their own past, which they may or may not be able to recover; hence the possibility of renaissances.

Traditions also forget the fundamental structure of their own constitution. For, while traditions are mechanisms to maintain the integrity of a teaching or the identity of a group over time (the Christian tradition is called to safeguard the deposit of faith from loss and deformation, and to incarnate it identically in ever-changing cultural situations), they also require difference and rupture. Theories of tradition tend to emphasize its identity-preserving function over its constitution through difference. The latter is the subject of the present book.

The Other in the Christian Tradition

In its self-understanding, the Christian tradition originates in an irruption of the divine Other, which radically transforms and reconfigures the world into which it breaks. The Exodus narrative of Moses's ascent on Mount Sinai represents an attempt to speak of the awesome encounter with the divine as a result of which laws are revealed that give the world a new structure, mediating the presence of the sacred Other. The Gospels speak of an even more dramatic irruption of God into the world, in the form of the incarnation. The incarnation challenges human reason at such a fundamental level that it is easy to see it as a form of madness; the "foolishness of the Cross" of which Saint Paul speaks (1 Cor. 1:18–25) epitomizes the fact that, in Christian thought and practice, reason finds its ultimate measure outside of itself, in a divine wisdom that exceeds the human horizon.

Vertically, then, the identity of the Christian tradition owes itself to the wholly Other who is its transcendent origin. Horizontally, it defines itself over against the Jewish roots from which it has historically arisen. Thus, it understands itself as the end of Judaism, in both senses of the term, that is, as the fulfillment of the prophecies of the Old Testament, but also as the supersession of a covenant now rendered old by Jesus's "better promises"

2

(Heb. 8:6). Jesus's word "I am come not to destroy, but to fulfill" (Matt. 5:17) has all the power of a Hegelian sublation: the law that is *aufgehoben* in the Christian message is at once maintained, elevated, and—as elevated—canceled. But just like Hegel's dialectic, the Christian sublation of its Jewish other was not always peaceful. In documents such as Saint Paul's epistle to the Galatians, we witness the painful process through which a Christian identity fashioned itself over against its Jewish roots.

One might think that the idea of fulfillment, which was so central to the emergence of Christianity from Judaism, also played a role in the encounter between Christianity and the Greco-Roman culture of its time. Certainly, Saint Paul's proclamation of the gospel at the Areopagus, with its temple dedicated to an unknown god (Acts 17:23), could be interpreted along these lines: the god who was still unknown to the pagans became incarnate in Jesus Christ, manifesting himself to those with an open heart. But this line of thought remained marginal. Rather, the church fathers' interpretation of the despoiling of the Egyptians as narrated in Exodus (3:21–22) functioned as paradigmatic for the Christian approach to non-Christian cultural and intellectual wealth. Since authentic truth always comes from God—whether those who have discovered it understand its source or not—it is the Christian prerogative and task to remove such truth from its imperfect owners in order to bring it to its fulfillment in a new synthesis.[3] This approach is as characteristic of Augustine's reading of Neoplatonism as it is of Aquinas's reception of Aristotelianism and, more recently, Christian attempts to appropriate modern and postmodern thought.

The identity that the Christian way of life and thinking bestows upon those who follow it can be described as disruptive, even transgressive, in relation to the worldly assumptions it challenges. The Nietzschean term "transvaluation of values" is not inappropriate in this context.[4] The word of the cross turns wisdom into foolishness, strength into weakness. The mystic who seeks God will find him only in a cloud of unknowing. After an experience that many biographers have taken to be mystical in nature,

---

3. See Augustine, *De doctrina christiana* 2.144–48, ed. and trans. R. P. H. Green, Oxford Early Christian Texts (Oxford: Clarendon, 1995), 124–27.

4. As Adolf von Harnack saw well when he turned Nietzsche against himself by describing the Christian faith as an *Umwertung aller Werte*; see his lecture "Wie soll man Geschichte studieren, insbesondere Religionsgeschichte? Thesen und Nachschriften eines Vortrages vom 19. Oktober 1910 in Christiana/Oslo," ed. Christoph Markschies, *Zeitschrift für neuere Theologiegeschichte* 2 (1995): 148–59, at 159.

Thomas Aquinas famously declared all he had written to be mere straw by comparison with what had been revealed to him: *Omnia que scripsi videntur michi palee respectu eorum que vidi et revelata sunt michi.*[5] But the reality of God and his actions do not confound merely on a contemplative and theoretical level; they throw into disarray our everyday lives and earthly loyalties. For those who do not value God more highly than their own fathers and mothers, brothers and sisters, even their own lives, are not worthy of being followers of Jesus (Luke 14:26). Whereas the Old Testament regarded progeny as a sign of God's blessing, the New Testament expresses a preference for celibacy: "He that is without a wife, is solicitous for the things that belong to the Lord, how he may please God. But he that is with a wife, is solicitous for the things of the world" (1 Cor. 7:32–33). In the Western church, celibacy and virginity—that is to say, the withdrawal from family ties, which entail the strongest earthly obligations—were long seen as the privileged sign of a life touched by the Other.

To understand the Christian tradition, then, it is necessary to investigate not only its positive content—its theories and practices in their historical development—but also the limits through which it has defined itself: above all, God, Judaism, and the world with its wisdom, its loyalties, its attachments. The limit is dialectically connected with its opposite—a situation Saint Paul captures in the Epistle to the Romans (chap. 7), in his reflections on the relationship between the law and sin. We know sin only because of the law, while the law exists only as long as we live according to the flesh, that is, in sin. Similarly, the limit reveals itself only through transgression, while transgression exists only in relation to some limit.

Transgression

But where have we strayed? We are now talking about the Christian tradition as linked in some way to transgression. This requires clarification.

First, we need to understand the term "transgression" not in its common moral sense, but etymologically. Etymologically, "to transgress" means nothing more than "to step across." Roman authors used the verb from which "transgress" is derived, *transgredi*, in precisely this sense, as they

---

5. Dominicus M. Prümmer, OP, and Marie-Hyacinthe Laurent, OP, eds., *Fontes vitae S. Thomae Aquinatis* (Toulouse: Privat, 1912–1937), 377.

talked about transgressing rivers and mountains.[6] In English, using "transgression" in a nonmoral sense requires some effort, since the word does not seem to be attested in the broader, more neutral meaning that it carries in Latin.

Yet, why make such an unnatural etymologizing effort? This question leads to a second point. Michel Foucault has written the following about our contemporary culture:

> [Transgression] is allied to the divine, or rather, from this limit marked by the sacred, it opens up the space where the divine functions. . . . In that zone which our culture affords for our gestures and language, transgression prescribes not the sole manner of discovering the sacred in its unmediated substance, but rather of recomposing it in its empty form, in its absence, rendered scintillating by that very fact. . . . Perhaps one day [transgression] will seem as decisive for our culture, as much part of its soil, as the experience of contradiction was at an earlier time for dialectical thought.[7]

Transgression, Foucault is arguing here, operates at the limit between the sacred and the profane. In stepping across that limit, transgression clears a space for experiencing the divine. Foucault, however, distances himself from traditional religion—while defining transgression in relation (but also in contradistinction) to it. Thus, he suggests, transgression plays a role in our culture that is analogous to what "the experience of contradiction"

6. See Charlton T. Lewis and Charles Short, *A Latin Dictionary* (Oxford: Clarendon, 1879), s.v. "transgredior."

7. Michel Foucault, "A Preface to Transgression," trans. Donald F. Bouchard and Sherry Simon, in *Essential Works of Foucault, 1954–1984*, ed. Paul Rabinow, vol. 2, *Aesthetics, Method, and Epistemology*, ed. James D. Faubion (New York: New Press, 1998), 69–87, at 75, 70, 72. I have corrected the English translation, in particular the second sentence, which Bouchard/Simon have mistranslated as follows: "In that zone which our culture affords for our gestures and speech, transgression prescribes not only the sole manner of discovering the sacred in its unmediated substance, but also a way of recomposing it in its empty form, its absence, through which it becomes all the more scintillating." Foucault's essay first appeared in 1963 in the journal *Critique* (vol. 19, nos. 195–96 [August/September 1963]: 751–69); the French text is now available in *Dits et écrits, 1954–1988*, ed. Daniel Defert, François Ewald, and Jacques Lagrange, 2 vols. (Paris: Gallimard, 2001), #13, 1:261–78, where the sentence in question reads: "Celle-ci, dans l'espace que notre culture donne à nos gestes et à notre langage, prescrit non pas [!] la seule manière de trouver le sacré dans son centenu immédiat, mais de le recomposer dans sa forme vide, dans son absence rendue par là-même scientillante [sic]" (262).

used to be for dialectical thought. In referring to "dialectical thought," Foucault does not have Hegel in mind. He is thinking of Christian mysticism, a surprisingly positive discussion of which appears on the very first page of the essay from which the text just quoted has been extracted, "A Preface to Transgression." His thesis is that, in the wake of the death of God that has rendered earlier forms of mysticism inaccessible, transgression has taken the place of the mystical ascent. What transgression discovers, however, is not God's unmediated substance, but rather the empty shell left by his absence. This experience, Foucault claims, is decisive for our culture.

Foucault's text suggests transgression as a link between traditional religion, in particular the Christian mystical tradition, and the postmodern, post-Nietzschean experience of the divine. This experience may be radically negative—indeed, it may be nothing but the experience of an absence—but still it expresses a longing for a "scintillating" beyond.

The methodology that justifies the conjunction of the terms "tradition" and "transgression" in the title of this study takes its inspiration from the old Christian practice of "pillaging" whatever intellectual possessions derive from God, thus pointing back to him, even if such explicit Christian use was not intended by the owners of the possessions.[8] The point pursued by this methodology is not to bring a reluctant Foucault posthumously back into the Christian fold, but to show that the brilliant theories and intellectual tools he developed can be put to fruitful Christian use.[9] If, in this dialogue, it turns out that there may be Christian answers to some of the burning questions of postmodern philosophy and culture—answers that take these questions seriously and let themselves be genuinely challenged, perhaps transformed by them—then that is all the better.

8. We will have an opportunity to examine this metaphor in detail in Chapter 3, pp. 89–99 below. For a stimulating reflection on its use in a contemporary Christian context, see Paul Griffith, "Seeking Egyptian Gold: A Fundamental Metaphor for the Christian Intellectual Life in a Religiously Diverse Age," *Cresset* 63, no. 7 (2000): 5–16.

9. Foucault himself described his work as a "tool-box." Lacking the talent, he said ironically, to produce anything of literary value, he tried in his books simply to produce tools, instruments, and weapons for others to use as they see fit: "De plus, je n'ai ni le talent ni le génie nécessaires pour fabriquer des œuvres d'art avec ce que j'écris. Alors je fabrique—j'allais dire des machines, mais ce serait trop à la Deleuze—des instruments, des ustensiles, des armes. Je voudrais que mes livres soient une sorte de *tool-box* dans lequel les autres puissent aller fouiller pour y trouver un outil avec lequel ils pourraient faire ce que bon leur semble, dans leur domaine." The quotation is from "Prisons et asiles dans le mécanisme du pouvoir," in *Dits et écrits*, #136, 1:1389–93, at 1391.

We now examine the philosophical context in which Foucault speaks of transgression.

Foucault's Nietzschean Roots

In the programmatic preface to his first major work, which appeared in 1961 under the title *Folie et déraison* ("Madness and Unreason"), Foucault placed his entire oeuvre prospectively under the auspices of Friedrich Nietzsche: "The following study might be only the first, and perhaps the easiest, in this long line of inquiry which, under the sun of the great Nietzschean quest, would like to confront the dialectics of history with the immobile structures of the tragic."[10] This sentence sounds surprisingly metaphysical, positing as it does an unchangeable tragic pattern underlying all of history. The later Foucault, for whom the *a priori* structures of thought and culture were subject to historical change, could not have written it.[11] But this is not a study of the development of Foucault's thought. What the author of *Folie et déraison* had in mind in speaking of the "immobile structures of the tragic" is that, following Nietzsche, "the tragic structure from which the history of the Western world is made is nothing other than the refusal, the forgetting, and the silent collapse of tragedy."[12] Nietzsche, of course, in his own youthful *Birth of Tragedy*, had suggested that, at the heart of the human experience, an opposition, a conflict, and a struggle work themselves out between the two forces that he named the Apollonian and the Dionysian. For the first, Apollonian, force, the art of the sculptor is paradigmatic, since sculpture—and Nietzsche is thinking primarily of sculpture in its classical Greek form—captures the world around it in beautiful, dream-like images that we contemplate from the distance of a pleasant gaze. The Dionysian, on the other hand, finds its quintessential expression in music, which pervades

10. Michel Foucault, *History of Madness*, ed. Jean Khalfa, trans. Jonathan Murphy and Jean Khalfa (London: Routledge, 2006), xxx; trans. amended. For the French text of this preface to the first edition (omitted in later editions), see *Dits et écrits*, #4, 1:187–95 (for this quotation, see 190). Foucault never renounced the Nietzschean inspiration of his oeuvre. In 1984, the year of his death, he still spoke of his *nietzschéisme fondamental* ("Le retour de la morale," in *Dits et écrits*, #354, 2:1515–26, at 1522).

11. The term "historical *a priori*" appears in the preface to *The Order of Things: An Archaeology of the Human Sciences* [no translator given] (New York: Vintage Books, 1994), xxii, where it is used interchangeably with *episteme*.

12. Foucault, *History of Madness*, xxx (*Dits et écrits*, 1:189).

and intoxicates us as it wants to absorb the listener into a "mysterious primordial unity" that threatens to undo the boundaries of subjectivity.[13] In the earliest Greek tragedies, the Dionysian force appeared in the form of the chorus of satyrs, beings half human, half beast.

The Apollonian, if left to dominate, creates a culture that is all pleasant surface, while the Dionysian, unfettered and unmediated, will drag civilization into a maelstrom where all individuality and distinction are erased. Nietzsche's claim in *The Birth of Tragedy* is that classical Greek civilization had discovered an ideal balance between the two forces. Then Socrates's philosophy, in conspiracy with the Euripidean theater, destroyed that balance, replacing it with the superficial, untragic worldview that has promoted an optimistic rationalism ever since. With its belief in unlimited progress and its penchant for "bourgeois mediocrity,"[14] the Socratic logocentrism has set the tone for all of Western history. But, Nietzsche warns, there is a price. The Dionysian has not been rooted out, but only driven underground, where it has continued to grow: "Dionysos now sought refuge in the depths of the sea, namely, in the mystical flood waters of a secret cult gradually spreading across the entire world."[15]

Nietzsche derived the evidence for his theory from his study of pre-Socratic and pre-Euripidean Greek civilization: its mythology, festivals, poetry, and theater, in which he found a more authentic expression of truth than in the philosophic tradition.

What one notices immediately about Nietzsche's theory is its fundamentally Hegelian character. Taking the Hegelian dialectic and turning it against itself represents a Hegelian refutation of Hegel, so to speak.[16] Hegel believed that, through the interplay of identity and difference, same and other, history works toward the absolute self-transparency and freedom

13. Friedrich Nietzsche, *The Birth of Tragedy and Other Writings*, ed. Raymond Geuss and Ronald Speirs, trans. Ronald Speirs (Cambridge: Cambridge University Press, 1999), #1, p. 18. "Mysterious primordial unity" translates *das geheimnissvolle Ur-Eine* (Nietzsche, *Werke. Kritische Gesamtausgabe*, ed. Giorgio Colli and Mazzino Montinari, Dritte Abteilung, vol. 1 [Berlin: de Gruyter, 1972], 26).

14. Nietzsche, *The Birth of Tragedy*, #11, p. 56 (the German has *bürgerliche Mittelmässigkeit*; Nietzsche, *Werke*, 73).

15. Nietzsche, *The Birth of Tragedy*, #12, p. 64. I have amended Speirs's translation to reflect the German text more closely: "... nämlich in die mystischen Fluthen eines die ganze Welt allmählich überziehenden Geheimcultus" (Nietzsche, *Werke*, 84).

16. "L'histoire de la philosophie posthégélienne peut être présentée ... comme une réfutation hégélienne du hégélianisme" (Alphonse De Waelhens, *La philosophie et les expériences naturelles*, Phaenomenologica 9 [The Hague: Nijhoff, 1961], 13).

Mosaic depicting a satyr at the Villa Romana del Casale, Sicily. Photograph courtesy of Dr. Michael Wilson, York, England.

of Spirit. Using Hegel's own categories of identity and difference, Nietzsche tells a radical counterstory: history is not the harmonious reconciliation of opposites in higher and higher syntheses, but rather the fateful oppression of difference. It does not, therefore, constitute a relentless march of progress; on the contrary, it represents decline from the unparalleled genius of the Greeks. What is more, the return of the Dionysian as it silently, subversively conquers the world could spell disaster.

From the 1961 preface to *History of Madness*, it is clear that Foucault, at least at this point in his intellectual itinerary, viewed his project as an extension and broadening of Nietzsche's thesis from *The Birth of Tragedy*.

While *Birth* formulated a daring philosophical hypothesis, and provided limited evidence for it from aspects of Greek civilization, it did not show how the suppression of the Dionysian that started with Socrates and Euripides has manifested itself in specific developments throughout the history of the West. This is what Foucault now sets out to do. He claims that Western civilization has defined itself through a series of binary oppositions, suppressing that which was not compatible with its shallow, optimistic, Apollonian view of reality. Foucault's list of examples begins with a paragraph on the division between the Occident and the Orient, which the "colonizing reason"[17] of the West has construed as its mysterious other, at once strange and attractive—perhaps, in a distant past, even its origin, which now lies on the other side of a limit. The list continues with the opposition between the wakeful world of appearances and the dream. Again, Western attitudes have oscillated between "derision"[18] of the world of dreams and the notion that it could hide deep truth. Then Foucault moves on to the history of sexual prohibitions. Unlike the divisions Orient/Occident and wakeful consciousness/dream, the topic of sexuality is explored at length in *The History of Sexuality*, a multivolume work composed toward the end of his life. (This fact shows that he did not simply abandon the project sketched in his 1961 preface, despite the different phases that scholars have identified in his oeuvre.)[19] His point in *The History of Sexuality* is that sexual prohibitions have functioned as much more than repressions of marginalized forms of desire; they have simultaneously encouraged an obsession with sexuality, which our contemporary culture burdens with the power of holding the secret of human existence.[20]

"Finally," Foucault writes, "and firstly, we must speak of the experience of madness."[21] Throughout the history of the West, he claims, reason has defined itself over against this other, variously conceived as hubris, madness, dementia, or unreason. These concepts exhibit significant differences in their relationship to reason. In particular, once madness comes to be conceived as unreason, *dé-raison*, the purview of rationality itself narrows.

17. Foucault, *History of Madness*, xxx (*Dits et écrits*, 1:189).

18. Foucault, *History of Madness*, xxx (*Dits et écrits*, 1:190).

19. On these phases—archaeology, genealogy, and problematization—one may read Thomas Flynn, "Foucault's Mapping of History," in *The Cambridge Companion to Foucault*, ed. Gary Gutting, 2nd ed. (Cambridge: Cambridge University Press, 2005), 29–48.

20. See especially *The History of Sexuality*, vol. 1, *An Introduction*, trans. Robert Hurley (New York: Vintage Books, 1990).

21. Foucault, *History of Madness*, xxx (*Dits et écrits*, 1:190).

It is in *Folie et déraison* that Foucault chronicles this development, which he argues is decisive for the modern experience and understanding of reason.

Foucault's examples in the 1961 preface are brief, but even his short characterizations bring out an aspect in his understanding of the dialectics of history at which Nietzsche only hinted, namely, the fact that the repressed other continues to define the positive pole of each binary opposition even after it has been relegated to the margins, to the other side of the limit. *The Birth of Tragedy* suggested that the Dionysian leads a subversive and dangerous existence even after the one-dimensional culture of the Apollonian is established; it is not simply wiped out. Yet Nietzsche did not go into any detail on the continuing dialectic of the Dionysian and the Apollonian—the "immobile structures of the tragic," as Foucault calls them. Foucault thus elaborates on Nietzsche not only by providing additional examples of the struggle between the Dionysian and the Apollonian, but also by sketching a theoretical framework for the enduring relationship between the two forces:

> One could write a history of *limits*—of those obscure acts (*gestes*), necessarily forgotten as soon as they are accomplished, through which a culture rejects something that will be the Outside (*l'Extérieur*) for it; and throughout the course of its history, this hollowed-out void, this white space by means of which it isolates itself, defines it as much as its values. For, these values it receives and maintains in the continuity of history; but in that region of which we want to speak, it exercises its essential choices, operating the division (*partage*) which gives it the face of its positivity; here the original depth where it forms itself is to be found. To question a culture about its limit-experiences (*expériences-limites*) is to question it in the confines of history, about a tearing-apart which is like the very birth of its history. In a tension that is continually in the process of resolving itself, there occurs the confrontation between the temporal continuity of a dialectical analysis and the unveiling of a tragic structure at the threshold of time.[22]

22. Foucault, *History of Madness*, xxix (*Dits et écrits*, 1:189); trans. amended. Colin Gordon rightly views this passage "as formulating, perhaps with unique explicitness, an ongoing dimension of inquiry within and beyond Foucault's own work" ("History of Madness," in *A Companion to Foucault*, ed. Christopher Falzon, Timothy O'Leary, and Jana Sawicki [Chichester, UK: Wiley-Blackwell, 2013], 84–103, at 89).

This passage offers an intriguing theory of the dialectical structure underlying the development of cultures—or, for our purposes, traditions. For to say that a culture "receives and maintains" certain values "in the continuity of history" sounds very much like a definition of tradition. Such a definition, however, leaves out a crucial element that "defines it as much as its values," namely, the "division which gives it the face of its positivity." In this division, a culture/tradition defines a limit to the core of its identity, an Outside that will function as its other. The act of relegating to the margins something that used to belong to the center, however, creates a "hollowed-out void" that will continue to haunt the center. There will be a tension that will continue to work itself out throughout the history of the culture that it defines. Yet this tension will not be at the surface—just like Nietzsche's Dionysus, who had sought refuge in the depths of the sea. This is because the culture defined dialectically through its positive values and its negative Outside will necessarily forget the initial division that created it.

To remain with Foucault's examples from the 1961 preface, the Occident forgets how much it depends on the Orient, its other, for its self-understanding. For instance, Plotinus is said by his biographer, Porphyry, to have developed serious interest in Persian and Indian thought; but what do we know about, and how much do we emphasize, the Eastern aspects of Neoplatonism, one of the main currents of the Western philosophic tradition?[23] At some point, we decided to separate the reality of the "objective" world from the shadow world of the dream, which used to be the locus of prophetic insight and divine revelation; yet objective reality continues to be haunted by the dream, which has reasserted its rights in Freud's psychoanalytic theory. Modern-day sexuality has constituted itself over against carefully distinguished species of sexual perversion; now these perversions are threatening the mainstream, as we witness the multiplication of sexual

---

23. On Plotinus's interest in Persian and Indian thought, as well as his participation in a military expedition to Mesopotamia, see Porphyry, "On the Life of Plotinus and the Order of His Books," in *Plotinus I*, trans. A. H. Armstrong, Loeb Classical Library 440 (Cambridge, MA: Harvard University Press; London: Heinemann, 1966), 1–85, at 8–11. In his brilliant study *Foucault et le christianisme* (Lyons: ENS Éditions, 2011), Philippe Chevallier suggests that the division Orient/Occident implicitly underlies the entire argument of the 1961 preface, in that the Orient stands for Dionysus and the tragic, while the Occident is associated with Christ and a *logos* seeking to overcome the reality of appearances in a transcendent otherworld. The early Foucault, Chevallier submits, hinted at the possibility of recovering a Christianity not yet affected by this division, one in which Christ and Dionysus were "images of each other" (Chevallier, 276).

identities. And, finally, modern reason has left behind the madman with his prophetic or demonic delusions. But madness returns in other forms, such as the epidemic of depression, which threatens the rationality of a society built on efficiency, consumption, and profit. So we attempt to medicate the threatening other away.

Part of the dialectical relationship between the Dionysian and the Apollonian, which—itself immobile in its tragic structure—underlies the history of the West, is the forgetting and silencing of the Dionysian other. The element constituted as the Outside has to find indirect, subversive ways to utter itself, between the lines, so to speak, as the language of the mainstream culture no longer has the right words available. In 1961, Foucault had not yet formulated his later view according to which there is no such thing as simply repressive power; nonetheless, he makes it very clear that any attempts to forget and silence the Outside will forever be accompanied by an irrepressible murmuring of the Other:

> The great work (*œuvre*) of the history of the world is indelibly accompanied by an absence of an *œuvre*, which renews itself at every instant but which runs, unchanged in its inevitable void, through the entire course of history—and from before history, because it is already present in the initial decision, as well as after it; because it will triumph in the last word uttered by history. The plenitude of history is possible only in the space, at once empty and populated, of all those words without language which, to everyone who lends his ear, make heard a muted noise from beneath history, the obstinate murmuring of a language which would speak *on its own*—without speaking subject and without interlocutor, folded in upon itself, a lump in its throat, crumbling away before having reached any formulation and returning without much ado to the silence from which it has never broken off. Charred root of meaning.[24]

Charred root of meaning: all meaning is grounded in an act of exclusion—a violent act of exclusion perhaps—that has defined the other as lying outside the purview of history; as incapable of engaging in meaningful acts, productive accomplishments; and therefore as falling short of human subjectivity. One is reminded of Hegel's exclusion, from his story of the unfolding of Spirit, of all those cultures that happened not to fit into the schema in which he attempted to capture the historical march toward Absolute

---

24. Foucault, *History of Madness*, xxxi–xxxii (*Dits et écrits*, 1:191); trans. amended.

Knowledge. Against this Apollonian optimism, Foucault asserts a different reality—a history that remains permanently marked by the brokenness of its origins.

It is only a small step from the "charred root of meaning" to the idea that a transgressive force looms in the "muted noise from beneath history," a force with the power to destabilize the beautiful edifice of the great works of history. But Foucault does not make that step in the Nietzschean context of the 1961 preface. He chooses to discuss transgression elsewhere, and in relation to none other than the sober Immanuel Kant.

Foucault's Critique of Kant

When, in the early 1980s, the editor of a new *Dictionnaire des philosophes* that was to be produced by the Presses universitaires de France approached Foucault's assistant François Ewald with the request for an entry on Foucault, it was a text by Foucault himself that ended up being submitted. Amusingly, the entry was signed by one Maurice Florence, abbreviated as "M.F.," a philosopher otherwise unknown in France. The entry begins with these words: "To the extent that Foucault fits into the philosophical tradition, it is the *critical* tradition of Kant . . . "[25]

Together with Nietzsche (read through a Heideggerian lens),[26] Kant was one of Foucault's main philosophical interlocutors, present in his work from the very beginning.[27] But Foucault's relationship with Kant was complex. He used Kantian methods—the *a priori*, in particular—while attempting to disentangle postmodern philosophy from the structural problems of the Kantian approach.[28]

25. Maurice Florence, "Foucault," trans. Robert Hurley, in *Essential Works of Foucault*, 2:459–63, at 459. As a matter of fact, the sentence quoted is the first in the *second* paragraph of the entry originally published in the *Dictionnaire des philosophes*; the first paragraph, however, is included neither in the *Dits et écrits* version of the text nor in its English translation in the *Essential Works of Foucault*. For the original entry, see *Dictionnaire des philosophes*, ed. Denis Huisman (Paris: Presses universitaires de France, 1984), 1:942–44. The *Dits et écrits* version is "Foucault," #345, 2:1450–55.

26. See "Le retour de la morale," 2:1515–26, at 1522: "Il est probable que si je n'avais pas lu Heidegger, je n'aurais pas lu Nietzsche." The entire context of this sentence is interesting, but too long to quote here.

27. Chevallier, *Foucault et le christianisme*, 278, puts it very eloquently: "le lien source de la pensée foucauldienne n'est pas d'abord la Forêt Noire ou Sils-Marie, mais bien Königsberg."

28. See n. 11 above for the notion of the "historical *a priori.*"

Until 1968, a doctorate in the humanities in France, the *doctorat ès lettres*, required two dissertations: a *thèse principale* and a *thèse complémentaire*. Foucault's principal thesis was *Folie et déraison*, whose 1961 preface we discussed in the previous section. For his complementary thesis, Foucault translated Kant's *Anthropology from a Pragmatic Point of View*, providing a detailed introduction. He later developed his complementary thesis into *The Order of Things*; the original text has become available only recently.[29]

Kant was very much on Foucault's mind when he wrote the "Preface to Transgression" in 1963. As we have already seen, the essay conducts its discussion of transgression in a conceptual space that is created by the juxtaposition of an older form of transgression, which was able to connect man with the divine, with post-Nietzschean transgression, which discovers the Absolute only in its absence. For the most part, Foucault's allusions to Christian mysticism remain vague in the "Preface"; they appear, for example, in a few references to the language and dialectics of "contradiction," that is to say, positive and negative theology.[30] The opening paragraph, however, is an exception in that Foucault directly addresses a particular aspect of Christian mysticism, namely, its relationship to sexuality: "[S]exuality never enjoyed a more immediately natural meaning, and it perhaps never knew a greater 'felicity of expression,' than in the Christian world of

29. Michel Foucault, *Introduction to Kant's "Anthropology,"* trans. Roberto Nigro and Kate Briggs (Los Angeles: Semiotext(e), 2008); French edition: E. Kant, *Anthropologie d'un point de vue pragmatique*, précédé de Michel Foucault, *Introduction à l'"Anthropologie,"* ed. Daniel Defert, François Ewald, and Frédéric Gros, Bibliothèque des textes philosophiques (Paris: Vrin, 2008). Béatrice Han has interpreted the introduction to *Anthropology* as the starting point of Foucault's oeuvre, where he defined the crucial problematic that was going to occupy him throughout his career; see her *Foucault's Critical Project: Between the Transcendental and the Historical*, trans. Edward Pile, Atopia: Philosophy, Political Theory, Aesthetics (Stanford: Stanford University Press, 2002), esp. chap. 1, pp. 17–37. Han contends that Foucault never managed to disentangle himself from the very structures he criticized, so much so that he "defeated himself from the very beginning" (37). She does not, however, pay any attention to transgression as a possible way out of the Kantian conundrum. By contrast, Chevallier, *Foucault et le christianisme*, 251–52, sees this avenue very clearly: from within the empirical, transgression seeks to access the very boundaries that make experience possible. For a critical discussion of Han's important book, see Gary Gutting's review in *Notre Dame Philosophical Reviews*, 2003.05.01 (http://ndpr.nd.edu/news/foucault-s-critical-project/, accessed December 27, 2017).

30. See "A Preface to Transgression," 72 (quoted above, n. 7) and 77 (= *Dits et écrits*, 1:269): "Would it be of help, in any case, to argue by analogy that we must find a language for the transgressive which would be what dialectics was, in an earlier time, for contradiction?"

fallen bodies and of sin. Its entire mysticism, its entire spirituality prove it, which were totally incapable of dividing the continuous forms of desire, of rapture, of penetration, of ecstasy, of that outpouring which has us faint: [this mysticism and this spirituality] felt that all of these movements were leading, without interruption or limit, right to the heart of a divine love of which they were the final outpouring and the source returning upon itself."[31] What a strange passage, coming from the pen of an avowed Nietzschean! It reads like an ode to Christian mysticism, tinged by a hint of nostalgia. For, despite the truth that medieval mysticism could be an intensely physical and even sexual experience,[32] one should not forget that medieval theologians viewed sex that was not mystically elevated as the *fomen peccatis*, the "tinder of sin."[33]

Foucault was more interested in Christian mysticism and familiar with its sources than is normally assumed. He spent the summer of 1950 studying Plotinus.[34] In an essay roughly contemporaneous with the "Preface to

31. Foucault, "A Preface to Transgression," 69 (*Dits et écrits*, 1:261). I have retranslated this passage to reflect Foucault's French more closely: "Jamais pourtant la sexualité n'a eu un sens plus immédiatement naturel et n'a connu sans doute un aussi grand 'bonheur d'expression' que dans le monde chrétien des corps déchus et du péché. Toute une mystique, toute une spiritualité le prouvent, qui ne savaient point diviser les formes continues du désir, de l'ivresse, de la pénétration, de l'extase et de l'épanchement qui défaille; tous ces mouvements, elles les sentaient se poursuivre, sans interruption ni limite, jusqu'au cœur d'un amour divin dont ils étaient le dernier évasement et la source en retour." For an excellent discussion of the "Preface to Transgression," see Chevallier, *Foucault et le christianisme*, 245–57. Mark D. Jordan offers a discussion of the essay in his *Convulsing Bodies: Religion and Resistance in Foucault* (Stanford: Stanford University Press, 2015), 19–26, but after a quick paraphrase focuses on its Bataillean context.

32. On this topic, one may consult the work of scholars like Carolyn Walker Bynum, *Fragmentation and Redemption: Essays on Gender and the Human Body in Medieval Religion* (New York: Zone Books, 1991), and Rachel Fulton Brown, *From Judgment to Passion: Devotion to Christ and the Virgin Mary, 800–1200* (New York: Columbia University Press, 2002).

33. See, for example, the standard textbook of scholastic theology, Peter Lombard's *Book of Sentences*, book II, dist. 30, chap. 8 through dist. 31, chap. 7 (*Sententiae in IV libris distinctae*, vol. 1 [Grottaferrata: Editiones Collegii S. Bonaventurae, 1971], 499–510).

34. See Daniel Defert, "Chronologie," in *Dits et écrits*, 1:13–90. On p. 18, under "juillet" (of 1950), we read: "Passe l'été à étudier Plotin." The "Chronology" is now also available in English translation, namely, in *A Companion to Foucault*, 11–83. As far as I can see, Foucault scholars have not paid any attention to Foucault's immersion in Plotinus, with the exception of Jeffrey Dirk Wilson, "Foucault as Inverted Neo-Platonist in 'A Preface to Transgression,'" paper delivered at the Sixty-Second Annual Conference of the Metaphysical Society of America in 2011 (http://www.metaphysicalsociety.org/2011/Session%20V.Wilson.pdf, accessed December 28, 2017).

Transgression" (1963) and relevant to its subject matter, "The Thought of the Outside" (1966), Foucault writes approvingly of the tradition of Pseudo-Dionysius: "It will one day be necessary to try to define the fundamental forms and categories of this 'thought of the outside.' It will also be necessary to try to retrace its path, to find out where it comes to us from and in what direction it is moving. One may well assume that it was born of the mystical thinking that has prowled the confines of Christianity since the texts of Pseudo-Dionysius: perhaps it survived for a millennium or so in the forms of negative theology."[35] So, on the one side of Foucault's discussion of transgression we have his suggestion that, in former times, there used to be an access to the divine, even to a divine love; for the mystical transgression of the "limit marked by the sacred" opened up a space where the divine could function.[36] On the other side is Foucault's description of transgression after the death of God—which, by the way, does not mean that God has somehow passed away, but that postmodern life occurs in a fundamentally god-less space.[37] This description has nothing triumphant about it; rather, it sounds dark and sad (which is also the mood of Nietzsche's own declarations of the death of God). Indeed, Foucault's description of postmodern sexuality, which he claims has become the locus where transgression plays itself out after the death of God, has an almost apocalyptic tone to it: "What characterizes modern sexuality from Sade to Freud is not its having found the language of its logic (*le langage de sa raison*) or of its nature, but, rather—and through the violence done by such languages—its having been 'denatured': cast into an empty space where it encounters nothing but the meager form of the limit, and where it has no beyond (*au-delà*), no prolongation, except in the frenzy that breaks it."[38]

35. Michel Foucault, "The Thought of the Outside," trans. Brian Massumi, in *Essential Works of Foucault*, 2:147–69; trans. amended in light of "La pensée du dehors," in *Dits et écrits*, #38, 1:546–67. *La pensée du dehors* can also be translated as "the thought *from* outside." This was Massumi's original translation in the version of the essay printed in *Foucault/Blanchot* (New York: Zone Books, 1987), 7–58. For an excellent interpretation of Foucault's thought as a form of negative theology, see James Bernauer, SJ, "The Prisons of Man: An Introduction to Foucault's Negative Theology," *International Philosophical Quarterly* 27, no. 4 (December 1987): 365–80.

36. See the text quoted above, n. 7.

37. See Foucault, "A Preface to Transgression," 71 (*Dits et écrits*, 1:263): "Not that this death should be understood as the end of his historical reign, or as the finally delivered judgment of his nonexistence, but as the now-constant space of our experience."

38. Foucault, "A Preface to Transgression," 69 (*Dits et écrits*, 1:261); trans. amended in light of the French: "Ce qui caractérise la sexualité moderne, ce n'est pas d'avoir trouvé, de

The theory that is intimated in this passage, read in conjunction with the sentences on Christian mysticism that immediately precede it, is at once Foucauldian and inspired by Georges Bataille. ("A Preface to Transgression" appeared in Bataille's own journal, *Critique*, which devoted a special issue to him after his death in 1962.) Bataille argued that the erotic is essentially a religious phenomenon, and vice versa: that religion is essentially erotic. Both religion and eros aim at the mystical experience of unified Being.[39] Foucault suggests that this continuity, which still existed in the tradition of Christian mysticism, broke at some point, with the consequence that modern sexuality no longer has any connection with the beyond; instead, it "encounters nothing but the meager form of the limit." This idea reflects the theory that we encountered in the preface to *Folie et déraison*: "One could write a history of *limits*." According to this theory, a culture defines itself through an original division in which an element that used to be part of the undifferentiated center becomes the Outside. Modernity, on this reading, created a sexuality devoid of transcendence—the divine having been marginalized in the "death of God." Foucault therefore concludes: "the language of sexuality has lifted us into the night where God is absent, and where all our actions are addressed to this absence in a profanation that at once identifies it, dissipates it, exhausts itself in it, and restores it to the empty purity of its transgression."[40]

To put this differently, before the death of God, transgression confronted the human being with the "limit of the Limitless"; this confrontation amounted to an experience of the "exteriority of being." In the postmodern world—that is to say, in the wake of Nietzsche and the death of God—the experience of the Limitless has been replaced by "an experience that is *interior* and *sovereign*." "But such an experience," Foucault adds, "for which the death of God is an explosive reality, discovers—as its secret and its light, [as] its intrinsic finitude—the limitless reign of the Limit, [and] the emptiness of this crossing [of the limit] where it spends itself and is found wanting."[41] Despite the nostalgic overtones of some of his remarks,

---

Sade à Freud, le langage de sa raison ou de sa nature, mais d'avoir été, et par la violence de leurs discours, 'dénaturalisée'—jetée dans un espace vide où elle ne rencontre que la forme mince de la limite, et où elle n'a au-delà et de prolongement que dans dans la frénésie qui la rompt."

39. See Georges Bataille, *Erotism: Death and Sensuality*, trans. Mary Dalwood (San Francisco: City Lights Press, 1986).

40. Foucault, "A Preface to Transgression," 70 (*Dits et écrits*, 1:262).

41. Foucault, "A Preface to Transgression," 71 (*Dits et écrits*, 1:263); trans. amended.

Foucault makes it quite clear that there is no possibility of a "return to a homeland or the recovery of an original soil."[42] The limit has changed its meaning, and so has transgression. If the thought of the Outside is still possible, that is to say, if it is possible to break out of the interiority of the sovereign subject, then the means to such transcendence can no longer be traditional Christian mysticism, which encountered the limit in the form of the Limitless. Rather, the thought of the Outside now has to confront the limit as such, and to think man in his radical finitude. (Finitude is a modern discovery, different from thinking man as made in God's image and likeness.) Can this movement of radical critique still produce an ontology, Foucault asks, that is to say, can there be "an understanding that comprehends both finitude and being"?[43]

The answer is: maybe. It is precisely Immanuel Kant who made an "opening . . . in Western philosophy when he articulated, in a manner that is still enigmatic, metaphysical discourse and reflection on the limits of our reason."[44] Remember, Kant's critique was meant to constitute the mere "prolegomena" to any future metaphysics! But then, Kant foreclosed this very opening by tying his critical enterprise to anthropology, that is to say, by making the critical question of limits a question regarding the limits and constitution of human reason. Foucault's entire *thèse complémentaire* was devoted to this problem, which at that point in his career he described in terms of "alienation."[45] Kant, who—as Foucault emphasizes—delivered lectures on anthropology during a period of twenty-five years (1772–1797), both before and after the publication of the *Critique*, tried to ground the *a priori* by means of an investigation into human nature. This approach resulted in insurmountable confusion and a vicious circle: human subjectivity, the seat of an *a priori* meant to capture the conditions for the possibility of experiencing objects (as well as the limits of such experience), becomes itself the

---

The French reads: "Mais une telle expérience, en laquelle éclate la mort de Dieu, découvre comme son secret et sa lumière, sa propre finitude, le règne illimité de la Limite, le vide de ce franchissement où elle défaille et fait défaut." The syntactic status of *sa propre finitude* is ambiguous. It could be an extension of the *comme* phrase (which is my interpretation, indicated by the insertion of "as"), but it could also be the first direct object of the verb *découvre*, in which case the translation would read: "discovers . . . its own finitude."

42. Foucault, "A Preface to Transgression," 75 (*Dits et écrits*, 1:267).

43. Foucault, "A Preface to Transgression," 75 (*Dits et écrits*, 1:267). Foucault himself uses the term "ontology," speaking of "une pensée qui serait, absolument et dans le même mouvement, une Critique et une Ontologie, une pensée qui penserait la finitude et l'être."

44. Foucault, "A Preface to Transgression," 76 (*Dits et écrits*, 1:267).

45. Foucault, *Introduction to Kant's "Anthropology,"* 123.

object of empirical inquiry. Already in the complementary thesis, Foucault submits that the "anthropological illusion," according to which it is possible to ground the *a priori* in empirical studies of human nature, constitutes the fundamental problem of contemporary philosophy.[46] A few years later, he makes this claim the centerpiece of his argument in *The Order of Things*, where he terms the Kantian knot of contemporary thought the "empirico-transcendental doublet": human subjectivity is what renders all experience possible transcendentally while itself being "subjected" to empirical investigation in the human sciences.[47] An inextricable confusion ensues.

It is worth pointing out that the empirico-transcendental doublet produces problems that are not of a merely abstract philosophical nature. Since Kant, the human being has been subjected to ever more detailed and intense empirical research. At the same time, the human sciences, in which this research is pursued, have increasingly turned from fundamental investigations of the human condition in disciplines such as psychology, sociology, anthropology, and linguistics, to areas of study whose principal goal is, as Foucault might say, to "normalize" populations so that they function as efficient workforces and eager consumers. To illustrate this point, consider a list of concentrations within the College of Human Sciences at Texas Tech University, culled from the college's website:[48]

- Addictive disorders and recovery studies
- Apparel design and manufacturing
- Community, family, and addiction sciences
- Family and consumer sciences extension education
- Human development and family studies
- Human sciences
- Interior design
- Nutritional sciences
- Personal finance
- Personal financial planning
- Restaurant, hotel, and institutional management
- Retail management
- Youth development

46. Foucault, *Introduction to Kant's "Anthropology,"* 122, 124.

47. Foucault, *The Order of Things*, 318.

48. http://www.depts.ttu.edu/hs/human_sciences/index.php, accessed November 15, 2017.

According to this model, the human sciences take care of it all: youth, the family (considered, it must be pointed out, in immediate conjunction with consumption), health, nutrition, and personal financial management. The latter is crucial for the retailer, who depends on consumers capable of paying their bills. Health and nutrition education keep the population sufficiently fit to work and consume. The hospitality industry, for its part, provides distraction from the economic cycle, while interior design educates the consumer's taste. Should anyone seek the door to the other side of this professionally managed society,[49] addiction counseling is available through those versed in "recovery studies."

If most of the time most of us do not see this bleak picture, this blindness—or forgetfulness—is due to the fact that we regard ourselves as "lords of the earth," as Heidegger puts it in his famous technology essay. We view ourselves as transcendental subjects who have everything technologically under control, and for whom the world has become nothing but a resource catering to human needs; nothing "stands over against" us anymore as an "ob-ject."[50]

In *The Order of Things*, published in 1966, Foucault attempts to cut through the Kantian knot by historicizing the transcendental—a Heideggerian move.[51] Consequently, he no longer identifies the subject as the seat of the *a priori*, but moves this function to historical structures he calls "*epistemes*." In *Folie et déraison* and the "Preface to Transgression"—and other work from the early 1960s—his solution is much more Nietzschean. Thus, the commentary on Kant's *Anthropology* ends with this sentence: "The trajectory of the question *Was ist der Mensch?* in the field of philosophy reaches its end in the response which both challenges and disarms it: *der Übermensch*."[52] Likewise, in the "Preface to Transgression," the one to awaken us from Kant's "confused sleep of dialectics and anthropology" (a delightful allusion to Kant's famous

49. The rock band The Doors released a song entitled "Break on through (to the Other Side)" as part of their debut album, *The Doors* (1967). Jim Morrison, the vocalist, died in 1971 from an overdose of heroin. He was only twenty-seven.

50. See Martin Heidegger, "The Question concerning Technology," trans. William Lovitt, in *Basic Writings*, ed. David Farrell Krell (San Francisco: HarperSanFrancisco, 1993), 311–41. The phrase "lord of the earth" occurs on p. 332.

51. See my essay "The Historicization of the Transcendental in Postmodern Philosophy," in *Die Logik des Transzendentalen. Festschrift für Jan A. Aertsen zum 65. Geburtstag*, ed. Martin Pickavé, Miscellanea Mediaevalia 30 (Berlin: de Gruyter, 2003), 701–13.

52. Foucault, *Introduction to Kant's "Anthropology*," 124.

"dogmatic slumber") is the philosopher of the Superman.[53] But he is keeping varied company:

> From the lessons on Homer to the cries of a madman in the streets of Turin, who can be said to have spoken this continuous language, so obstinately the same? Was it the Wanderer or his shadow? The philosopher or the first of the nonphilosophers? Zarathustra, his monkey, or already the Superman? Dionysus, Christ, their reconciled figures, or finally this man right here? The breakdown of philosophical subjectivity and its dispersion in a language that dispossesses it while multiplying it within a space created by its absence is probably one of the fundamental structures of contemporary thought.[54]

The solution to the Kantian problem, then, consists in the retrieval of the language of madness that spoke before the creation of the subject. For the subject, sovereign and rational, owes its existence to the binary divisions that the preface to *Folie et déraison* describes as the crucial limits by which a culture defines itself. An investigation of those divisions and those limits uncovers the "charred root of meaning"—the exclusion that made the subject possible, made meaning possible, and history.

Nietzsche allowed himself to be spoken by such a language, so much so that many oppositions that have come to define the cultural space of the West collapsed as he wrote—like the division between the philosopher and the nonphilosopher, between wisdom and madness, between pagan gods and the Christian God—until his oeuvre finally broke down, becoming nonoeuvre in the last letters and postcards, which in a kind of "holy frenzy" he signed variously as "Dionysos" and as "The Crucified."[55]

---

53. Foucault, "A Preface to Transgression," 78 (*Dits et écrits*, 1:267).

54. Foucault, "A Preface to Transgression," 79 (*Dits et écrits*, 1:270).

55. On the religious significance of Nietzsche's final "transgressive transformation" (216), see Bruce Ellis Benson, *Pious Nietzsche: Decadence and Dionysian Faith* (Bloomington and Indianapolis: Indiana University Press, 2008), 215–16. The reference to "holy frenzy" occurs on p. 215.

Return to Transgression

What have we learned from our consideration of the philosophical context in which the early Foucault discusses transgression?[56] The most important point is doubtless the ontological meaning of transgression for Foucault.[57] Foucault is not interested in this topic primarily because, assuming the posture of the avant-garde intellectual, he wants to challenge and overthrow the bourgeois ethics of mid-century France. Transgression, he declares explicitly, "must be detached from its dubious association with ethics if we want to *think* it, and to think *from* it and *in the space* it denotes; it must be liberated from the scandalous or subversive, that is, from anything that is driven by the power of the negative. Transgression does not seek to oppose one thing to another, nor does it let anything slip into the game of mockery or seek to shake the solidity of foundations."[58] As we have already seen, Foucault feels highly ambiguous about a superficially "liberated" sexuality. Instead, he views transgression as a possible solution to a philosophical problem—namely, how to break out of the Kantian subjectivity and rediscover the Outside, Being, even the divine. This rediscovery requires a testing of the limits through which the sovereign subject has defined itself. Some of these limits may, in fact, have an ethical significance. It is part of the brilliance of Foucault's oeuvre that he is capable of showing the practical implications of large theoretical problems. To offer only one

56. One of the earliest English contributions to Foucault scholarship, Charles G. Lemert and Garth Gillan's *Foucault: Social Theory as Transgression* (New York: Columbia University Press, 1982), suggested that transgression remained a central theme throughout Foucault's oeuvre. There is truth to this idea, although it runs counter to the now-established view according to which Foucault's works fall into clearly distinguishable phases. Also see the following note.

57. Diogo Sardinha speaks of the *sens ontologique* of transgression in his excellent essay, "L'éthique et les limites de la transgression," *Lignes*, no. 17 (2005): 125–36. Sardinha emphasizes the coherence of Foucault's oeuvre, arguing that "l'expérience littéraire du début des années soixante et le déplacement vers l'Antiquité propre aux années quatre-vingt appartiennent à un même univers problématique, qu'on pourrait appeler celui des limites de l'être et leur rapport à l'éthique" (126).

58. Foucault, "A Preface to Transgression," 74 (*Dits et écrits*, 1:265–66). I have retranslated this passage from the French text, adding the italics for clarification: ". . . pour essayer de la penser, pour penser à partir d'elle et dans l'espace qu'elle dessine, il faut la dégager de ses parentés louches avec l'éthique. La libérer de ce qui est le scandaleux ou le subversif, c'est-à-dire de ce qui est animé par la puissance du négatif. La transgression n'oppose rien à rien, ne fait rien glisser dans le jeu de la dérision, ne cherche pas à ébranler la solidité des fondements."

example from Foucault's early research, the treatment to which the center of society, the so-called mainstream, subjects the marginalized madman reflects a certain understanding of what reason is—and vice versa, modern psychiatric practice undergirds a particular form of rationality. Philosophy therefore has an ethical and even political dimension—something of which Foucault was acutely aware, as is evidenced by his social and political activism—but this does not mean that transgression cannot be treated as being, first and foremost, an ontological issue. After the death of God, can transgression still give us access to the Other?

CHAPTER 1

The Irruption of the Divine

The narrative of Moses's ascent on Mount Sinai not only stands at the center of the book of Exodus, but it became—in Walter Brueggemann's words—the "paradigm for all future covenantal confrontations" between God and his people.[1] Indeed, throughout the Jewish and, later, the Christian tradition, Exodus 19 has served as a model of how the immanent and profane world comes into contact with the transcendent and sacred. In the New Testament, the Letter to the Hebrews contains one of the sustained reflections on the new covenant and its difference from the old, Mosaic one. Almost point by point, the author of Hebrews uses the Exodus narrative as a framework within which to imagine the new covenant: "For you are not come to a mountain that might be touched, and a burning fire, and a whirlwind, and darkness, and storm. . . . But you are come to Mount Sion, and to the city of the living God, the heavenly Jerusalem, and to the company of many thousands of angels" (Heb. 12:18 and 22).[2]

Beyond Scripture itself, the history of the reception of Exodus 19 includes the use that Pseudo-Dionysius the Areopagite made of the passage. In his *Mystical Theology*, he rereads the Mount Sinai narrative as setting the pattern not so much for the covenantal encounter between God and his people as for the individual's mystical ascent to the hidden God. The authority Dionysius enjoyed can only have amplified the resonance that the narrative had in Christian ears.

1. Walter Brueggemann, "The Book of Exodus," in *The New Interpreter's Bible* (Nashville: Abingdon, 1994), 1:834.

2. On the relationship between Exod. 19 and Heb. 12, see Brevard S. Childs, *The Book of Exodus: A Critical, Theological Commentary* (Philadelphia: Westminster, 1974), 376–78.

A much less well-known yet fascinating adaptation of Exodus 19 occurred in the nascent scholastic movement of the twelfth century. It is to be found in the first continuous gloss—the so-called Pseudo-Peter of Poitiers gloss—on Peter Lombard's famous *Book of Sentences*, the standard textbook of scholastic theology. The Pseudo-Peter of Poitiers gloss was by no means an insignificant text, being used as an introduction to systematic theology from the time of its creation in the 1160s until at least the early fourteenth century. This gloss interprets the biblical narrative of Moses's ascent on Mount Sinai as an allegory of the structure and history of scriptural interpretation itself, in the process shedding much light on the role of transgression in the constitution of the biblical tradition.

But first, we must examine some essential features of Exodus 19 itself.

The Mount Sinai Narrative

From the literary point of view, the Mount Sinai narrative is of an "extreme difficulty," as Brevard Childs has noted: "In spite of almost a century of close, critical work many of the major problems have resisted a satisfactory solution."[3] One of these main problems lies in the fact that Moses is depicted as ascending Mount Sinai three times, even within Exodus 19 (and the ascents and descents resume in chapter 24; Moses returns from the mountain only in chapter 34). This repetition could be due to the different sources that flow together in the narrative of the ascents, since the text as it appears canonically in Exodus 19 already constitutes a sixth-century to fourth-century rereading of a tradition reporting a thirteenth-century event.[4] Alternatively, God could have summoned Moses onto the mountain twice in order to give him instructions on how to prepare for the crucial third encounter, which culminates in the dispensation of the law. Given the historical distance, however, biblical scholars have judged any "precise reconstruction" of what happened to be "impossible."[5] Although what is being recounted is deeply anchored in the tradition, we cannot apply modern standards of historical verification to the narrative. This elusiveness of origins so frustrates the modern Western mind that many

---

3. Childs, *The Book of Exodus*, 344.

4. See Brueggemann, "The Book of Exodus," 1:680.

5. Cornelis Houtman, *Exodus*, Historical Commentary on the Old Testament, vol. 2 (Louvain: Peeters, 1996), 433.

exegetes seek refuge in strategies of interpretation that are *prima facie* opposed, but share a common goal: namely, to eliminate the ambiguity of the scriptural text. Thus, fundamentalists will insist on the historical accuracy of the narrative in every detail, while adherents of the historical-critical method tend to interpret away any "hard" reality. Erich Zenger, for example, considers the stories surrounding Mount Sinai as literary projections, into a single event, of Israel's long spiritual experience of living in God's presence.[6] There may therefore have been no encounter between God and Moses on the mountain. Both strategies are ultimately rationalist, rejecting as they do the notion that reason could be grounded in anything other than itself and the "facts" that it recognizes as its domain. "But facts," as Alasdair MacIntyre wittily remarked, "like telescopes and wigs for gentlemen, were a seventeenth-century invention."[7] Tradition follows a different logic: charred root of meaning, again.

That origins keep withdrawing is something of which the writers of Exodus 19 are acutely aware, for although the passage narrates a theophany, God's presence is never depicted as being unmediated. Indeed, strictly speaking, we are not dealing with a theo*phany* at all, to the extent that this word indicates a coming forth into the light (the meaning of the verb φαίνω). For God appears in Exodus 19 only as a voice, or as a speaker, remaining hidden to the eye: "The Lord said to him: Lo, now I will come to thee in the darkness of a cloud, that the people may hear me speaking to thee, and may believe thee for ever" (19:9). Furthermore, the cloud in which God appears (also in 24:15–18) represents only one level of mediation, an outer layer, as it were; for the cloud itself is due to the fire whose form God has assumed: "And all mount Sinai was on a smoke: because the Lord was come down upon it in fire, and the smoke from it as out of a furnace" (19:18). There are hints that Moses himself may have seen more of God than this fire, especially during his forty-day sojourn at the top of the mountain. Thus, at one point, God is said to have shown him his back (33:23). Even Moses, however, could not look God in the face: "Thou canst not see my face: for man shall not see me and live" (33:20).

The theophany that is narrated in Exodus 19 is accompanied by terrifying and dangerous signs of God's might: thunder, lightning, and the

---

6. See Erich Zenger, *Israel am Sinai. Analysen und Interpretationen zu Exodus 17–34* (Altenberge: CIS-Verlag, 1982); quoted in Houtman, *Exodus*, 433.

7. Alasdair MacIntyre, *Whose Justice? Which Rationality?* (Notre Dame: University of Notre Dame Press, 1988), 357.

deafening sound of trumpets (19:16 and 19:19). "And all the mount was terrible" is how the biblical text sums up the overwhelming experience of the people gathered at the foot of the mountain (19:18). The distance between the holy Other and the profane is further emphasized by God's injunction to Moses to "let [the people] wash their garments" (19:10), that is to say, to have them engage in a ritual of cleansing. In ancient Israel (as in the premodern world more generally), clothes were not what they are today, that is to say, a more or less arbitrarily chosen external appearance unrelated to the human reality beneath; rather, they were profoundly expressive of the social and religious status of their wearer. Clean clothes meant cleansed people.[8] The cleanliness necessary for the encounter with the Lord also includes abstention from sexual relations: "come not near your wives" (19:15).

As if this demarcation of the sphere of the divine from the world of everyday life were not sufficient, the pericope that we are analyzing commands Moses to set up boundaries around the mountain, the sacred place where the earth comes into contact with heaven: "And thou shalt appoint certain limits to the people round about, and thou shalt say to them: Take heed you go not up into the mount, and that ye touch not the borders thereof: every one that touches the mount dying he shall die" (19:12). The theme of the limits and the mortal risk associated with crossing them is repeated several times (19:13, 21, and 24). The danger of transgressing the boundaries around the mountain is such that anyone who has violated the injunction not to step over the limits must be killed from afar, lest others subject themselves to the same peril. Or perhaps the violator has become unclean, with the risk that the curse he has attracted could communicate itself to others: "No hands shall touch him, but he will be stoned to death, or shall be shot through with arrows: whether it be beast, or man, he shall not live" (19:13). Note that even animals must stay away from the mountain. They too are included in the created order that must keep a distance from its all-powerful Maker. Toward the end of chapter 19, Moses repeats and confirms the order he has received: "And Moses said to the Lord: The people cannot come up to mount Sinai: for thou didst charge, and command, saying: Set limits about the mount, and sanctify it" (19:23).

8. See Houtman, *Exodus*, 450, who cites Anton Jirku, "Zur magischen Bedeutung der Kleidung in Israel," *Zeitschrift für die alttestamentliche Wissenschaft* 37, no. 1 (January 1918): 109–25. For a more recent, in-depth treatment of the significance of clothes in the Old Testament, see Claudia Bender, *Die Sprache des Textilen. Untersuchungen zu Kleidung und Textilien im Alten Testament*, Beiträge zur Wissenschaft vom Alten und Neuen Testament 177 (Stuttgart: Kohlhammer, 2008).

That which is holy (*sanctus*), then, is also that which it is forbidden, under sanction (from *sancio, sanxi, sanctus*), to transgress. Even coming into God's presence from afar requires purification: the clothes that have been soiled in one's everyday activities must be washed to indicate one's readiness to transcend the profane order. Sexual activity must be avoided. And yet, despite these preparations for the reception of God's word, his presence—even his veiled, mediated presence—is terrifying, like a natural disaster. Those who ignore the warning not to come close face certain death. The entire scenario depicted in Exodus 19 not only conveys the hiddenness of God—the Origin, the Other, the Outside—but also resonates with fear, violence, and death. Again, Foucault's diagnosis, that the roots of meaning are "charred," appears apt, even if the act of exclusion in Exodus 19 originates in God himself: God excludes the people from approaching him.

And yet, how can the holy and transcendent enter into the profane world unless some act of transgression—once again, literally understood as the act of stepping across, *trans-gredi*—provides a mediation between the two spheres? The answer that Exodus provides is twofold. God is the primary transgressor, so to speak, insofar as he "come[s] down in the sight of all the people upon mount Sinai" (19:11; cf. 19:18, 20). In fact, however, God never addresses the people directly, but speaks only to Moses: "that the people may hear me speaking to thee, and may believe thee for ever" (19:9). The result of this double transgression is the law—the Ten Commandments, which chapter 20 reveals as the content of the Lord's discourse to Moses. The Ten Commandments themselves are followed by much more detailed legal and religious instructions, including those for the establishment of the tabernacle. God's extraordinary and terrifying self-showing, then, the irruption of the divine, leads to a mediated presence of the divine—mediated by Moses, but also by the law, which, with its repeated command of "Thou shalt not," appears to spell out in detail the primary interdict, which is simply not to overstep the boundary between the sacred and the profane.

In the book of Exodus, chapter 19 belongs to a broader dynamic within which God's people are first liberated from Pharaoh, then encounter their Lord covenantally at Mount Sinai, and finally prepare a dwelling for the holy in their midst by executing the instructions Moses received for the establishment of the tabernacle.[9] In this dynamic, but also in the complex

---

9. See Brueggemann, "The Book of Exodus," 1:682–83.

literary mosaic that makes up the Exodus text, scriptural scholars have found evidence for a certain tension between prophetic and priestly elements—the former being connected with the liberation of God's people and his dramatic presence at Sinai, the latter with the conventional stabilization, one could say, of this presence in and through the tabernacle. This tension, however, does not have to become a contradiction, if one views the tabernacle as the fulfillment of the covenantal encounter itself.[10]

As already noted, chapter 19 forms a particularly close unity with chapter 24, which has Moses ascend Mount Sinai once again, both to seal the covenant with God in a meal and to receive further revelations during a forty-day stay on the top of the mountain, in the Lord's presence. Like chapter 19, chapter 24 "contains a whole series of compositional problems which have called forth a great divergence of opinion."[11] It is clear, however, that the narrative of Exodus 24 differs from the earlier one in a number of respects. Most significantly for our purposes, it includes others—notably Moses's brother Aaron, Aaron's sons Nadab and Abihu, as well as Joshua and the seventy elders of Israel—in the ascent: "And he said to Moses: Come up to the Lord, thou, and Aaron, Nadab, and Abiu, and seventy of the ancients of Israel, and you shall adore far off" (24:1).[12] There is a certain ambiguity, however, in that the very next verse seems "to reverse categorically the instructions" just given, as Brevard Childs has noted:[13] "And Moses alone shall come up to the Lord, but they shall not come nigh: neither shall the people come up with him" (24:2). It may be possible to smooth out this tension—as the commentary tradition has done—by assuming different levels of ascent, which in turn implies different levels of hierarchy and mediation. Thus, later in chapter 24, Moses orders the seventy elders to stay behind as he climbs further toward the top of the mountain to meet the Lord: "Wait ye here till we return to you" (24:14).

The narration of Moses's return from Mount Sinai in Exodus 34 indicates that the encounter with the Lord brought about physical alterations to Moses's appearance. According to Jerome's Vulgate translation, his face

10. As does Childs, *The Book of Exodus*, 537–52. On p. 540, he writes: "The glory of God which once covered Mount Sinai fills the tabernacle. The cloud representing the presence of God now accompanies Israel above the tabernacle on her journey. The tabernacle serves as a portable sanctuary of the presence of God[,] whose covenant will have been made known at Sinai. What happened at Sinai is continued in the tabernacle."

11. Childs, *The Book of Exodus*, 499.

12. Exod. 19:24 mentions Aaron as accompanying Moses in the ascent.

13. Childs, *The Book of Exodus*, 500.

had become "horned" (*cornuta*); more modern translations follow the Septuagint, which describes Moses's face as "glorified" (δεδόξασται), or shining with glory. Jerome's rendering, albeit no longer the preferred version, is by no means absurd, as the Hebrew root he translated as "horned"—קרן (*qrn*)—occurs dozens of times in the Old Testament, and in each case means "horn."[14] Indeed, recent scholarship has vindicated Jerome's choice, since in the iconography of the ancient Near East, horns were associated with divine power and the king who represented it.[15] The art historian Ruth Mellinkoff even declared that the "history of religions could almost be written as the history of horned gods and goddesses."[16] It would make sense that after Moses's encounter with the Lord, his appearance transgressed the normal limits of the human gestalt, rendering him transhuman, more-than-human. His satyr-like appearance had become so strange to the people of Israel that they "were afraid to come near" (34:30). To hide his terrifying transformation, Moses therefore had to veil his face when he interacted with his people (34:33, 35). We note three points from this episode: first, God's presence is so powerful that his chosen messenger, Moses, is physically transformed or even deformed by the encounter; second, just as God veils himself in fire and in a cloud, lest anyone behold his face and die, so Moses in his mediating role ends up having to conceal his face, because God remains overwhelming even in the mediated reflection of his messenger's appearance; third, Moses's transformation has introduced an element of alienation between him and his people, who react to his altered appearance with fear.

In sum, then, this is the structure that Exodus lays out for the relationship between God and his people: first, God is the Other, the Outside, who is terrifying in his difference. Failing to respect the infinite distance between God and his creation means death, as transgressing the limits discussed in Exodus 19 carries a mortal penalty. But how are God and his people going to meet and communicate to conclude the covenant? Mediation is necessary. This mediation begins with God's own initiative, which consists in making himself visible, through created veils, and above

---

14. Following Jerome's translation, the "horned Moses" became a tradition in medieval art and thought; see Ruth Mellinkoff, *The Horned Moses in Medieval Art and Thought* (Berkeley: University of California Press, 1970).

15. This is the argument Thomas Römer makes at the beginning of his inaugural lecture at the *Collège de France: Les cornes de Moïse. Faire entrer la Bible dans l'histoire*, Leçons inaugurales du Collège de France (Paris: Collège de France/Fayard, 2009), 3–6.

16. Mellinkoff, *The Horned Moses*, 3.

Horned Moses receiving the Law in a fourteenth-century manuscript of the *Somme le Roi* (MS. Lille, Bibliothèque municipale, 116, fol. 3v).

all audible, on Mount Sinai.[17] For his people, the reception of God's commands requires preparation; through purification, they need to separate themselves from their profane lives, at least to an extent. Furthermore, just

17. Did the people hear God's unmediated voice? Exod. 19:19 mentions sounds of the horn getting louder and louder as God and Moses converse. Did the horn drown out the conversation, or was God's voice so powerful as to be heard over the sounds of the horn? For a discussion, see Houtman, *Exodus*, 456–57.

as God transgresses the boundaries between the sacred and the profane by appearing on the top of the mountain—which symbolically mediates between the high and the low—so Moses is summoned to transgress the limits drawn around the mountain in order to encounter the Lord in the cloud at the top. According to some verses, especially in Exodus 24, Moses is allowed to bring a select group of priests (like Aaron), assistants (Joshua), and elders with him as he ascends Mount Sinai—but only up to a point. The final encounter with the Lord, at the summit, has Moses stay in the cloud in solitude for forty days.

The result of Moses's encounter with the Lord is the law, which regulates the relationship between the sacred and the profane in various levels of detail, reaching from the Ten Commandments to instructions for worship, diet, and many other aspects of everyday life.

Pseudo-Dionysius on the Mystical Ascent

We were talking about the elusiveness of origins. Pseudo-Dionysius the Areopagite was one of the most influential authors in the Christian tradition, of subapostolic authority, but no one knows his identity—except negatively: he was not, scholars definitively ascertained at the dawn of the twentieth century, Dionysius the Areopagite, Saint Paul's disciple from the Acts of the Apostles (17:34).[18] Quoting extensively from Proclus (412–485), Pseudo-Dionysius must have composed his writings toward the end of the fifth or beginning of the sixth century. He may have been a Syrian monk.[19] Why did the author of the Dionysian corpus put on this veil? The most likely explanation is that he wished to disappear behind his writings, just

18. One of the decisive contributions was by Hugo Koch, who showed Pseudo-Dionysius's dependence on Proclus in painstaking detail; see his book, *Pseudo-Dionysius Areopagita in seinen Beziehungen zum Neuplatonismus und Mysterienwesen*, Forschungen zur Christlichen Litteratur- und Dogmengeschichte 1 (Mainz: Franz Kirchheim, 1900). Doubts regarding the authenticity of the Dionysian corpus go back as far as Nicholas of Cusa, who expressed consternation at the fact that this great authority was unknown to the church fathers! For references to Cusa, Lorenzo Valla, and Erasmus (the latter two provided more detailed arguments), see Pseudo-Dionysius Areopagita, *Über die Mystische Theologie und Briefe*, trans. Adolf Martin Ritter, Bibliothek der griechischen Literatur 40 (Stuttgart: Hiersemann, 1994), 4–6.

19. Ritter provides a critical overview of recent attempts to identify Pseudo-Dionysius with a known historical figure; research in this regard has, however, remained inconclusive. See *Über die Mystische Theologie*, 8–19.

as Moses disappeared in the cloud at the summit of Mount Sinai, there to exist for forty days in God's presence. Effacing his self in writing—it has been suggested—was part of his spiritual practice.[20]

That it was Pseudo-Dionysius's ultimate goal to emulate Moses's ascent is evident in the following passage from *Mystical Theology*:

> This, at least, is what was taught by the blessed Bartholomew. He says that the Word of God is vast and miniscule, that the Gospel is wide-ranging and yet restricted. To me it seems that in this he is extraordinarily shrewd, for he has grasped that the good cause of all is both eloquent and taciturn, indeed wordless. It has neither word nor act of understanding, since it is on a plane above all this, and it is made manifest only to those who travel through foul and fair, who pass beyond the summit of every holy ascent, who leave behind them every divine light, every voice, every word from heaven, and who plunge into the darkness where, as scripture proclaims, there dwells the One who is beyond all things.
>
> It is not for nothing that the blessed Moses is commanded to submit first to purification and then to depart from those who have not undergone this. When every purification is complete, he hears the many-voiced trumpets. He sees the many lights, pure and with rays streaming abundantly. Then, standing apart from the crowds and accompanied by chosen priests, he pushes ahead to the summit of divine ascents. And yet he does not meet God himself, but contemplates, not him who is invisible, but rather where he dwells. This means, I presume, that the holiest and highest of the things perceived with the eye of the body or the mind are but the rationale (λόγους) which presupposes all that lies below the Transcendent One. Through them, however, his unimaginable presence is shown, walking the heights of those holy places to which the mind at least can rise. But then he [Moses] breaks free of them, away from what sees and is seen, and he plunges into the truly mysterious darkness of unknowing. Here, renouncing all that the mind may conceive, wrapped entirely in the intangible and the invisible, he belongs completely to him who is beyond everything. Here, being neither oneself nor someone else

20. For a detailed interpretation of Dionysius's pseudonymity as mystical practice, see Charles M. Stang, *Apophasis and Pseudonymity in Dionysius the Areopagite: "No Longer I"* (Oxford: Oxford University Press, 2012). An article-length condensation of the same author's argument is available in "Dionysius, Paul and the Significance of the Synonym," in *Re-Thinking Dionysius the Areopagite*, ed. Sarah Coakley (Chichester, UK: Wiley-Blackwell, 2009), 11–25.

(οὔτε ἑαυτοῦ οὔτε ἑτέρου), one is supremely united to the completely unknown by an inactivity of all knowledge, and knows beyond the mind by knowing nothing.[21]

To make sense of this dense passage, we need to place it within the contexts in which it belongs: first, the context of the Pseudo-Dionysian corpus of writings; second, the biblical context of the Mount Sinai narrative, as well as its reception in the New Testament; third, the context of Dionysius's Neoplatonic sources; fourth, the context of the intellectual and religious milieu in, for, and perhaps against which Pseudo-Dionysius wrote. Even if we bracket the fourth context here, because of the difficulties of reconstructing it, and regard Dionysius's Proclean roots as well established, considering the first two contexts will already shed much light on our text.

Paul Rorem has described *The Mystical Theology* as "a brief summary or even the climax of Dionysian thought."[22] As such, the treatise assumes knowledge of the other writings in the corpus, especially *The Divine Names* and the two *Hierarchies*. Of course, the extract we just quoted, from the end of chapter 1, also presupposes the context of *The Mystical Theology* itself.

We understand the term "theology" as designating a methodically built intellectual edifice that summarizes our knowledge of God in a systematic way—just as biology renders a systematic and scientific account of the various forms of life. This is not how Pseudo-Dionysius employs the term.[23] Where our translation has the phrase "the Word of God," the Greek text reads θεολογίαν, which is literally understood as the *logos* not *on*, but rather *of*, the *theos*. The immediately following reference to the gospel makes this quite clear. God, then, Dionysius claims, speaks of himself both in many words and in none. He has revealed himself to his people in the texts of Scripture, yet the "good cause of all" about whom we can

---

21. Pseudo-Dionysius, *The Mystical Theology*, in *The Complete Works*, trans. Colm Luibheid, Classics of Western Spirituality (Mahwah, NJ: Paulist Press, 1987), 133–41, at 136–37 (chap. 1, no. 3). For the Greek text, see *Corpus Dionysiacum II*, ed. Günter Heil and Adolf Martin Ritter, 2nd ed., Patristische Texte und Studien 67 (Berlin: de Gruyter, 2012), p. 143, l. 8–p. 144, l. 15.

22. Paul Rorem, *Pseudo-Dionysius: A Commentary on the Texts and an Introduction to Their Influence* (Oxford: Oxford University Press, 1993), 183.

23. See René Roques, "Note sur la notion de *theologia* selon le Pseudo-Denys l'Aréopagite," *Revue d'ascétique et de mystique* 25 (1949): 200–212; reprinted in the author's *Structures théologiques. De la gnose à Richard de Saint-Victor*, Bibliothèque de l'École des hautes études, Section des sciences religieuses 72 (Paris: Presses universitaires de France, 1962), 135–45.

legitimately form affirmations in both philosophical and biblical terms ultimately transcends all words and intelligibility. Note that we are not imposing this absolute transcendence on God for extrinsic, philosophic reasons (because Proclus tells us that the One is beyond all knowledge, for example); rather, Scripture itself attests to it—notably, in the Mount Sinai narrative.

The Mount Sinai narrative must, however, not be taken out of the context in which *theologia* is both of many *logoi* and of none. Thus, even the mystical ascent is a moment in a larger whole. The whole may culminate in the ascent, yet it is more than just the ascent. In the Dionysian corpus, this dialectical relationship between "positive" and "negative" theology is reflected in the balance between *The Divine Names* and the *Hierarchies*, on the one hand, and *The Mystical Theology*, on the other.

Moreover, reading *The Mystical Theology* against the backdrop of the other Dionysian writings suggests a liturgical context for Dionysius's adaptation of the Mount Sinai narrative. Louis Bouyer, in particular, has emphasized this point, speaking of "the Christian liturgy, and more precisely still, the Byzantine liturgy of the Eucharist," as the "fundamental place of Dionysius's thought."[24] More recent scholars like Paul Rorem have elaborated on Bouyer's insight.[25] When we read about Moses in *The Mystical Theology*, therefore, we should keep in mind the hierarch who leads the liturgy in *The Ecclesiastical Hierarchy*. Just as Moses must first submit to purification, so the hierarch must wash his hands before the liturgical celebration. When in our passage Moses "pushes ahead to the summit of divine ascents," accompanied only by chosen priests, this further advance corresponds to the way in which the hierarch and his priests approach the altar. Likewise, when in the Mount Sinai narrative Moses moves beyond the audible trumpets and visible lights toward the level of contemplation,

24. Louis Bouyer, "'Mystique.' Essai sur l'histoire d'un mot," *La Vie spirituelle, Supplément* no. 9 (May 15, 1949): 3–23, at 21: "Il convient ici d'insister en effet sur ce second lieu de la 'mystique' aréopagitique, lequel est à vrai dire le lieu fondamental de la pensée de Denys: la liturgie chrétienne, et plus définiment encore la liturgie byzantine de l'Eucharistie."

25. "Pseudo-Dionysian 'mysticism' is intimately related to the liturgy," Rorem writes in *Biblical and Liturgical Symbols within the Pseudo-Dionysian Synthesis*, Studies and Texts 71 (Toronto: Pontifical Institute of Mediaeval Studies, 1984), 142. Similarly, Alexander Golitzin declares: "The *ascensus montis Dei* is at the same time an *ingressus ad altare Dei*, a movement into the living core of the Christian mystery: to Christ in heaven, on the altar, and in the heart" (*Mystagogy: A Monastic Reading of Dionysius Areopagita*, Cistercian Studies Series 250 [Collegeville, MN: Liturgical Press, 2013], 40).

we should think of the hierarch, who knows how to interpret the Scriptures according to their spiritual meaning. Moses's final ascent into the darkness of unknowing evinces the third power of the ecclesiastical hierarchy, which is the power of perfection.[26]

Several commentators have noted the absence of love in the mystical ascent as Pseudo-Dionysius describes it. Indeed, love is absent not only in the passage on which we are commenting, but there is no mention of it in the entire *Mystical Theology*. Jan Vanneste is the scholar who has drawn attention most emphatically to what seems to be a love-less, intellectual form of mysticism that is more reminiscent of pagan Neoplatonism than of authentic Christian spirituality.[27] But here, too, replacing the treatise in the Dionysian corpus as a whole may relieve some anxieties. In fact, *The Divine Names* treats goodness as God's most important name. This goodness in turn calls forth love as the appropriate response from his creation: "And so it is that all things must desire, must yearn for, must love, the Beautiful and the Good."[28] Nevertheless, it is undeniable that the mystical ascent as *The Mystical Theology* envisages it emphasizes intellectual ascesis more than growth in love.[29]

But then, one has to admit that Moses's ascent on Mount Sinai—which, after all, serves Pseudo-Dionysius as the paradigm for the mystical experience—seems to have no place for love either. Nevertheless, the New Testament account of God, with its emphasis on the loving God, is subtly present in Dionysius's adaptation of the Mount Sinai narrative. Most significantly, the violent aspects of the vetero-testamentary episode have disappeared altogether: the repeated threats that anyone transgressing the

26. See Rorem, *Biblical and Liturgical Symbols*, 140–42, and *The Ecclesiastical Hierarchy*, chap. 5.1: "Concerning the Clerical Orders, Powers, Activities, and Consecrations" (*The Complete Works*, 233–39).

27. See Jan Vanneste, SJ, *Le mystère de Dieu. Essai sur la structure rationnelle de la doctrine mystique du pseudo-Denys l'Aréopagite*, Museum Lessianum, Section philosophique 45 (Bruges and Paris: Desclée de Brouwer, 1959). Father Vanneste summarized the gist of his argument in the following English article: "Is the Mysticism of Pseudo-Dionysius Genuine?," *International Philosophical Quarterly* 3 (1963): 286–306.

28. Pseudo-Dionysius the Areopagite, *The Divine Names*, chap. 4, #10, in *The Complete Works*, 79.

29. A point that Vanneste emphasizes—indeed, overemphasizes—in repeatedly insisting on how "cold" the portrayal of mystical theology is in Dionysius; see "Is the Mysticism of Pseudo-Dionysius Genuine?," 292, 295. Vanneste's argument, ultimately, is that in *The Mystical Theology* there are no signs of the kind of personal mystical experience that only a bestowal of supernatural grace could explain.

limits around the mountain will perish; the emphasis on the mortal danger of encountering God too closely; and the fact that even Moses returns in some way disfigured, or at least transformed in a frightful way, from the top of the mountain. As a consequence, one could say that Dionysius's version of the Mount Sinai narrative redefines the transgressive register. What is being overstepped, in Dionysius's account, are not physical boundaries, but rather intellectual limitations, that is to say, the inability of the human mind to grasp God conceptually. These limitations are left behind in a purgation of the human mind through a process of negation: every concept that the human mind believed gave it a hold on God must be renounced. The final chapter of *The Mystical Theology* teaches a progressive conceptual ascesis that culminates in the renunciation of any human language, whether positive or negative, in relation to God:

> Again, as we climb higher we say this. It is not soul or mind, nor does it possess imagination, conviction, speech, or understanding. . . . It cannot be grasped by the understanding since it is neither knowledge nor truth. It is not kingship. It is not wisdom. It is neither one nor oneness, divinity nor goodness. . . . It is not sonship or fatherhood, and it is nothing known to us or to any other being. It falls neither within the predicate of nonbeing nor of being. . . . [I]t is both beyond every assertion, being the perfect and unique cause of all things, and, by virtue of its preeminently simple and absolute nature, free of every limitation, beyond every limitation; it is also beyond every denial.[30]

Together with all its concepts and logic, whether affirmative or negative, the human intellect must eschew any desire to shape thoughts actively, giving itself over in total passivity "to him who is beyond everything." This subjection of the mind—this transformation of the subject into subject —deprives the self of its boundaries: "Here, being neither oneself nor someone else, one is supremely united to the completely unknown by an inactivity of all knowledge, and knows beyond the mind by knowing nothing."[31] In this sense, we are indeed dealing with a transgression here. But, by comparison with the Mount Sinai narrative, the transgression has been

---

30. Pseudo-Dionysius the Areopagite, *The Mystical Theology*, chap. 5, in *The Complete Works*, 141.

31. Pseudo-Dionysius the Areopagite, *The Mystical Theology*, chap. 5, in *The Complete Works*, 141.

internalized. It is now a transgression of self, rather than an overstepping of physical boundaries.

If there is any danger to such a renunciation of self, Pseudo-Dionysius adverts to it only indirectly and discreetly: "But see to it," he writes, fictionally addressing Saint Timothy, "that none of this comes to the hearing of the uninitiated (τῶν ἀμυήτων), that is to say, to those caught up with the things of the world, who imagine that there is nothing beyond instances of individual being and who think that by their own intellectual resources they can have a direct knowledge of him who has made the shadows his hiding place."[32] The idea that the mystical ascent and the negative theology with which it is connected are not to be revealed to people of insufficient intellectual purity is inherent in the very term "mystical." The Greek word μυστικός suggests something that is mysterious and hidden because only the μύσται, those initiated into the secret, have been granted access. In the context of the pagan mystery cults, the word designated in particular the secret of the rite itself, rather than any doctrinal content.[33] The term carries a different but still related meaning in New Testament passages where the revelation of the gospel is seen as inaccessible to nonbelievers. Matthew 13:11 is an example: "Because to you it is given to know the mysteries (μυστήρια) of heaven: but to them it is not given" (cf. Mark 4:11 and Luke 8:10). In the Pauline epistles, however, "mystery" receives the more banal sense of a deep religious truth, and does not appear to have any "exclusive" connotations (as in Eph. 3:9; 6:19; Col. 1:26).

In Pseudo-Dionysius, by contrast, the talk about "mystery" retains some of these connotations, as is clear from his use of the term ἀμύητος to designate the kind of person to whom his teachings should not be disclosed. The "limits" from the Mount Sinai narrative, then, have not disappeared, although their transgression is no longer associated with violence. In fact, it remains unclear what happens if the mysteries *are* revealed to the uninitiated. Perhaps the ἀμύητοι would simply fail to understand, just as those outside the community of his followers fail to penetrate Jesus's parables (Mark 4:11). But it is important not to cast pearls before swine,

---

32. Pseudo-Dionysius the Areopagite, *The Mystical Theology*, chap. 1, #2, in *The Complete Works*, 136; *Corpus Dionysiacum II*, p. 142, ll. 12–15. Luibheid translates τῶν ἀμυήτων as "of the uninformed," a phrase that fails to convey the connection of the term with the initiation into religious mysteries.

33. As Bouyer stresses, in order to distinguish the Christian use of the term from its pagan roots; see "'Mystique.' Essai sur l'histoire d'un mot," 6.

"lest perhaps they trample them under their feet, and turning upon you, they tear you" (Matt. 7:6).

Concerning transgression, one important aspect of the Exodus account seems to have completely disappeared in the interpretation that *The Mystical Theology* offers. In discussing the Exodus narrative, we called God the "primary transgressor," in that he takes the initiative to cross the boundaries between the sacred and the profane, showing himself—even though through multiple veils—at the summit of Mount Sinai. The Lord, furthermore, calls Moses repeatedly to meet him at the mountaintop. In Pseudo-Dionysius's adaptation, on the other hand, there is no reference at all to a divine initiative. It might appear, therefore, that the ascent of the mystic is driven entirely by the logic of negation, that is, by intellectual purification. Again, one could object that such a reading ignores the liturgical context of *The Mystical Theology*. This objection seems valid; what is more, Dionysius's emphasis on the passivity of the one who enters the darkness of unknowing at least implies that the initiative in this encounter is all on God's side.

Pseudo-Dionysius does bring out strongly another dimension of the Mount Sinai narrative, namely, the hierarchy of people who are called to the mountain. The Exodus story distinguishes three groups, with some ambiguities as well as differences between chapters 19 and 24:

1. The general people of Israel, who are not allowed to proceed beyond the limits (according to Exod. 19:24, this group includes the priesthood);
2. Moses, Aaron, Nadab, Abihu, and the seventy elders of Israel, who are allowed to ascend the mountain up to a certain point (Exod. 24:9 has the complete list, whereas Exod. 19:24 mentions only Aaron as accompanying Moses, leaving it unclear up to what point); and
3. Moses himself, who completes the ascent to the summit and meets the Lord in the cloud.

The Mystical Theology modifies this list, updating it to reflect the realities of the Christian community and liturgy.

1. In the first place, there is a division between those who have undergone purification and those who have not. As already indicated, the purification in question echoes the washing of the hands by the hierarch celebrating the liturgy; but there was also a general purification for all the people.

2. Then, Moses leaves behind the "crowds" and begins his ascent in the company of "chosen priests." Those having received ordination can hardly be excluded from a Christian hierarchy, or simply be assimilated to the crowds of laypeople, which is why they quietly take the place of Moses's closest relatives and associates. Dionysius makes sure to clarify that this group gets to see only where God "dwells"; that is to say, the members of the group grasp only the *logoi* of creation that point to its Creator. This interpretation takes care of Exodus 24:10, where the biblical text asserts of Moses and those accompanying him: "And they saw the God of Israel."

3. Finally, Moses "breaks free" of his company, proceeding into the cloud of unknowing.

In the Exodus account of the ascent, Moses returns from the mountaintop with the law; the objective of his encounter with the Lord is covenantal and communal. Again, we find Pseudo-Dionysius silent on this issue. But if we take the liturgical context of the passage seriously, we should understand that the hierarch, whom Moses has come to symbolize for Dionysius, exercises a teaching function. As part of his role as the liturgical mediator between the Lord and his people, the hierarch is called to exegete the Scriptures in light of the ineffable transcendence of God that the mystical union has revealed to him. It would be a large mistake, therefore, to read the Dionysian account of the mystical union in modern subjective terms, as a "psychological experience considered solely or primarily in its subjectivity."[34] There is a personal element in the mystical union, to be sure, to the extent that it involves a specific self and soul; the meaning of the union, however, transcends the individual.

For a theory of tradition, the comparison between the Exodus narrative and its Pseudo-Dionysian adaptation yields several insights. In essence, we witness a work of translation, in its broad sense of a transference of meaning from one historical situation to another. Thus, Moses becomes the hierarch; the ascent of Mount Sinai symbolizes the progress of Christian intellectual ascesis; the cloud in whose veil God appears assumes the meaning of his fundamental unknowability by the human intellect; and so forth. This work of translation is driven not only by the individual lit-

---

34. Bouyer, "'Mystique.' Essai sur l'histoire d'un mot," 21–22: "S'il en est ainsi, on comprend finalement que la 'mystique' chez les Pères ne se réduise jamais à une expérience psychologique considérée seulement ou premièrement dans sa subjectivité."

erary and religious imagination of Pseudo-Dionysius but also by a vast hermeneutic mechanism that has its roots in the Gospels—in particular, the Gospel according to Matthew, where Jesus appears as the new Moses. (The relationship, more generally, between the Old Testament and its "fulfillment" in the New will occupy us in the next chapter.) Furthermore, in treating Moses's life, or an episode from it, as symbolizing the soul's journey to God, Pseudo-Dionysius was preceded by other writers in the Greek tradition—most famously, Gregory of Nyssa.[35]

Dionysius's translation is not, and cannot be, seamless: as in any such work of cultural adaptation, emphases shift, misunderstandings generate new meanings, and elements of the original are forgotten. Thus, we have noted how the meaning of the limits, and therefore of transgression, changes between the two texts. In the Exodus account, we are dealing with physical limits around a mountain, and the transgression of these limits is a physical overstepping as well. Therefore, the consequences of such overstepping are bluntly physical also: death or—in the case of Moses, who alone is allowed into God's presence—some kind of bodily disfigurement. In *The Mystical Theology*, Pseudo-Dionysius endows the limits and the transgression with a new spiritual significance, while the death that, in Exodus, follows the transgression is perhaps still echoed in the effacing of the self that occurs at the mystical summit. The way in which Moses's contact with God removes him from the ordinary Israelites is taken up in the "mystical" character of the Pseudo-Dionysian teaching: "See to it that none of this comes to the hearing of the uninitiated." As for elements of the original story that disappear in its Dionysian version, the exclusion of the priests among the ordinary people who are forbidden to cross the limits seems most significant.

We now turn to another, later adaptation of the Mount Sinai narrative.

The Pseudo-Peter of Poitiers Gloss

Pseudo-Peter of Poitiers was not Peter of Poitiers. Who he was, exactly, we do not know, just as we have no precise information on the identity of the author of the corpus of writings long attributed to Dionysius the Areopagite. Pseudo-Peter of Poitiers, however, did not deliberately claim the

---

35. See Gregory of Nyssa, *The Life of Moses*, trans. Abraham J. Malherbe and Everett Ferguson, Classics of Western Spirituality (New York: Paulist Press, 1978).

identity of another. Rather, as with many other texts in the age of the manuscript, his gloss on the *Book of Sentences* circulated under an incorrect name because of a copyist's error, or some similar accident in the transmission of the work. It is certainly instructive to what extent the foundation and growth of a tradition are subject to "pure historical contingency," to cite an expression by Alasdair MacIntyre.[36] A tradition is not the product of self-transparent subjectivity. Its sources are obscure, often being hidden, beyond recovery, in the fog of history. We already made a similar observation in relation to the book of Exodus.

The Pseudo-Peter of Poitiers gloss on the *Book of Sentences* was a minor but nonetheless pedagogically influential text. The first continuous commentary on Peter Lombard's standard theology textbook, its successive "editions," as we would say, served as an introduction to Peter Lombard's work from the 1160s until at least the first decades of the fourteenth century.[37] During the long period of its use, it helped shape the minds of countless theologians.

The Pseudo-Poitiers gloss interprets the Mount Sinai narrative in its prologue, which provides a traditional *accessus* to the *Book of Sentences*, that is to say, an introduction that answers certain basic questions about topics such as the author, subject matter, structure, method, intention, audience, and usefulness of the work.[38] The allegorical interpretation of Exodus occurs as the prologue deals with the audience of the *Sentences*:

> Now the Master composed this book for three kinds of people, namely, for the faint-hearted (or those fleeing), for the lazy ones, and for the blasphemers. All of these are sufficiently prefigured in the Old Testament. In fact, according to the commandment of the Lord limits had been established by Moses around Mount Sinai, which it was not lawful for the people to cross, lest they see the Lord and perish. When the Lord called and Moses ascended the mountain, Hur, Aaron, Joshua, and the seventy (who were to receive of his spirit) followed him right to the limits. However, as Moses was staying with the Lord on the mountain, Hur, Aaron, and the seventy went back, fatigued by the tedium of the divine

---

36. The term is from MacIntyre, *Whose Justice? Which Rationality?*, 354.

37. See Marcia L. Colish, "The Pseudo-Peter of Poitiers Gloss," in *Mediaeval Commentaries on the "Sentences" of Peter Lombard*, vol. 2, ed. Philipp W. Rosemann (Leiden and Boston: Brill, 2010), 1–33 (see 11 for a mention of the gloss in 1316).

38. See the classic treatment of this subject by Edwin A. Quain, SJ, *The Medieval Accessus ad Auctores* (New York: Fordham University Press, 1986).

waiting. Only Joshua remained by the limits, anxious for the return of his master. The following could have occurred, [although] it is not reported that many of the people perished after crossing the limits.

The mountain that Moses ascended is mystically understood as Sacred Scripture, which exists in the immovable stability of both Testaments. It is protected so that it is not lawful to contradict it. The limits set around the mountain are mystically understood as the explanations of the saints, whose footsteps we are obliged to follow, lest we cross the limits that our fathers have set. By Moses, who ascended the mountain when God called, those are mystically understood who in the early church ascended through great divine inspiration to the eminence of the Sacred Page—such as Paul and the other apostles, who as the Holy Spirit dictated [to them] penetrated the profound and obscure [dimensions] of Sacred Scripture. Besides them, however, there are those who ascend right to the limits, yet neither cross them nor turn back out of lack of confidence—such as the eager doctors who apply themselves tenaciously to the thorough examination of Sacred Scripture. They are signified by Joshua. [Then] there are those who come right to the limits, but turn back tired—namely those who, considering the large number of books of the Sacred Page, lose confidence in themselves and therefore return to the other faculties, like dogs to vomit [see Prov. 26:11 and 2 Pet. 2:22]. Those are called faint-hearted or given to flight; they are indicated figuratively by Hur, Aaron, and the seventy. There are others who do not even reach the limits; who, *entangled with secular businesses* [2 Tim. 2:4], do not study or ask anything about Sacred Scripture. They are the lazy ones, signified by those who did not even venture to leave the camp. [Again,] there are others who cross the limits and perish, like the heretics who esteem the explanations of the saints less than their own inventions. They are the blasphemers, signified by those who perhaps perished after crossing the limits.

It is for these three kinds of people that the Master composed this book: for the faint-hearted or those given to flight, in order to call them back by means of the brevity of the work; for the lazy ones, to spur them on through the easiness of the work; [and] for the blasphemers, to refute them by the authorities of the saints.[39]

---

39. For the Latin text on which this translation is based, see the appendix. The present book does not address the question of the sources of the prologue. Since an article that Raymond-M. Martin, OP, published in 1931, we know that the Pseudo-Poitiers text relies

Why the most influential theology textbook of the Western tradition is here considered to have been composed as a kind of remedial tool for those at the margins of the learned community—or even of orthodoxy—is an interesting question, but not one on which we can dwell in the present context. Let us only say that, even in the twelfth century, theology as we understand it—that is to say, as a branch of learning systematically representing our knowledge of all things divine—had not yet consciously constituted itself as a discipline. The masters and students in the schools of the nascent scholastic movement studied what they called *sacra pagina*, the "Sacred Page," theological reflection still being conceived as nothing but commentary in the margins of God's Word. In fact, that is how the *Book of Sentences* itself began: as scriptural commentary, which then gradually assumed a more systematic and independent shape.[40] This is why the author of the Pseudo-Peter of Poitiers gloss views Peter Lombard's work as nothing that possesses value in itself. The function it serves is auxiliary: to help those who are either too afraid or too lazy to study the Sacred Page, and to rebut others whose lack of orthodoxy renders them unworthy of approaching Scripture.

With great precision, the author of the Pseudo-Peter of Poitiers gloss maps his "mystical" interpretation onto the text of Exodus. The mountain, we learn, corresponds to Sacred Scripture. The limits around it signify the limits of orthodox interpretation as the fathers of the church have defined it. Moses stands for inspired writers who, going beyond the fathers, were able to penetrate the most profound and obscure levels of the biblical text—like Saint Paul and the other apostles who composed letters to elucidate the gospel. Joshua (whom Exod. 24:13 mentions in passing as accompanying Moses in his ascent) is associated with those interpreters of Scripture who proceed right to the limits of interpretation, without ever overstepping them. Aaron, Hur (who is mentioned in Exod. 24:14), and the seventy take on a decidedly negative connotation as they come to signify those readers of Scripture who do not go far enough, losing confidence in their ability to approach the sacred text. The people staying in the valley are just too lazy to attempt a serious reading of the Sacred Page at all. Finally, those who "perhaps" perished

heavily on a prologue to the *Sentences* attributed to Peter Comestor; see Raymond-M. Martin, OP, "Notes sur l'œuvre littéraire de Pierre le Mangeur," *Recherches de théologie ancienne et médiévale* 3 (1931): 54–66.

40. See Philipp W. Rosemann, *Peter Lombard*, Great Medieval Thinkers (New York: Oxford University Press, 2004), 43–53.

after transgressing the limits (the gloss says "perhaps" because the biblical text does not include an account of lives actually lost) correspond to heretical interpreters of Scripture, who stray from the tradition of the fathers.

Now let us unpack this interpretation in more detail.

1. *Scripture as Sacred Place.* The Pseudo-Poitiers gloss imagines Scripture as being just as immovable and stable as Mount Sinai: the letter of the Word of God is unchangeable like the rocks that form this mountain. The sacredness of Mount Sinai, however, is not simply due to the fact that it is an impressive part of God's creation; it is the place of a special encounter between God and his people. Following the logic of the allegory, then, Scripture is envisaged here not only statically as an immovable mountain, but also dynamically as the locus where God meets the readers of his Word. God's Word is not simply "given" in Scripture, but it reveals itself only to those willing to make the ascent to it. Without such an effort, it remains "obscure," as our text says, a series of dead letters. The Pseudo-Poitiers gloss thus conceives of Scripture as a revealing of God in the verbal sense, an unveiling that occurs only in the process of interpretation.

This dynamic meaning of revelation is nothing unusual or unique to the text we are discussing. The history of theology has long established that medieval thinkers tended to consider revelation not in its global sense—Scripture as revelation—but rather in terms of individual acts: God reveals himself to an attentive member of his church who is engaged in the kind of interpretative effort that the Pseudo-Poitiers gloss has in mind.

It is not a coincidence that the gloss refers to the "mystical" understanding of Scripture. As Joseph Ratzinger pointed out in his controversial *Habilitationsschrift, revelatio* is a term that medieval thinkers applied both to the manner in which God becomes accessible to those profoundly—"mystically"—contemplating his Word, and to God's self-revelation in the mystical ascent. More than that, interpreting Scripture mystically is an indispensable step in the ascent toward the cloud of unknowing, an ascent that, having gone through Scripture, finally transgresses it.[41]

41. On the notion of revelation in early scholastic theology, see Joseph Ratzinger, *The Theology of History in St. Bonaventure*, trans. Zachary Hayes, OFM (Chicago: Franciscan Herald Press, 1989), esp. 57–59, 86–94. Because it was so controversial—almost costing him his academic career—the full text of the pope's *Habilitationsschrift* has become available only recently: Joseph Ratzinger, *Offenbarungsverständnis und Geschichtstheologie Bonaventuras. Habilitationsschrift und Bonaventura-Studien*, Gesammelte Schriften 2 (Freiburg im Breisgau:

2. *The Meaning of the Limits.* In the Exodus narrative, Moses is both the one on whom God calls to establish boundaries around Mount Sinai and the one who is authorized to transgress the same boundaries in order to meet the Lord at the top. The Pseudo-Poitiers gloss appears to assign these two roles to distinct groups of people, respectively the church fathers and the authors of the apostolic letters.

a. Insofar as Moses ascends the mountain, he is seen as prefiguring "Paul and the other apostles, who as the Holy Spirit dictated [to them] penetrated the profound and obscure [dimensions] of Sacred Scripture." Why is Paul singled out here as one of the New Testament authors? The allegory makes sense only if we assume a distinction between a core of New Testament texts that existed before Paul and others were given the opportunity, by divine inspiration, to penetrate it. This core must be identical with the Gospels, in which Jesus, the Son, appears in person (albeit veiled in human flesh), just as the Father (veiled in a cloud) appeared to Moses on the mountaintop. Again, just as the Lord spoke to his people only through the mediation of Moses, who recognized and responded to God's call, so the Gospels require the mediation of the apostles, who, as Jesus's first followers, recognized him as the Son of God and were therefore in a position to reveal his message to others. This revelation occurred in the apostolic letters.

b. In Exodus, the limits separating the sacred mountain from the profane world of everyday life are due to an order the Lord himself issues. This appears different in the Pseudo-Poitiers gloss, which associates them with the church fathers; there is no mention of a divine initiative in their establishment. This difference requires a nuanced interpretation. First, although the limits show themselves only in the process of interpretation, that process does continue to be guided by divine assistance—after all, the church fathers fulfill a function whose Old Testament analogue is carried out by Moses at God's direct command. Moreover, and as already indicated, the early scholastic notion of *revelatio* was more dynamic than the modern one. Revelation does not occur, in the medieval understanding, once and for all in the static letters of a closed canon of Scripture; rather, it is an unveiling of God's scriptural message as it is unfolded in successive generations of readers. The fathers, in particular, are "indissolubly connected with Scripture," as Ratzinger has noted. "There is as yet no boundary line

---

Herder, 2009). This text treats the meaning of *revelatio* in scholastic theology, and especially in Bonaventure, in comprehensive detail.

drawn between Scripture and the Fathers.... They are the bearers of a new spiritual 'revelation,' without which the Scriptures simply would not be effective as revelation."[42]

Against this background, it may be best to amalgamate the two groups that we have distinguished following the lead of the gloss. For a coherent interpretation, we need to include in the group of "saints, whose footsteps we are obliged to follow," not only the fathers of the church but also the authors of the apostolic letters. It is these groups together who define the limits of interpretation on the basis of an inspired reading of what is most "profound and obscure" in the Scriptures.

There is a divinely sanctioned boundary, then, both in Exodus and in the Pseudo-Poitiers gloss, but the precise way in which this boundary operates varies in the two cases. In the former, the limit is defined at a precise moment, once and for all; in the latter, the process of interpretation generates the limit organically, and insofar as the process of interpretation may lead to further revelation of the divine, it is not clear that the limit, though real, is in principle unchangeable. Of course, even in the Exodus narrative, especially in the version of chapter 24, the limit is portrayed as being less than absolute, in that it allows a larger group of people to transgress.

3. *The Significance of Transgression.* This leads us to the significance of transgression in the Pseudo-Poitiers adaptation of the Exodus passage. Exodus places repeated emphasis upon the deadly danger of transgression; the Pseudo-Poitiers gloss is less emphatic, but it completes the Exodus account by imagining that transgressions actually occurred around Mount Sinai, leading to the death of the transgressors.[43] The physical death that the twelfth-century text imagines punished those who violated the boundary parallels the spiritual death that the heretics incur whose scriptural interpretation fails to be in accordance with the tradition of orthodoxy. Exodus paints in vivid colors the danger of the boundary even for someone authorized to cross it, such as Moses, for God's appearance is accompanied by signs of his overwhelming might and leaves the one who encountered him physically altered. There is much less emphasis on the frightfulness of the encounter at the top of the mountain in the Pseudo-Poitiers gloss. This

42. Ratzinger, *The Theology of History,* 79–80.

43. The text makes it very clear here that it is going beyond the Exodus account. The first sentence where the death of the transgressors is mentioned states, in less than perfect Latin, *potuit et esse haec non legatur,* which must mean something like "This could have been [although] it is not read [in Exodus]." Later in the passage we hear of those who "perhaps" (*forte*) perished when they crossed the limit.

is to be expected, because what the "saints" meet at the top of the mountain is not God himself, but the gospel account of his incarnation—in other words, God's presence is more mediated. This mediation naturally renders the original drama of the irruption of the divine less frightful.

Let us note, nonetheless, that in the Exodus narrative, just as in its twelfth-century adaptation, a foundational act of transgression occurs, and necessarily so. Moses would not have received the law had he not followed the Lord's call to climb to the mountaintop, leaving the limits around Mount Sinai behind. The tradition of scriptural interpretation as the Pseudo-Poitiers gloss depicts it is founded in the transgression of the normal limits of interpretation by a group of people whom the Holy Spirit inspires in their exploration of the *profunda et obscura sacre scripture*.

4. *The Hierarchy of Mediation.* The Pseudo-Poitiers gloss views the interpretation of Scripture as transmitted in a tradition that involves multiple layers of mediation. Jesus's voice as heard in the Gospels is first reflected upon by the apostolic letters, then further interpreted by the church fathers. These exegetes determine the limits of orthodoxy, which the "eager doctors" accept as they assimilate what has been handed down. Even this assimilation, which is depicted as docile rather than foundational, requires a certain degree of courage. The fainthearted, after all, find Scripture too daunting to approach. Note that the interpretation of Scripture always remains in authorized hands; there is no room in our gloss for the modern notion according to which the ordinary faithful have direct access to God's Word.

To conclude, the value of the Pseudo-Peter of Poitiers gloss consists in the fact that it articulates the structure of biblical interpretation on the basis of Scripture itself, by reading a specific scriptural passage at a metalevel as conveying not only a particular content (namely, the events at Mount Sinai) but also the way to approach that content, and all biblical content. The scriptural passage that the author of the gloss has chosen for his "mystical" reading depicts, appropriately, the foundation of the covenant, that is to say, of God's relationship with his people through the law.

Scripture, in the account given by the twelfth-century gloss, is the sacred locus of an encounter with God. In Scripture, God offers us his Word, but hearing it requires the effort of an ascent. Because God appears to us only veiled, Scripture is fundamentally obscure. To penetrate this obscurity is a dangerous task, so that it can be accomplished only by mediators who are inspired by God himself. These mediators form a hierarchy, but they also form a chronological succession: first Paul and the apostles, then the church fathers, then the "eager doctors" of the schools. Our text is remarkable in that it exhibits an inchoate awareness of the role of time and history in the transmission of texts and ideas. The mediators provide a bridge between the sacred obscurity of God's Word and its reception in the profane world of everyday existence—just as Moses's encounter on Mount Sinai brought the law down into the valley, from the dark cloud in which Moses found God at the summit.

Transgression is a condition for the possibility of this mediation. Earlier, we called God the primary "transgressor": he takes the initiative to show himself on the mountain, just as he takes the initiative to become incarnate, suspending the boundaries between the human and the divine in his Son. Human beings respond to God's transgression by one of their own. Thus, Moses is called to cross the limits and meet the Lord on the mountain, an experience that transforms him into a satyr-like, frightful creature. The mystical ascent as Pseudo-Dionysius envisages it culminates in a breakdown of the boundaries of the human subject: the mystical union. Thus, the irruptions of the divine into the human world are dangerous—so dangerous that everyday folk need to be protected from them lest they die. Only the chosen few are called to transgress the limits—or to establish them in the first place, as Moses did by promulgating the law and the church fathers did by defining standards of interpretation. Ordinary people will die—physically or spiritually—if they transgress these limits. Why? Because the limits define the very structures in which human beings live. In the Old Testament, the acceptance of God's law in the covenant defines a new community; it constitutes the identity of Israel. Likewise, the reading of Scripture creates the community of the Christian tradition, through which those belonging to this tradition understand themselves. Heretics stand outside.

CHAPTER 2

The Incarnate God as the New Moses

The incarnation was an even more dramatic irruption of the divine Other than Moses's encounter with the Lord on Mount Sinai. It involved more than the Lord descending on a mountain to speak to his prophet, who had to overstep certain limits to reach the summit. The incarnation involved the transgression of the boundary between the human and the divine, indeed the fusion of the two, in the person of Jesus, the God-man. God himself paid the price for this transgression—death, which the Son suffered upon the cross. In the crucifixion, God embraced and redeemed man in his most abject and broken condition. We will see, however, that the cross did not free the human being from the yoke of violence, except in an eschatological sense; for the Christian is called to follow Christ on the path of self-sacrifice.

The historical circumstances in which the incarnation occurred—in a Jewish man who lived in the Roman Empire at the time of Augustus and Tiberius—helped determine the ways in which the God-man and the religious community that formed around him defined their identity. Presented as the new Moses in the Gospel according to Saint Matthew, Jesus said about himself that he had "not come to destroy, but to fulfill" (Matt. 5:17) the covenant of the Old Testament. The notion of fulfillment entails a complex—and, one is tempted to say, fateful—interplay of identity and difference, continuity and transgression, between Jesus's message and its Jewish roots. As for the religious and philosophical values of the Greco-Roman world, Saint Paul's word of the "foolishness of the cross" suggests a radical rejection, but here, too, the situation is more complex than it might first appear to be.

The New Moses

The fact that Jesus came to fulfill the old covenant, as the promised Messiah, is evident throughout the New Testament, but it is brought out particularly clearly and deliberately in the Gospel according to Saint Matthew. It was composed between AD 80 and AD 100 by a Jewish author deeply rooted in his tradition for whom it was crucial to show that Jesus, although he was "destabilizing" this tradition, did not destroy and abolish it, but rather brought it to completion. Studying the way in which Matthew presents Jesus as a new Moses, Dale Allison summarized his findings in these words: "Thus the newness we encounter in Matthew is that of completion, and it always gives us a *déjà vu*: there is repetition and the past lives on."[1] Building upon Allison's textual analyses, we can point out several ways in which Matthew's Gospel lets us see Jesus's life and death in light of the Mosaic precedent.

1. In a first, central respect Jesus repeats Moses's life by radicalizing the office of prophet. Moses was called to encounter the Lord on Mount Sinai, where he came close to him, perhaps saw God's "back" but not his face. Above all, Moses heard God's voice. Jesus, on the other hand, *is* God's face. There is no "encounter" between the Father and the Son; there is identity: Jesus is God become visible.

Despite this visibility, God remains veiled even in the incarnation, just as the Lord appeared to Moses as fire, and in a cloud. Because the veil that God uses in the incarnation is human nature itself, it is possible to mistake Jesus for a mere man. This of course happened, both in Jesus's own time and throughout history: God took the risk of not being recognized even when he was seen face-to-face, in his Son. A hymn in the Letter to the Philippians speaks eloquently of the way in which God lowered himself in taking the "habit" of a man:

> [Christ Jesus] who being in the form of God, thought it not robbery to
> be equal with God;
> But emptied himself (ἐκένωσεν), taking the form of a servant (δούλου),
> being made in the likeness of men, and in habit (σχήματι) found
> as a man.
> He humbled himself, becoming obedient unto death, even to the death
> of the cross. (Phil. 2:6–8)

---

1. Dale C. Allison Jr., *The New Moses: A Matthean Typology* (Minneapolis: Fortress, 1993), 273. The reference to the "destabilizing tradition" is on the same page.

Some medieval theologians took verse 7—"in habit found as a man," *habitu inventus ut homo*—as evidence of the so-called "*habitus* theory of the incarnation," according to which Christ wore man like a piece of clothing.[2] While this theory has fallen out of favor, it does not have to be read as failing to do justice to the reality of the union between God and man. One needs to bear in mind what clothing used to be in the ancient world (and in fact, was until fairly recently): a revelation of the identity of its wearer.[3] The passage in Philippians certainly does not see an incompatibility between Christ's taking on the habit of a man and the reality of his self-humiliation.

In Jesus, God's "emptying" of himself, his *kenōsis*, was extreme; yet it was not without precedent. God already "lowered" himself by speaking to Moses on the mountain—a situation for which we have used the term "transgression" to designate God's overstepping the boundary between the divine and the created world. In meeting Moses, however, the Lord, as it were, just barely crossed this boundary; in Jesus, he immersed himself in the material world, becoming united with it. This extreme transgression culminated in the cross, where Jesus was executed like a slave—for the word δοῦλος, which the Douay-Rheims version tactfully renders as "servant," did mean "slave" in the ancient world.[4] Moses, we recall, also had to pay a physical price for meeting the Lord: perhaps he became horned. Whatever happened to him, his appearance became sufficiently terrifying and unbearable to his fellow Israelites that he had to cover his face. Jesus's crucified body was totally mangled; that is the price he paid for assuming man, and man's burden.

Two millennia of familiarity with descriptions and depictions of the crucifixion have rendered us immune to the horrors of this punishment. An entire tradition built on Christ's redeeming death on the cross has largely forgotten what the cross was, historically. It was not a symbol of

2. Peter Lombard summarizes the *habitus* theory in his *Book of Sentences*, adducing evidence for it from Augustine and Hilary; see *The Sentences*, book 3, trans. Giulio Silano, Mediaeval Sources in Translation 45 (Toronto: Pontifical Institute of Mediaeval Studies, 2008), dist. 6, chaps. 4–5 (pp. 28–30). For further discussion of the *habitus* theory, forcefully defended in the school of Peter Lombard, see Lauge Olaf Nielsen, *Theology and Philosophy in the Twelfth Century: A Study of Gilbert Porreta's Thinking and the Theological Expositions of the Doctrine of the Incarnation during the Period 1130–1180*, Acta theologica danica 15 (Leiden: Brill, 1982), 279–361.

3. On this point, see note 8 in Chapter 1.

4. For an insightful discussion of δοῦλος, one may read the detailed entry in Gerhard Kittel's *Theological Dictionary of the New Testament*, ed. and trans. Geoffrey W. Bromiley, vol. 2 (Grand Rapids: Eerdmans, 1964), 261–79 (278–79 treat Phil. 2:7).

ecclesiastical power nor an objet d'art. Let us remind ourselves that the Romans generally reserved crucifixion for criminals who were noncitizens. Indeed, according to Martin Hengel, "in most Roman writers crucifixion appears as the typical punishment for slaves."[5] Although crucifixion was frequent in imperial Rome, the writers of the period talked about it rarely and reluctantly: the unspeakable suffering that it inflicted was a taboo, something that could not fully be assimilated into language.[6] Commentators on Scripture, too, have noted the brevity with which this central event of the Gospel is dispatched. In Matthew 27, the actual crucifixion occurs somewhere between verse 31 (the soldiers "led him away to crucify him") and verse 35 ("after they had crucified him . . ."). The lines in between pass over the details that would have been involved in the nailing of the Lord to the cross. The crucifixion occurs between the lines, so to speak, in a space marked by silence.[7] Like other victims of crucifixion, Jesus died naked, as Matthew 27:35 narrates: "And after they had crucified him, they divided his garments, casting lots." It is uncertain whether the loincloth that is traditional in depictions of the crucifixion corresponds to historical reality.[8] "By the public display of a naked victim at a prominent place," Hengel explains, "crucifixion . . . represented his uttermost humiliation, which had a numinous dimension to it."[9] This is the heart of the Christian tradition:

5. Martin Hengel, *Crucifixion in the Ancient World and the Folly of the Cross* (Philadelphia: Fortress, 1977), 51. Hengel's short but incisive volume has recently been updated by the painstakingly detailed research of John Granger Cook, *Crucifixion in the Mediterranean World*, Wissenschaftliche Untersuchungen zum Neuen Testament 327 (Tübingen: Mohr Siebeck, 2014).

6. Hengel writes (*Crucifixion*, 38): "Crucifixion was widespread and frequent, above all in Roman times, but the cultured literary world wanted to have nothing to do with it, and as a rule kept quiet about it." Cook, after assembling comprehensive evidence from literary and archaeological sources—Roman, Greek, and Hebrew/Aramaic—comes to the conclusion that "the Gospel accounts are the most extensive of any that have survived antiquity" (*Crucifixion*, 452).

7. Davies and Allison comment: "On the matters of what sort of cross was used to crucify Jesus and how he was fastened upon it Matthew is mute. This betrays more than a lack of morbid curiosity. The dearth of details bespeaks a positive distaste for this most barbarous of ancient tortures" (W. D. Davies and Dale C. Allison Jr., *A Critical and Exegetical Commentary on the Gospel according to Saint Matthew*, vol. 3 [Edinburgh: T. & T. Clark, 1997], 613).

8. Cook, *Crucifixion*, 427, has found evidence suggesting that victims of crucifixions were sometimes entirely nude, but on other occasions may have been wearing some type of undergarment.

9. Hengel, *Crucifixion*, 87. On the distinction between (natural) nakedness and the degrading state of exposure that follows the removal of clothes, in particular with reference to

the God-man tortured to death in public, naked, like a slave, in a situation of ineffable humiliation and horror. Charred root of meaning.

Hengel does not elaborate on his remark according to which crucifixion—and he means crucifixion as such, not just in Jesus's case—had a "numinous dimension" to it. What can be numinous about a spectacle of cruelty and death? The answer is that the sickening sight of a crucifixion confronts the observer with the abject, understood as a phenomenon that lies so totally outside the boundaries of subjectivity, and is so unassimilable to the subject, that it is experienced as wholly Other. The expression "wholly Other" comes from Rudolf Otto, who in his classic analysis of the sacred described the *mysterium tremendum* as fundamental to the experience of the divine. "Aghast" is the term Otto's English translator chose to capture something of the effects of the *mysterium tremendum*, of which Otto wrote: "The awe or dread may indeed be so overwhelmingly great that it seems to penetrate to the very marrow, making the man's hair bristle and his limbs quake."[10] This must have been the effect of a crucifixion.[11]

---

the Old Testament, see Claudia Bender, *Die Sprache des Textilen. Untersuchungen zu Kleidung und Textilien im Alten Testament*, Beiträge zur Wissenschaft vom Alten und Neuen Testament 177 (Stuttgart: Kohlhammer, 2008), 133–47.

10. Rudolf Otto, *The Idea of the Holy: An Inquiry into the Non-Rational Factor in the Idea of the Divine and Its Relation to the Rational*, trans. John W. Harvey, 2nd ed. (Oxford: Oxford University Press; London: Humphrey Milford, 1950), 16. For "aghast," see p. 14, and for "wholly Other," see p. 25. The notion of the abject is explored by Julia Kristeva, *Powers of Horror: An Essay on Abjection*, trans. Leon S. Roudiez (New York: Columbia University Press, 1982).

11. To see something of this effect today, and to grasp how the *mysterium tremendum* can be at the root of a religious quest, one can open the pages of a recent biography of Georges Bataille: Michel Surya, *Georges Bataille: An Intellectual Biography*, trans. Krzysztof Fijalkowski and Michael Richardson (London: Verso, 2002). The illustrations printed at the center of the volume (between pp. 274 and 275) include four photographs of a Chinese execution by means by *lingchi*, or cutting to pieces. In commenting on these images, Surya (pp. 93–95) reproduces the standard (and Bataille's own) account, according to which one of these photographs first came into Bataille's possession in 1925, and was to haunt him for the rest of his life. Again following the standard account, the photographs show the execution of a certain Fuzhuli, who assassinated a Mongolian prince. As Timothy Brook, Jerôme Bourgon, and Gregory Blue (*Death by a Thousand Cuts* [Cambridge, MA: Harvard University Press, 2008], 222–42) have recently demonstrated, however, the photographs depict the torture and death of another, unidentified man. Furthermore, there are so many other inaccuracies in Bataille's account that Brook, Bourgon, and Blue question the authorship of parts of *Les larmes d'éros*, the 1961 work that culminates in the *lingchi* photographs. They offer an interpretation of the *lingchi* photographs in the context of an earlier work, *L'expérience intérieure* (1943), where they say the "tormented man . . . figures as a sort of substitute for the crucified Christ during meditations that approximate the visiting of the stations of the Cross" (233).

In discussing the way in which God's in-mattering in the incarnation constitutes a radicalization of his theophany on Mount Sinai, we can go one step further in considering the Eucharist. As is most evident in the crucifixion, in the incarnation God took on the form of a slave, subjecting himself to human misunderstanding—to the risk, that is, of not being recognized as God. If this risk was a reality in the incarnation, it is even more acute in the Eucharist, which goes beyond even the incarnation in crossing the boundary between Creator and creation. For in the Eucharist, God veils himself in the accidents of bread and wine; that is the habit he wears, to use the language of Philippians. Given the quotidian humbleness of the eucharistic species—food and drink—it is very easy indeed not to see through the veil.[12]

Just as in the crucifixion, there appears a dimension of the abject in the Eucharist. Let me illustrate this claim. One of the standard questions in scholastic discussions of eucharistic theology was, *Quid sumit mus?* What does the mouse eat in case crumbs from the Eucharist drop to the ground undetected, and are left there for vermin to consume? Answers to this question varied; most tellingly perhaps, Peter Lombard in the *Book of Sentences* acknowledged its existence but refused to discuss it. He must have sensed its jarring inappropriateness: Can God be eaten by mice? Appalled by the idea, the Lombard curtly declared: "It may also be truly said that the body of Christ is not received by brute animals, even when they appear to do so. What, then, does a mouse receive? What does it eat? God knows!"[13] This was not to be the last word on the issue, however. In fact, the great scholastic commentaries of the thirteenth century went far beyond the "mouse" question in weighing the most appalling scenarios. Even mentioning them makes one recoil: What if, for instance, the

12. I have developed this line of thought in an article on Jean-Luc Marion; see "Postmodern Philosophy and J.-L. Marion's Eucharistic Realism," in *The Mystery of Faith: Reflections on the Encyclical Ecclesia de Eucharistia*, ed. Maurice Hogan, SSC, and James McEvoy (Blackrock, Co. Dublin: Columba Press, 2005), 224–44; republished with corrections in *Transcendence and Phenomenology*, ed. Peter M. Candler Jr. and Conor Cunningham (London: SCM, 2007), 84–110.

13. Peter Lombard, *The Sentences*, book 4, trans. Giulio Silano, Mediaeval Sources in Translation 48 (Toronto: Pontifical Institute of Mediaeval Studies, 2010), dist. 13, chap. 1, no. 8 (p. 68). For scholarly discussion of the "mouse" problem, one may consult Artur Michael Landgraf, *Dogmengeschichte der Frühscholastik*, vol. III/2, *Die Lehre von den Sakramenten* (Regensburg: Pustet, 1955), 207–22; and, more recently, Gary Macy, "Of Mice and Manna: Quid Mus Sumit as a Pastoral Question," *Recherches de théologie ancienne et médiévale* 58 (1991): 157–66.

Eucharist is vomited up, or thrown into a latrine?[14] These possibilities indicate the extent to which God has emptied himself, entering into the region of the abject.

To complete this first part of our discussion of the "new Moses," we note that the elements of terror that threatened God's people in the Mount Sinai narrative—the thunder, the lightning, the trumpets, the limits drawn around the mountain that were accompanied by threats of death, Moses's horns—have in the incarnation been transferred onto the God-man himself. On Mount Sinai, the root of meaning is charred because God is terrifying in his might; on Calvary, God himself is horribly suffering. Not least for that reason, Jesus can say, "For my yoke is sweet and my burden light" (Matt. 11:30): he is the one who carried the cross.

2. We move on to another mountain, a lighter one to talk about. This is the mountain where Jesus pronounced the Sermon on the Mount. Dale Allison, not an uncritical commentator on the Moses typology, found much evidence to support the traditional association of the mountain of Jesus's preaching with Mount Sinai: "Jesus is the Moses-like Messiah who proclaims the eschatological will of God on a mountain typologically equated with Sinai."[15] Again, there are crucial differences, which flow from the primal one already discussed, namely, the difference between the office of the prophet and the mission of the Son of God. Most importantly, whereas Moses received the law from the Lord, Jesus proclaims the new law on his own, divine authority. Still, there is a kind of transmission occurring: in the case of Moses, from the Lord to the people of Israel; in Jesus's case, from the Father in whose name he speaks (Matt. 11:27), to the "little ones" (Matt. 11:25) in his audience.

What the relationship is between the old law and the new, together with the meaning of the "fulfillment," is a matter we will take up in a separate section.

3. In terms of the Moses typology in Matthew, one passage stands out in its explicitness, and that is the narrative of the transfiguration in chapter 17.[16] Jesus takes Peter, James, and John to a "high mountain" (17:1), where he is "transfigured" or, more literally, metamorphosed (μετεμορφώθη; 17:2):

14. Bonaventure's *Sentences* commentary provides an example of this type of discussion. For the issue of throwing up the Eucharist, see *Liber IV Sententiarum*, Opera theologica selecta 4 (Quaracchi: Collegium S. Bonaventurae, 1949), dist. 13, art. 2, qu. 2 (pp. 294–97); the latrine appears in dist. 9, art. 2, qu. 4 (pp. 198–99).

15. Allison, *The New Moses*, 185.

16. Allison examines Matt. 17:1–8 in *The New Moses*, 243–48.

his face becomes shining like the sun, and his clothes turn white like light (or like snow, following the manuscript tradition reflected in the Vulgate).[17] Then Moses and Elijah appear—Elijah, who, according to Jesus himself, had already returned in John the Baptist (11:14), thus fulfilling the prophecy of Malachi (Mal. 4:5). This leaves Jesus as the new Moses. This parallel is confirmed as we read on: "And as he was yet speaking, behold a bright cloud overshadowed them. And lo, a voice out of the cloud, saying: This is my beloved Son, in whom I am well pleased: hear ye him" (Matt. 17:5). The Lord once again speaks from within the veil of a cloud, and just as in Exodus, he urges his people (here represented by the three disciples) to hear his messenger—who in this case is his own Son. And another significant difference: after the disciples "fell upon their face, and were very much afraid" (17:6)—this echoes the threatening circumstances of the Lord's appearance on Mount Sinai—Jesus declares, "Arise, and fear not" (17:7). There is no need for fear because violence and death have been subsumed in the cross.

But at this point, the crucifixion has not yet occurred! Commentators think that the transfiguration narrative may represent the transposition, into a pre-Easter scene, of the experience of the resurrected Jesus. But even if one does not follow this compositional theory, there is no doubt that the "transfiguration story anticipates the eschatological events of the resurrection and the parousia of Jesus."[18] In the overall dynamic of the Gospel narrative, then, the story powerfully contrasts the suffering of the Son of Man on the cross with the "revelation of Jesus as belonging to the divine world."[19] We have so far emphasized the horrific and humiliating nature of Jesus's death on the cross—the charred root of meaning of the Christian tradition. There would be no meaning and no tradition, however, if the cross had been the last word in Jesus's life: someone claiming to be the Son of God would have been tortured to death by the Romans. It is the fact that, through Jesus, God reached into the depths of his fallen creation in order

17. The author of Matthew does not follow the tradition of associating *qeren* from Exod. 34:29 with horns. Why not? He knew Hebrew, but quoted the Old Testament both from Septuagint and from non-Septuagint Greek sources (see W. D. Davies and Dale C. Allison Jr., *A Critical and Exegetical Commentary on the Gospel according to Saint Matthew*, vol. 1 [Edinburgh: T. & T. Clark, 1988], 29–33). Perhaps he just followed the LXX version, but we cannot attempt to resolve this question here.

18. As M. Eugene Boring writes in "The Gospel of Matthew," in *The New Interpreter's Bible* (Nashville: Abingdon, 1994), 8:366.

19. Boring, "The Gospel of Matthew," 8:363.

to bring it back to him—to redeem it—that makes the death on the cross the root of religious meaning and hope.

"I Am Not Come to Destroy . . ."

Jesus's famous word, that he has come not to destroy but to fulfill the law, sums up one of the essential aspects of the Gospel according to Saint Matthew and, indeed, of the Christian message: namely, that Jesus is the Messiah who fulfills the prophecies of the Old Testament. As we have seen, throughout his text, the author of Matthew presents Jesus typologically as the new Moses—as someone repeating, and in repeating completing, central stages in the life of the first lawgiver.

In the text of Matthew, the fulfillment passage (5:17–18) occurs within the Sermon on the Mount (chaps. 5–7), where it is preceded by the beatitudes and followed by specific examples that illustrate how the new law fulfills the old. Let us consider this context first. Chapter 5 opens with the following verse: "And seeing the multitudes, he went up into a mountain, and when he was set down, his disciples came unto him" (5:1). Note the hierarchy intimated in this opening sentence: the assembled multitude of people prompts Jesus to ascend the mountain, but he preaches to them via his disciples, who are his primary audience. "And opening his mouth, he taught them, saying: Blessed are the poor in spirit: for theirs is the kingdom of heaven" (5:2–3). Several additional beatitudes follow. What does it mean that the "poor in spirit"—those who are aware of their humble status as God's children, and who are perhaps materially poor as well—own the kingdom of heaven? Several commentators have drawn attention to the indicative tense ("theirs *is* [ἐστιν] the kingdom of heaven"), which suggests neither a command nor a future wish, but rather a fact. Jesus—Davies and Allison explain—is "conscious of being the eschatological herald who has been anointed by God and given the Spirit":[20] out of this authority he *declares* the poor in spirit, the meek, those who mourn, etc., to be blessed. We are dealing with what modern linguists have called a "performative speech act": an utterance that effects what it says.[21] Again, the beatitudes are not "wishful thinking," nor do they urge Jesus's followers to adopt certain ethical guidelines, but they are—to quote M. Eugene Boring—"prophetic

---

20. Davies and Allison, *A Critical and Exegetical Commentary*, 1:438–39.
21. See Boring's commentary in "The Gospel of Matthew," 8:177.

declarations made on the conviction of the coming-and-already-present kingdom of God."[22]

The word "blessed" (μακάριος) also occurs in several Old Testament passages that express similar beatitudes, like Job 5:17 ("Blessed is the man whom God correcteth") or Psalm 1:1 ("Blessed is the man who hath not walked in the counsel of the ungodly"). "Blessed" does not simply mean "happy" in a worldly sense, but rather conveys that a particular individual is God-pleasing, and stands in God's grace (as opposed to being cursed). Jesus, who is God, is able to make such a statement on his own authority. This authority is emphasized at the very end of the Sermon on the Mount: "For he was teaching them as one having power, and not as the scribes and Pharisees" (Matt. 7:29).

The beatitudes precede 5:17–18; the verses that follow are of a different character. Juxtaposing commandments from the old law with Jesus's expectations regarding the conduct of his followers, they give content to the idea of fulfillment. The antitheses begin thus:

> For I tell you, that unless your justice abound more than that of the scribes and Pharisees, you shall not enter into the kingdom of heaven. You have heard that it was said to them of old: Thou shalt not kill. And whosoever shall kill shall be in danger of the judgment. But I say to you, that whosoever is angry with his brother, shall be in danger of the judgment. And whosoever shall say to his brother, Raca, shall be in danger of the council. And whosoever shall say, Thou fool, shall be in danger of hell fire. (5:20–22)

The untranslated, probably Aramaic word *raca* in this text is worth brief consideration. *Rêqā* (ריקא or ריקה) is roughly synonymous with "fool," so that it does not add to the meaning of the passage. It may have possessed a particular emotional tinge that made it difficult to translate.[23] More significantly, however, *raca* allows the reader to glimpse through the Greek surface of the text to the historical situation it narrates. The reader suddenly realizes that Jesus, whose speech is being reported, did not speak Greek but (primarily) Aramaic. As we noted in discussing the Mount Sinai narrative, the origins withdraw—Jesus, whose words

---

22. Boring, "The Gospel of Matthew," 8:177.
23. This was argued by Gerhard Mussies, "The Use of Hebrew and Aramaic in the Greek New Testament," *New Testament Studies* 30 (1984): 416–32, esp. 424–25.

seemed so immediate and lively as we started reading the Sermon on the Mount, now appears veiled in Greek. Indeed, some biblical commentators feel that the antitheses themselves are Matthew's literary device (or, in this particular context, let us use the more precise phrase: a literary device employed by the author of Matthew). Others have argued that the startling nature of the antithetical form, which "is not found in Scripture outside of Matthew 5," is original, indicating Jesus's supreme authority to reshape the law.[24]

But what is the meaning of this first antithesis (and, by implication, of the five that follow)? Clearly, we are dealing with a radicalization of the old law. The sixth commandment prohibits murder, that is to say, the gravest possible form of physical injury to a fellow human being. Jesus goes further in demanding that no one harm his brother (or sister) at all, not even by uttering an insult. Such a demand doubtless challenges the old law, which it shows to be insufficient. We could even use our word "transgression" to describe this challenge (there is a "stepping beyond" the old law involved here), although the term "transcendence" is more intuitive: it conveys that whatever "transgression" may be occurring is in an upward, ascending direction. The antithesis of the sixth commandment is certainly not suggesting any violation or contradiction of the law. As Davies and Allison have put it, "Anyone who followed the words of Jesus in 5.21–48 would not find himself in violation of any Jewish law."[25]

If we remind ourselves of the other five antitheses, we are left in no doubt over the radical nature of what Jesus expects of his followers: (1) Jesus radicalizes the commandment not to commit adultery in the exhortation to avoid even lustful glances (5:27–30); (2) the Old Testament regulates divorce; Jesus prohibits divorce, "excepting for the cause of fornication" (5:32); (3) Jesus reinterprets the third commandment, not to take the Lord's name in vain, by demanding no swearing whatsoever (5:33–37); (4) Jesus replaces the vetero-testamentarian law of retaliation, "an eye for an eye," with the commandment not to retaliate, ever, for any injustice suffered, but willingly to turn the other cheek, and to go the extra mile (5:38–42); (5) finally, it is not sufficient, Jesus declares, to love one's neighbor and one's brother—even the tax collectors and heathens do this—but we must love our enemies, do good to them, and pray for them (5:43–48). We must, in other words, empty ourselves, just as Jesus was to empty himself on the

---

24. For this discussion (and the quotation), see Boring, "The Gospel of Matthew," 8:188.
25. Davies and Allison, *A Critical and Exegetical Commentary*, 1:507.

cross. The list ends, and culminates, in the impossible commandment: "Be you therefore perfect, as also your heavenly Father is perfect" (5:48).

An interesting bit of manuscript evidence testifies to the fact that Christians have always, from very early on in the tradition, asked themselves how on earth they could be expected to be perfect. In verse 22, "whosoever is angry with his brother" (πᾶς ὁ ὀργιζόμενος τῷ ἀδελφῷ αὐτοῦ), some ancient manuscripts have inserted "without cause" (εἰκῇ).[26] One understands the impulse! Still, the addition misses the point of the sentence, and of the series of antitheses as a whole: they are uncompromising.

The perfection demanded of Jesus's disciples and followers is, in a certain sense, no longer of this world. The antitheses have to be read against the background of the beatitudes, that is to say, Jesus's preceding performative blessing: because you have received God's grace, because you already are his children—Jesus seems to be saying—you can be expected to act in ways that are characteristic of the kingdom. Jesus's demands are transgressive, in that they upset the values that govern the world. The law of retaliation, for example, makes sure that no one "gets away" with crime—that the economy of debt and repayment is upheld. Where would we be if the burglar who broke into my house did not receive his just sentence, but if I gave him my car as well? In chapters 6 and 7, we should add, Jesus spells out in greater detail how he understands his radicalization of the law in real-life situations.

In keeping with the impulse that was behind the added little word εἰκῇ in verse 22, the tradition has defused the transgressive character of Jesus's radicalization of the law. This is a statement of fact, not a criticism. The promised second coming took longer than expected; the number of Christians increased; persecution ceased; Christians eventually moved into roles of political, economic, and military power: Who can command an army while turning the other cheek? The church therefore decided that Jesus's revaluation of values in the Sermon on the Mount applied only to those seeking perfection by keeping the evangelical counsels in a consecrated life; for the rest of us, the commandments suffice.

We now have enough background and context to examine 5:17–18:

> Do not think that I am come to destroy the law, or the prophets. I am not come to destroy, but to fulfill. For amen I say unto you, till heaven and earth pass, one jot, or one tittle shall not pass of the law, till all be fulfilled.

26. See Davies and Allison, *A Critical and Exegetical Commentary*, 1:512n4.

The Douay-Rheims version renders both πληρῶσαι from verse 17 and γένηται from verse 18 with forms of the same English verb, "to fulfill," and this although the Vulgate distinguishes them (*adimplere* versus *fiant*). To preserve the distinction in English, γένηται could have been translated as "is accomplished" or "has come to pass." If philologically a distinction is lost in the Douay-Rheims text, theologically its choice was correct. For the fact that verse 17 speaks of "the law, or the prophets" indicates that the fulfillment at issue concerns at once the old law and the Old Testament as a whole. Jesus has come to fulfill the prophecies of the Old Testament; he is the Messiah. Furthermore, verse 18 places the law in the context of the end-times: not even the smallest elements of the law will lose their force "till heaven and earth pass." Jesus's fulfillment of the law, then, is eschatologically tied to the fullness of time, which will not be reached until all of God's promises are fulfilled. The verb πληρόω is frequently used in the New Testament in this eschatological sense, which signifies the coming to pass of God's promises as salvation history moves to completion.[27] In this perspective, Jesus's radicalization of the law appears as a crucial stage in the historical realization of God's will.

Given the extreme importance of Matthew 5:17 for the relationship between the Old Testament and the New—indeed, for the relationship between Christianity and its Jewish roots—it is not surprising that the interpretation of the verse is controversial. Davies and Allison have distinguished nine different types of readings.[28] One difficulty concerns a fact we encountered above: since Jesus did not preach in Greek, the question arises as to what Hebrew or Aramaic term πληρῶσαι translates (if there is a historical, pre-Easter core to the story). The central issue, however, boils down to this: Is Jesus fulfilling the law by obeying it perfectly and bringing out its inner meaning, God's original intent, or is he fulfilling the law by transcending it?[29]

27. See the entry "πληρόω" in Gerhard Friedrich, *Theological Dictionary of the New Testament*, ed. and trans. Geoffrey W. Bromiley, vol. 6 (Grand Rapids: Eerdmans, 1968), 286–98, esp. 295–97.

28. In one particularly ingenious interpretation, Henrik Ljungman submitted that Jesus's fulfillment of the old law is its unification in the one commandment to love God and neighbor. The whole of the law is present, fully and undiminished, in that one principle. See Ljungman, *Das Gesetz erfüllen. Matth. 5,17ff. und 3,15 untersucht*, Lunds Universitets Årsskrift, N.F., Avd. 1, Bd. 50, Nr. 6 (Lund: Gleerup, 1954).

29. See Davies and Allison, *A Critical and Exegetical Commentary*, 1:485–86.

A glance at a few passages outside the immediate context of 5:17 may be useful here.

Matthew 12:1–14 relates the story of how Jesus's disciples harvest some corn on a Sabbath, with the result that the Pharisees accuse them (and Jesus himself) of breaking the fourth commandment. Jesus has two responses, one of which is clearly inner-Jewish: there are some exceptions to the Sabbath law, like the ritual activities of priests (12:5) or even secular emergencies, such as the need to rescue a sheep (12:11). There is nothing transgressive in these explanations. But Jesus also says: "For the Son of Man is Lord even of the sabbath" (12:8). This is not a Jewish answer, but one that unambiguously affirms Jesus's authority over the law.

Matthew 15:1–20 is particularly interesting for our discussion, not least because this pericope explicitly addresses the disciples' "transgression" of the law: "Then came to him from Jerusalem scribes and Pharisees, saying: Why do thy disciples transgress (παραβαίνουσιν, *transgrediuntur*) the tradition of the ancients? For they wash not their hands when they eat bread. But he answering, said to them: Why do you also transgress (παραβαίνετε, *transgredimini*) the commandment of God for your own tradition? For God said . . ." (15:1–4). We have seen the significance of ritual cleanliness in the context of the Mount Sinai narrative: cleaning one's garments or, in this case, one's hands acknowledges the boundary between the soiled world of everyday life and the purity of the sacred realm. Ritual cleanliness, thus, is not a small matter. Why, then, do the disciples not wash their hands before eating? Jesus answers the Pharisees by means of a rebuttal: you are transgressing the law too! He is alluding, it seems, to the Pharisees' attempts to shield their wealth from the requirement to support their parents, which amounts to a breach of the fifth commandment.[30] This counterattack does not in fact respond to the accusation. (Some commentators point out that washing one's hands before eating was not actually part of the Torah, so that the Pharisees did not read the tradition correctly.)[31] The real response comes in verse 11 (and is repeated in vv. 17–20): "Not that which goeth into the mouth defileth a man: but what cometh out of the mouth, this defileth a man."

---

30. This is Boring's explanation in "The Gospel of Matthew," 8:332–33: "Verses 4–6 picture the Pharisees as interpreting the Torah in such a way as to provide an escape hatch for their members who had aging parents they did not wish to support. They could declare (some of) their property to be dedicated to the Temple, and thus not available to provide for their own parents in their time of need." Mark 7:9–13 is clearer on the issue than Matthew's adaptation.

31. See Boring, "The Gospel of Matthew," 8:331–32.

The structure of this response is similar to what we discovered in connection with Matthew 12. First, Jesus provides an inner-Jewish rebuttal; then, the register becomes more radical and transgressive. Matthew 15:11 does nothing less than challenge Jewish dietary prescriptions: what matters is not what goes into the mouth, but what comes out of it. The notion of cleanliness is interiorized in this teaching: Jesus presents a pure heart—one free from thoughts of murder, adultery, fornication, theft, false testimony, and blasphemy—as much more important than external cleanliness.[32] Is it rash to conclude that Jesus is not scandalized by certain "transgressions" of the old law; indeed, that he encourages them? I think not.

Note also the revealing way in which the term "tradition" (παράδοσις) appears in 15:2 and 3: tradition is not seen as an absolute value, an infallible guide to truth, but rather as subject to distortion and misinterpretation. If tradition causes one to "transgress the commandment of God," it may in turn need to be transgressed.

One final illustration of what fulfilling the law may mean is in Matthew 5:17. Matthew 10:34–37 formulates Jesus's demand that following him takes precedence over the commandment to honor one's father and mother: "Do not think that I came to send peace upon earth: I came not to send peace, but the sword. For I came to set a man at variance against his father, and the daughter against her mother, and the daughter in law against her mother in law. And a man's enemies shall be they of his own household. He that loveth father or mother more than me, is not worthy of me; and he that loveth son or daughter more than me, is not worthy of me." Discipleship, we learn, can come at the price of war within one's family, which is a particularly hard cross to bear, given the closeness—and, according to the fifth commandment, the sacredness—of family ties. A parallel passage in Luke 14:26 is equally stark: "If any man come to me, and hate not his father, and mother, and wife, and children, and brethren, and sisters, yea

---

32. Here, I find it hard to agree with Boring's attempts to preserve the "Jewishness" of Jesus's teachings. Boring goes so far as to write that the pericope in question "is not a comprehensive pronouncement nullifying the laws of the Torah regarding ritual defilement, such as the food laws. It is, rather, a thoroughly biblical and Jewish mode of declaring the relative importance of the inner commitments of the heart . . . over against the ritual commandments, which are still not abolished" ("The Gospel of Matthew," 8:333). This is not how the tradition has understood this passage and its parallel in Mark 7:1–23. Saint Paul already felt that the only reason not to eat meat was in order not to upset those who still followed Jewish dietary laws (Rom. 14:14–23).

and his own life also, he cannot be my disciple." Jesus asks his disciples for nothing less than total self-sacrifice, which includes sacrificing one's family ties. The Son of Man, we could say, adapting a verse cited earlier, is Lord even of the family.

Shockingly, the passages just quoted reintroduce violence into the very heart of the Christian message. The violence and death that (in post-Easter perspective) Christ has taken upon himself and overcome return in the life of his followers. They will have to take up his cross, "be crucified with Christ" (Χριστῷ συνεσταύρωμθαι), as Saint Paul puts it (Gal. 2:19; cf. Rom. 6:6). Suffering is not over, except in eschatological perspective.

The Incident at Antioch

Even in Matthew, the "Jewish" Gospel that presents Jesus as the new Moses, we have come across passages which suggest that fulfilling the law could mean more than simply completing it. To be sure, every text that we have quoted to suggest a more transgressive dimension can be interpreted differently—"tamed," so to speak—given the many voices that flow together in the Gospels: Jesus's voice, the voices of the (uncertain) inspired authors, the voices of contemporary opponents, and the voices of Old Testament writers echoed in allusions and quotations. Would the ability to pierce through these layers of meaning, to the clarity of a one-dimensional teaching, not be the literary equivalent of seeing God face-to-face? Such immediacy is not given to us in this life. Interpretation and its uncertainties are a mark of living, as the medievals said, *in via*.[33]

If we turn to texts outside of the Gospels, we discover additional evidence of how Jesus's early followers were struggling to understand the meaning of his fulfillment of the law. A Christian community formed that began to define its identity, which always also means defining what one is *not*. So boundaries were becoming a problem, and the problem acquired a name: "Judaizing."

The verb "to Judaize" (ἰουδαΐζειν) is a *hapax legomenon* in the New Testament, where it occurs only in Galatians 2:14.[34] The context is an episode

33. On these difficult hermeneutical issues, all I can do is refer the reader to the classic small book by Raymond E. Brown, *The Critical Meaning of the Bible* (Mahwah, NJ: Paulist Press, 1981).

34. Kittel offers a short entry on ἰουδαΐζειν that adverts to the one use of the word in the Septuagint (Esther 8:17). See Gerhard Kittel, *Theological Dictionary of the New Testament*,

that has come to be known as the "incident at Antioch," in which two of the apostles, Paul and Peter, clashed publicly over the observance of Jewish rites in the Christian community. Antioch, where Paul is reported to have spent an entire year preaching (Acts 11:26), was an important center in the early church—so much so that Christians were first called by that name in Antioch (11:26). In more modern parlance, the events at Antioch must have been crucial for the formation of a Christian identity.[35] This identity formation involved exclusion, as it must.

In the opening verses of the Epistle to the Galatians, which is usually dated to the period between AD 50 and AD 56, we find an agitated Paul justifying himself: his teaching derives not from men, but from God himself! Paul's defensive posture quickly turns more aggressive, as he pronounces those disagreeing with him to be anathema:

> Paul, an apostle, not of men, neither by man, but by Jesus Christ, and God the Father, who raised him from the dead, And all the brethren who are with me, to the churches of Galatia. Grace be to you, and peace from God the Father, and from our Lord Jesus Christ. . . . I wonder that you are so soon removed from him that called you into the grace of Christ, unto another gospel. Which is not another, only there are some that trouble you, and would pervert the gospel of Christ. But though we, or an angel from heaven, preach a gospel to you besides that which we have preached to you, let him be anathema. As we said before, so now I say again: If any one preach to you a gospel, besides that which you have received, let him be anathema. (Gal. 1:1–3 and 6–9)

Ἀνάθεμα (or ἀνάθημα) is a word that the Septuagint employed to translate the Hebrew term חרם (ḥerem). In a first sense, ḥerem signifies items set

---

ed. and trans. Geoffrey W. Bromiley, vol. 3 (Grand Rapids: Eerdmans, 1965), 383. Gilbert Dagron, "Judaïser," *Travaux et Mémoires* 11 (1991): 359–80, offers reflections on the use of the term in Byzantine theology. For further literature on the topic, one may consult the footnotes in Róbert Dán, "'Judaizare'—the Career of a Term," in *Antitrinitarianism in the Second Half of the 16th Century*, ed. Róbert Dán and Antal Pirnát, Studia humanitatis 5 (Budapest: Akadémiai Kiadó; Leiden: Brill, 1982), 25–34.

35. James D. G. Dunn describes the Antioch incident as "an important watershed . . . in the development of Christian self-understanding" (*Jesus, Paul, and the Law: Studies in Mark and Galatians* [Louisville, KY: Westminster John Knox Press, 1990], 159). The following discussion is indebted to Dunn's fine treatment of the issue. Still useful, as well, is the older commentary by Ernest De Witt Burton, *A Critical and Exegetical Commentary on the Epistle to the Galatians* (Edinburgh: T. & T. Clark, 1977; first published in 1920).

apart for sacred use, indicating the division between the sacred and the profane (Lev. 27:28 is an example). The "tak[ing] out of ordinary human circulation"[36] that *herem* implies can, however, also acquire a meaning that seems diametrically opposed to the first: namely, not exclusion *for* God, but exclusion *from* God and his community. In this sense, *herem* and, with it, ἀνάθεμα express that something is accursed, that is, delivered over to the divine wrath to be destroyed. That is what Paul believes happens to those perverting the gospel of Christ—nay, that is what Paul commands in the imperative form: ἀνάθεμα ἔστω. What happened in the young community of followers of Christ (the Antioch incident is usually dated to the 40s of the first century) to occasion this violent reaction?

In the community at Antioch, Peter habitually ate with gentiles (Gal. 2:12). That is to say, he practiced table fellowship with non-Jews who were drawn into the nascent community of Jews who were followers of the gospel of Christ. During this period, just a few years after Jesus's death and resurrection, "Christianity" did not yet exist; what existed was a Jewish sect that believed in Jesus's promises. This sect (like more traditional forms of Judaism) attracted gentiles as well, and in some places did so in large numbers. Naturally, the "Jesus sect" adhered to Jewish traditions including, not least, the laws concerning unclean foods and ritual purity that governed the table fellowship. On the most likely interpretation, the table fellowship at Antioch that included gentiles had by no means abandoned the relevant Jewish customs; James Dunn surmises that in the gentiles' "table-fellowship with the Jewish believers, in particular pork was not used, and when meat was served care had been taken to ensure the beast had been properly slaughtered."[37] Yet a certain slackening may have occurred to accommodate the gentile members who had joined the group. This is when a delegation arrives with a message from James in Jerusalem (the center of Judaism)—and the message demands stricter observance of the laws.[38] Peter complies, withdrawing from the table fel-

36. Gerhard Kittel, *Theological Dictionary of the New Testament*, ed. and trans. Geoffrey W. Bromiley, vol. 1 (Grand Rapids: Eerdmans, 1964), 354.

37. Dunn, *Jesus, Paul, and the Law*, 154.

38. This is Dunn's interpretation. Richard B. Hays interprets the situation differently: the group from Jerusalem objected to any close association with gentiles, quite independently of whether the Torah was observed. See Hays, "The Letter to the Galatians," in *The New Interpreter's Bible*, 11:232. Michele Murray has suggested that Paul's main adversaries in Galatians were not observant Jews pressuring gentiles to "Judaize," but rather gentile converts to the gospel who underwent circumcision in order to escape persecution,

lowship with the gentiles, and taking with him the other Jewish members of the group. The action from Jerusalem and Peter's compliance with it trigger a public clash between Peter and Paul:

> But when Cephas was come to Antioch, I withstood him to the face, because he was to be blamed. For before that some came from James, he did eat with the Gentiles: but when they were come, he withdrew and separated himself, fearing them who were of the circumcision. And to his dissimulation the rest of the Jews consented, so that Barnabas also was led by them into that dissimulation. But when I saw that they walked not uprightly unto the truth of the gospel, I said to Cephas before them all: If thou, being a Jew, livest after the manner of the Gentiles, and not as the Jews do, how dost thou compel the Gentiles to live as do the Jews? (Gal. 2:11–14)

"Πῶς τὰ ἔθνη ἀναγκάζεις ἰουδαΐζειν;" How can you, by abandoning their group, force the gentiles to embrace a strict interpretation of Jewish laws—that is, to "Judaize"—when you have, in the practices of the table fellowship, already recognized that such Judaizing is not required by the gospel? Not only are you not faithful to the gospel, Paul charges, but clearly you are not being honest either: the whole thing smacks of hypocrisy—for the Greek word that Douay-Rheims renders as "dissimulation" is ὑπόκρισις. By submitting to the demands of the Jerusalem delegation, Peter is acting against both the truth and his own convictions.

There had never been a question, in the Jesus sect, whether or not its Jewish members should continue to follow the law: they were Jews, and lived as such in practice. The Antioch incident initially concerned nothing more than the enforcement of Jewish laws for gentile members of the group. The incident produced the effect, however, of crystallizing Paul's thoughts on the relationship between covenantal nomism and justification through faith. Perhaps, he discovered, they were "not two complementary emphases, but were in direct antithesis to each other."[39] This insight finds

---

and who urged fellow gentiles to do the same, that is to say, to "play a Jewish game." See Murray, *Playing a Jewish Game: Gentile Christian Judaizing in the First and Second Centuries CE*, Studies in Christianity and Judaism 13 (Waterloo, ON: Wilfrid Laurier University Press, 2004), 29–41. A shortcoming in Murray's interesting argument is the fact that she treats Christianity as an established identity, whereas Paul's letter is part of the struggle in which such an identity first arose.

39. Dunn, *Jesus, Paul, and the Law*, 162.

expression in the Epistle to the Galatians. In a passage like the following one, a Christian identity begins to emerge, marked by the word "not": "But knowing that man is not (οὐ) justified by the works of the law, but by the faith of Jesus Christ; we also believe in Christ Jesus, that we may be justified by the faith of Christ, and not (οὐκ) by the works of the law: because by the works of the law no flesh shall be justified (οὐ δικαιωθήσεται πᾶσα σάρξ)" (Gal. 2:16). The boundaries are becoming clearer here than in Jesus's word of "fulfillment," which could suggest the absence of negation. But let me venture an interpretation: in its larger context within the New Testament, the Matthean language of fulfillment can be understood in terms of Hegel's notion of *Aufhebung*, usually translated into English as "sublation." In German, the verb *aufheben* has three meanings: (1) "to lift up, to raise";[40] (2) "to cancel";[41] (3) "to preserve."[42] Meanings 2 and 3 are antithetical; their reconciliation lies in meaning 1: something can simultaneously be canceled out and preserved only if the cancellation entails the preservation of the canceled element at a higher level. *Aufhebung* is a central term in the logic of Hegel's system, whose unfolding depends on the sublation of opposed elements at a higher level. Thus, for example, the concepts of "being" and "nothing" are sublated in the notion of "determinate being"; earlier forms of philosophical thought are sublated in Hegel's system.[43]

Hegel's sublation, just as Matthew's fulfillment, is driven by negation. If there is no opposition, no sublation is able to occur. Likewise, the neotestamentary context of the language of fulfillment suggests that the law's

40. As in, "Sie hat das Buch vom Boden aufgehoben."
41. As in, "Es wurde beschlossen, das Gesetz aufzuheben."
42. As in, "Heb das gut für mich auf!"
43. The examples are from the entry on "sublation" in Michael J. Inwood, *A Hegel Dictionary* (Oxford and Malden, MA: Blackwell, 1992), 283–85 (at 284). The young Hegel himself interprets Matt. 5:17 as a sublation of (objective) law and (subjective) inclination. In *The Spirit of Christianity and Its Fate*, he writes: "This spirit of Jesus, a spirit raised above morality, is visible, directly attacking laws, in the Sermon on the Mount, which is an attempt, elaborated in numerous examples, to strip the laws of legality, of their legal form. The Sermon does not teach reverence for the laws; on the contrary, it exhibits that which fulfils the law but annuls it as law and so is something higher than obedience to law and makes it superfluous. . . . This expanded content we may call an inclination so to act as the laws may command, i.e., a unification of inclination with the law whereby the latter loses its form as law. This correspondence with inclination is the πλήρωμα of the law; i.e., it is an 'is,' which . . . is the synthesis of subject and object, in which subject and object have lost their opposition" (in *Early Theological Writings*, trans. T. M. Knox, Works in Continental Philosophy [Philadelphia: University of Pennsylvania Press, 1971], 212 and 214).

preservation, in and through Jesus's gospel, entails a completion and radicalization that is not free from an element of annulment. In some passages, this negative element makes a very subtle appearance; in others, especially in many Pauline texts, it is quite explicit. Among the many Pauline passages that emphasize the opposition between the law, works, and the flesh on the one hand, and faith, grace, and love on the other, the following one from Galatians stands out because of its audacious rereading of the Mount Sinai narrative:

> Tell me, you that desire to be under the law, have you not read the law? For it is written that Abraham had two sons: the one by a bondwoman, and the other by a free woman. But he who was of the bondwoman, was born according to the flesh: but he of the free woman, was by promise. Which things are said by an allegory. For these are the two testaments. The one from mount Sina, engendering unto bondage, which is Agar: For Sina is a mountain in Arabia, which hath affinity to that Jerusalem which now is, and is in bondage with her children. But that Jerusalem, which is above, is free: which is our mother. . . . Now we, brethren, as Isaac was, are the children of promise. But as then he, that was born according to the flesh, persecuted him that was after the spirit; so also it is now. But what saith the scripture? *Cast out the bondwoman and her son; for the son of the bondwoman shall not be heir with the son of the free woman.* (Gal. 4:21–30)

The strategy that Paul deploys here is quite remarkable: he attempts to dispossess the Jews of Antioch who insisted on having the gentiles "Judaize" of their own scriptural heritage. Or has the object of his attack already become much broader, including now "all those that desire to be under the law"? That would be all faithful Jewish people. The manner in which Paul moves quickly from the incident at Antioch—which was characterized not by an opposition between those following the law and others who did not, but involved, rather, a much more nuanced dispute over levels of adherence—suggests that he is in the process of constructing "hermeneutic Jews," to use an expression by Jeremy Cohen.[44] Paul's Jews are no longer real people, of flesh and blood, but constructs helping the emerging Christian community to define itself.

44. Jeremy Cohen, *Living Letters of the Law: Ideas of the Jew in Medieval Christianity* (Berkeley and Los Angeles: University of California Press, 1999), p. 3 with n. 3.

Paul's attack makes the shocking charge that those who desire to be under the law do not even understand it. They suffer from a "form of illiteracy,"[45] because reading requires going beyond the letter of the law—which is precisely what they are refusing to do. Only those who have freed themselves from the shackles of the letter, by embracing the promise of Jesus's death and resurrection, are capable of grasping the allegorical depths of the Old Testament. Specifically, in this case, the biblical narrative of Abraham's two wives in Genesis 16 has an allegorical dimension. The two wives— one, Sarah, free; the other, Hagar, a "bondswoman" or slave (παιδίσκη)— and their offspring signify the two Testaments. The covenant initiated on Mount Sinai has engendered its people into slavery (εἰς δουλείαν). The "Jerusalem that now is"—in other words, the Jerusalem represented by James's emissaries—stands in that lineage of unfreedom. But there is another Jerusalem, a free one, which lives according to the gospel. This is the Jerusalem that Paul represents. As for the other Jerusalem, the slavish one, it must be "cast out." Ἀνάθεμα ἔστω!

The incident at Antioch and everything that would follow it in the history of Jewish-Christian relations are the quintessential illustration of Foucault's theory of the significance of the Outside in the constitution of cultural identity. Let us remind ourselves of a text quoted in the introduction:

> One could write a history of *limits*—of those obscure acts (*gestes*), necessarily forgotten as soon as they are accomplished, through which a culture rejects something that will be the Outside (*l'Extérieur*) for it; and throughout the course of its history, this hollowed-out void, this white space by means of which it isolates itself, defines it as much as its values. For, these values it receives and maintains in the continuity of history; but in that region of which we want to speak, it exercises its essential choices, operating the division (*partage*) which gives it the face of its positivity; here the original depth where it forms itself is to be found. To question a culture about its limit-experiences (*expériences-limites*) is to question it in the confines of history, about a tearing-apart which is like the very birth of its history. In a tension that is continually in the process of resolving itself, there occurs the confrontation between the temporal continuity of a dialectical analysis and the unveiling of a tragic structure at the threshold of time.[46]

---

45. David Nirenberg, *Anti-Judaism: The Western Tradition* (New York: Norton, 2013), 83.
46. Quoted in the introduction, p. 11 above.

This is what we see in Galatians: the tearing apart that leads to the birth of the history of Christianity. Paul rejects "all those that desire to be under the law," creating a division between an inside and an outside that used not to exist; for, after the Antioch incident (and similar events in the "Jesus sect"), the Jews became the Other over against whom "Christians" were able to define their identity. It is not a coincidence that, as we noted, Christians first received that name at Antioch.

Foucault notes that the ejection of the Other creates a "hollowed-out void" and "white space" that will remain at the center of the culture that has defined itself through the division, and "give it the face of its positivity." This is, again, exactly the situation that has characterized Jewish-Christian relations throughout the centuries. Christianity did not eject Judaism from the center of a once undifferentiated identity, then to forget about the division and leave it alone. Rather, throughout its history, it has been preoccupied with its difference from Judaism. Already in the New Testament, the struggles between the Jesus sect and the "other" Jews from whom it began to divide itself left traces of what the biblical scholar Luke T. Johnson has called "anti-Jewish slander."[47] The incident at Antioch is only a particularly striking example. It is one thing to replace this polemic in its historical and rhetorical context—as biblical scholarship does—and thus to some extent to defuse it. It is another matter to study its *Wirkungsgeschichte*, as the Germans would say: the history of its effects. This *Wirkungsgeschichte* is alarming, as most recently David Nirenberg has shown in his book *Anti-Judaism: The Western Tradition*.[48] It is difficult to doubt Nirenberg's thesis, which traces the anti-Semitism of the twentieth century to its ultimate roots, the anti-Judaism of the New Testament. As the Western Christian tradition developed, the Jew functioned as a hermeneutic tool that allowed a changing center to define its identity over an imaginary Other. The word "imaginary" indicates that "Jews" simply came to stand for anything that one did *not* want to be. In patristic and medieval Christianity, the Jew was generally the one who clung to the letter of the law, which kills, rather than embracing the spirit, which gives life (2 Cor. 3:6).[49] Christian scriptural hermeneutic was a huge enterprise devoted to rereading the Old Testament allegorically

47. See Luke T. Johnson, "The New Testament's Anti-Jewish Slander and the Conventions of Ancient Polemic," *Journal of Biblical Literature* 108 (1989): 419–41.

48. Cited in note 45 above.

49. For a series of contemporary theological interpretations of the spirit/letter antithesis, see Paul S. Fiddes and Günter Bader, eds., *The Spirit and the Letter: A Tradition and a Reversal* (London: Bloomsbury, 2013).

in light of the New—to put it negatively, to wrestle their scriptural heritage from the Jews.[50] As the Byzantinist Gilbert Dagron has phrased it, in Christian exegesis the vetero-testamentary past became "at once oppressive and empty, carrying every meaning and never sending back anything but an echo of Christian history."[51] The Jew had congealed into a stereotype, no doubt, but he remained a figure of religious significance. In the secular age, the Jew became a figure in philosophic battles. Thus, for Kant, the Jew was the one who submitted to an external law, instead of correctly (that is, like Kant) viewing morality as the inner product of human reason. Hegel then argued that Kant himself was afflicted by the spirit of Judaism. And Hegel's contemporary Heine—himself of Jewish origin, no less—criticized the otherworldliness of the Jews, who failed to appreciate the beauty of the material world, unlike the colorful Egyptians, Babylonians, and Greeks. Schopenhauer, who hated Hegel (and everyone else), scribbled "Jew" in the margins of texts by rival philosophers from the idealist school.[52] Heidegger regarded the Jew as symbol and cause of the uprootedness of modern cosmopolitan life, torn from the soil where authentic thinking is possible.[53] One may find these theories interesting, or bizarre, or wrongheaded; what one should not forget, however, is that in the background of the intellectual anti-Judaism, from the patristic-medieval theories of supersession to Heidegger's philosophic anti-Semitism, there was always violence: "small" pogroms and persecutions punctuated the entire history of the Christian West, before they culminated in the final catastrophe of the Holocaust.

Much soul-searching after the Holocaust has caused the contemporary church to rethink its reading of Paul, and of the relationship between the Old and the New Testament. In his commentary on Galatians, Richard Hays warns us not to twist "Paul's good news into a pretext for violence."[54] The Pontifical Biblical Commission now recognizes the inherent, nonsub-

---

50. On this topic, the work of Henri de Lubac remains essential; see, in particular, *Medieval Exegesis*, vol. 1, *The Four Senses of Scripture*, trans. Mark Sebanc, Ressourcement: Retrieval and Renewal in Catholic Thought (Grand Rapids: Eerdmans, 1998), chap. 5: "The Unity of the Two Testaments" (225–67). Also useful: James Samuel Preus, *From Shadow to Promise: Old Testament Interpretation from Augustine to the Young Luther* (Cambridge, MA: Belknap Press of Harvard University Press, 1969).

51. Dagron, "Judaïser," 379.

52. All these examples are taken from chapter 12 of Nirenberg's *Anti-Judaism*, entitled "Philosophical Struggles with Judaism, from Kant to Heine" (387–422).

53. See Peter Trawny, *Heidegger and the Myth of a Jewish World Conspiracy*, trans. Andrew J. Mitchell (Chicago: University of Chicago Press, 2016).

54. Hays, "The Letter to the Galatians," 11:195.

lated value of the Jewish Scriptures. While Christians cannot and should not be forced to "Judaize" in the original sense of Galatians, they ought to recognize that the Jewish reading of the Hebrew Scriptures is "irreducible" in its legitimacy:

> The horror in the wake of the extermination of the Jews (the *Shoah*) during the Second World War has led all the Churches to rethink their relationship with Judaism and, as a result, to reconsider their interpretation of the Jewish Bible, the Old Testament. It may be asked whether Christians should be blamed for having monopolized the Jewish Bible and reading there what no Jew has found. Should not Christians henceforth read the Bible as Jews do, in order to show proper respect for its Jewish origins?
>
> In answer to the last question, a negative response must be given for hermeneutical reasons. For to read the Bible as Judaism does necessarily involves an implicit acceptance of all its presuppositions, that is, the full acceptance of what Judaism is, in particular, the authority of its writings and rabbinic traditions, which exclude faith in Jesus as Messiah and Son of God.
>
> As regards the first question, the situation is different, for Christians can and ought to admit that the Jewish reading of the Bible is a possible one, in continuity with the Jewish Sacred Scriptures from the Second Temple period, a reading analogous to the Christian reading which developed in parallel fashion. Both readings are bound up with the vision of their respective faiths, of which the readings are the result and expression. Consequently, both are irreducible.[55]

How can one hold that the Christian sublation of the Old Testament is legitimate and (from the Christian point of view) necessary while also maintaining that a Jewish reading of the Bible remains possible? We will address this question in our fourth chapter, on the development of traditions.

Let us return to Foucault's theory of the Outside for one final consideration. To the application of Foucault's theory to Galatians—and, more generally, to the emergence of Christianity as a separate identity—one could object that what Paul does in his letter to the Galatians and in other bibli-

---

55. Pontifical Biblical Commission, *The Jewish People and Their Sacred Scriptures in the Christian Bible* (Boston: Pauline Books and Media, 2003), no. 22. I am grateful to Fr. John Bayer, OCist for this reference.

cal texts is not an "obscure act, forgotten as soon as it was accomplished." We have the letter, after all, as part of the scriptural canon. Nonetheless, the church fathers found strategies to interpret away the embarrassing account "where Paul openly condemned Peter for hypocrisy."[56] Clement of Alexandria, for example, argued that the Cephas to whom Galatians refers was not Saint Peter the apostle, while Origen maintained that the whole disagreement was simulated.[57] Only the Reformation awakened Galatians from centuries of interpretive forgetfulness, finding in Paul's attack on Peter a foreshadowing of its own struggles with the Roman Church and its practice of selling indulgences.[58]

56. Dunn, *Jesus, Paul, and the Law*, 129.

57. See Dunn, *Jesus, Paul, and the Law*, 129, and especially Franz Overbeck, *Ueber die Auffassung des Streits des Paulus mit Petrus in Antiochien (Gal. 2, 11ff.) bei den Kirchenvätern* (1877), now available in *Werke und Nachlaß*, vol. 2, *Schriften bis 1880*, ed. Ekkehard W. Stegemann and Rudolf Brändle (Stuttgart and Weimar: J. B. Metzler, 1994), 221–334. Overbeck, a Protestant theologian, is best known as Nietzsche's faithful friend, but he was also the author of a significant body of theological work devoted to the early church.

58. See Martin Luther, *Lectures on Galatians (1535)*, trans. Jaroslav Pelikan, *Luther's Works* 26–27 (Saint Louis: Concordia, 1963–1964).

CHAPTER 3

The Christian Tradition in the Pagan World

As we continue considering the horizontal dimension in the constitution of the Christian tradition—that is to say, its identity-and-difference in relation to the culture into which the irruption of the divine occurred—we turn to the Greco-Roman world. One aspect of this world we have already encountered: the crucifixion. How could a punishment of such abhorrent violence exist in a sophisticated civilization, whose accomplishments in literature, philosophy, politics, law, and many other fields have profoundly shaped the Western tradition? As important and troubling as the question is, we cannot attempt to answer it here. What we do know is that "spectacles of death"—to cite the title of a book by Donald G. Kyle—were central to ancient Rome, and that they took many different forms, including the gladiator games.[1] In the crucifixion, God transformed one of the most horrific of these deadly spectacles into the cause of our salvation and a reason for hope.

This was as difficult to believe for Jews as it was for gentiles. The God of overwhelming power who called Moses on Mount Sinai amidst thunder and lightning could not have become incarnate, let alone be crucified. Within the context of the Roman Empire, crucifixion did not merely contradict religious and philosophic assumptions about the nature of divinity; rather, it was designed to cause and symbolize a total loss of even human dignity. Education in antiquity pursued the "development of perfection of the human self"—that was the practical goal of wisdom. The "maximum degradation" that a death on the cross entailed, exposing the victim in a distorted position of naked helplessness while causing him to lose all mental and bodily control, stood as the total negation of everything wisdom

1. See Donald G. Kyle, *Spectacles of Death in Ancient Rome* (London: Routledge, 1998).

and human perfection implied.[2] It is no wonder, then, that Paul describes the cross as a "stumbling block" to the Jews, "and unto the Gentiles foolishness" (1 Cor. 1:23). To understand this comment more fully, however, we should take its context in Paul's mission to Corinth into account, at least briefly.

The Foolishness of the Cross

Corinth was a city that thrived through trade. Located by the isthmus that links the Peloponnesian peninsula to the rest of Greece, it profited from the fact that shippers of goods from the eastern Mediterranean to Rome could avoid the hazards of the open sea by having their goods portaged across the isthmus, which is only a couple of miles wide. This geographic advantage brought Corinth a steady influx of traders, travelers, and sailors, which created what we would call a "multicultural" society. Archaeologists have found evidence of shrines and temples that were associated with Greek and Egyptian religion, as well as the Roman imperial cult. A Jewish community existed at Corinth too, and even a temple dedicated to "all the gods," lest any god be denied recognition.[3]

The atmosphere created by the confluence of these elements made Corinth, in the words of J. Paul Sampley, into the ancient equivalent of "Sin City."[4] There were trade and travel, a vibrant social fabric, and considerable wealth, but there was no deeply rooted culture. The division between the rich and the poor was large.

This is the picture that is reflected in Saint Paul's First Epistle to the Corinthians, composed in the early 50s. If at Antioch the Apostle had to deal with religious divisions over the Jewish heritage of the emerging Christian community, at Corinth the unrest in the "Jesus sect" was socially motivated. There were moral problems as well: "It is absolutely heard," writes Paul, "that there is fornication among you, and such fornication as the like

2. The quotations and ideas are from the fine essay by John M. G. Barclay, "Crucifixion as Wisdom: Exploring the Ideology of a Disreputable Social Movement," in *The Wisdom and Foolishness of God: First Corinthians 1–2 in Theological Exploration*, ed. Christophe Chalamet and Hans-Christoph Askani (Minneapolis: Fortress, 2015), 1–20, esp. 6 ("maximum degradation") and 9 ("development and perfection . . .").

3. I have adapted this description of Corinth from J. Paul Sampley, "The First Letter to the Corinthians," in *The New Interpreter's Bible* (Nashville: Abingdon, 2002), 10:773–74.

4. Sampley, "The First Letter to the Corinthians," 10:775.

is not among the heathens" (1 Cor. 5:1). This is why chapter 5 of the epistle begins a long series of exhortations regarding moral shortcomings. Many of these sins are sexual in nature, but others concern economics and degraded social relations among believers in general. In chapter 6, for example, Paul admonishes the community to abstain from lawsuits against each other: "I speak to your shame. . . . Brother goeth to law with brother, and that before unbelievers" (6:5–6). The community not only fails to live up to the Sermon on the Mount—"Why do you not rather take wrong?" Paul asks (6:7)—it also takes its disputes out into the world, where judgments will be made upon the basis of secular principles and laws. Furthermore, such use of the courts to resolve disputes reflected, as well as exacerbated, economic rifts, because the law served the interests of the wealthy. Sampley has noted that, in the Greco-Roman world, "only the wealthy, only the very powerful few who sat atop the steep social pyramid," were in a position to initiate civil court cases.[5]

Having sketched out the situation to which Paul speaks in First Corinthians, we turn back to his word regarding the foolishness of the cross. The passage is very strong, repeating the word "foolishness" (μωρία) and its cognates over and over:

> For the word of the cross, to them indeed that perish, is foolishness; but to them that are saved, that is, to us, it is the power of God. For it is written: *I will destroy the wisdom of the wise, and the prudence of the prudent I will reject* [cf. Isa. 21:14]. *Where is the wise? Where is the scribe? Where is the disputer of this world* [cf. Isa. 33:18]? Hath not God made foolish the wisdom of this world? For seeing that in the wisdom of God the world, by wisdom, knew not God, it pleased God, by the foolishness of *our* preaching, to save them that believe. For both the Jews require signs, and the Greeks seek after wisdom: But we preach Christ crucified, unto the Jews indeed a stumbling-block, and unto the Gentiles foolishness: But unto them that are called, both Jews and Greeks, Christ the power of God, and the wisdom of God. For the foolishness of God is wiser than men; and the weakness of God is stronger than men. For see your vocation, brethren, that *there are* not many wise according to the flesh, not many mighty, not many noble: But the foolish things of the world hath God chosen, that he may confound the wise; and the weak things of the world hath God chosen, that he may confound the strong.

5. Sampley, "The First Letter to the Corinthians," 10:853–64.

And the base things of the world, and the things that are contemptible, hath God chosen, and things that are not, that he might bring to naught things that are: That no flesh should glory in his sight. (1 Cor. 1:18–29)[6]

No one-dimensional interpretation of this pericope will do justice to its layers of meaning. The foolishness of the cross and the wisdom of the world (ἡ σοφία τοῦ κόσμου) are juxtaposed at several levels.

1. First, there is the socioeconomic level already discussed, which reflects the conditions and tensions within the Corinthian community to whom Paul's letter is addressed: "For see your vocation, brethren, that there are not many wise according to the flesh, not many mighty, not many noble." Drawing attention to the fact that the Corinthian community is largely composed of believers of low social status, Paul reminds its few wealthy members that God has shaken up the values of this world. These values do not count in the church; they have been suspended or even annulled. Did Jesus himself not die the death of a slave? There is a first "transvaluation of values" in this dimension of the passage.[7]

2. The second transvaluation comes in the juxtaposition of worldly wisdom with the foolishness of the faith, and of Paul's preaching the faith. Those who put their trust in the knowledge that they have acquired regarding the workings of the world will be disappointed, while those whom God has called will be saved. The emphasis on God's call (κλῆσις, v. 26; cf. 24) is crucial here: wisdom and prudence come from an effort of the subject to shape himself or herself—to acquire the right habits, as Aristotle would put it, in a community of (secular) virtue—whereas God's call is gratuitous. It has the power to save even the lowliest fool who answers the call.

3. God's call transgresses and annuls not only the division of the rich and the poor but—and here we are reminded of the central problem of the Epistle to the Galatians—also the division between Jews and gentiles. Equally shocked by the cross, albeit for different reasons, Jews and non-Jews are united in God's call. Or, to phrase this more accurately, the Jew/non-Jew distinction is annulled and replaced by a new one: believer versus nonbeliever.

4. "The Greeks seek after wisdom, but we preach Christ crucified": in this fourth antithesis, we can discern a repudiation not only of the kind

---

6. The Douay-Rheims Bible italicizes not only quotations from the Old Testament but also words not found in the Vulgate, such as "our" and "there are" in this text from First Corinthians.

7. Sampley, "The First Letter to the Corinthians," 10:811.

of worldly wisdom that would have characterized the wealthy members of the Corinthian church, but also of the more theoretical kind typically associated with the Greek philosophical tradition. Saint John Chrysostom interpreted the passage along these lines in his homilies on First Corinthians: "For Plato is cast out, not by some other wiser philosopher, but through an unlearned fisherman."[8] In this perspective, it would appear that God's foolishness is a direct negation of philosophical wisdom.

5. But this is not the case. While Paul speaks of God's foolishness, he also emphasizes that this divine "mania" is not simply opposed to wisdom. Rather, it constitutes a form of hyperwisdom, just as God's weakness on the cross must properly be understood as a hyperpower: "For the foolishness of God is wiser than men; and the weakness of God is stronger than men." Theologians in the Eastern tradition like Pseudo-Dionysius the Areopagite have therefore interpreted the foolishness of First Corinthians in accordance with an apophatic theology, which negates positive attributes of the Godhead insofar as they reflect the limitations of creaturely language and thought; at another, higher, and properly ineffable level these attributes return, being reaffirmed. The foolishness of the cross, then, is taken to annul wisdom as ordinarily understood while pointing to the unspeakable transcendent wisdom that is properly God's. This is how Pseudo-Dionysius elucidates the ascription of "foolishness" to God in *The Divine Names* (note, incidentally, the reference to Saint Paul as Dionysius's teacher):

> This is something which was marvelously grasped by that truly divine man, my teacher and yours and the light of our common instructor. For this is what he said: "The foolishness of God is wiser than men." Those words are true not only because all human thinking is a sort of error when compared with the solid permanence of the perfect divine thoughts but also because it is customary for theologians to apply negative terms to God, but contrary to the usual sense of deprivation.... Therefore let us supremely praise this foolish "Wisdom," which has neither reason nor intelligence, and let us describe it as the Cause of all intelligence and reason, of all wisdom and understanding.[9]

8. John Chrysostom, *In hom. 4 ad I Corinthios*, cited and translated by Andrew Louth, "Maximus the Confessor on the Foolishness of God and the Play of the Word," in Chalamet and Askani, *The Wisdom and Foolishness of God*, 89–99 (at 92).

9. Pseudo-Dionysius the Areopagite, *The Divine Names*, in *The Complete Works*, trans. Colm Luibheid, Classics of Western Spirituality (Mahwah, NJ: Paulist Press, 1987), chap. 7, no. 1, pp. 105–6.

The point of view from which Paul is able to declare the annulment and transcendence of worldly wisdom (in both its practical and more theoretical forms), together with the annulment and transcendence of worldly divisions (rich/poor, Jew/gentile), is eschatological: "This therefore I say, brethren; the time is short; it remaineth, that they also who have wives, be as if they had none; And they that weep, as though they wept not; and they that rejoice, as if they rejoiced not; and they that buy, as though they possessed not; And they that use this world, as if they used it not: for the fashion of this world passeth away" (1 Cor. 7:29–31). In the next verse, the passage continues with the verse we quoted in the introduction: "He that is without a wife, is solicitous for the things that belong to the Lord. . . ."[10]

"The time is short," says Paul, expecting the Lord to return soon. In the meantime, the reality of the world is not so much negated as suspended. The Corinthians are advised to live in the mode of the "as if not" (ὡς μή). Yes, it is preferable not to have a wife rather than having one—but it doesn't matter, in the end, as long as one lives *as though* one were not married. Similarly, it is surely preferable for a rich person to sell everything he or she has and give it to the poor, as the Lord himself commanded (Matt. 19:16–24); failing this determination and commitment, however, one should at least live *as if* one owned nothing. As Paul explains in Romans (4:17), it is God's call that brings this parallel world into existence; for God "quickeneth the dead; and calleth those things that are not, as those that are." (The Douay-Rheims version is a little obscure here in its literalness: "καλοῦντος τὰ μὴ ὄντα ὡς ὄντα" can also be rendered as "calls that which is not as though it were.") At the same time, God annihilates that which is; to recall our Corinthians passage: "And the base things of the world, and the things that are contemptible, hath God chosen, and things that are not, that he might bring to naught things that are" (1 Cor. 1:28).[11]

Paul's theology of the "as if"[12] indicates a certain softening of how the

10. See the introduction, p. 4 above.

11. In *God without Being*, Jean-Luc Marion interprets Rom. 4:17 and 1 Cor. 1:28 in terms of a Dionysian apophatic theology. God's calling of that which is not as though it were indicates a suspension of the ontological difference; in other words, for Marion, the difference between being and nonbeing does not point to Being, but to a "God without Being" who is Goodness and Love. See Marion, *God without Being*, trans. Thomas A. Carlson, Religion and Postmodernism (Chicago: University of Chicago Press, 1995), 83–102.

12. I am using this term advisedly. It would be an interesting task to compare Paul's theology of the "as if" with Hans Vaihinger's philosophy of the "as if," which was inspired, not by Scripture, but by Kant and Nietzsche. See Vaihinger, *The Philosophy of "As If": A System*

emerging Christian community read God's call, at least by comparison with many Gospel passages (which, of course, from a literary point of view, postdate the Pauline epistles). A passage like Matthew 10:34–37 ("I came not to send peace, but the sword"), considered in the previous chapter,[13] suggests that following Jesus requires a radical departure from the values of the world: a genuine transgression. For Paul, writing after Jesus's death and resurrection, in a state of readiness for the second coming, God's call puts the world into suspense. We should live *as though* the kingdom had already arrived; but it has not.

A New Socrates

If the message of the cross confounds the wise because the foolishness of God is wiser than men, what does this mean for the Christian attitude toward the Greek tradition of "seeking wisdom" (σοφίαν ζητεῖν; 1 Cor. 1:22)? Following Pseudo-Dionysius's interpretation, one would expect that philosophy (φιλο-σοφία) is suspended in Saint Paul's new world of the "as if" because "all human thinking is a sort of error when compared with the solid permanence of the perfect divine thoughts" (*Divine Names*). Surely, mere philosophy is incapable of capturing the logic of the cross (ὁ λόγος ... ὁ τοῦ σταυροῦ; 1 Cor. 1:18), which plays havoc with the principle of non-contradiction. Either God is wise or God is nonwise (that is, foolish): "hyperwisdom" is not a philosophical category. Neither is the notion that non-beings can be called "as if" they were beings: something either is, or it is not.

The Acts of the Apostles capture Paul's approach to philosophy in the story of his address at the Areopagus. Biblical scholars point out that, unlike Pauline letters like Galatians or First Corinthians, about whose historical authenticity there is no doubt, the Acts are closer in literary form (and in date) to the Gospel narratives. Thus, rather than aiming to provide an account of historical events and to intervene in them, the author of Acts (Luke, according to tradition) selects episodes from the earliest history of the church, which he interprets, synthesizes, and embellishes. To put this more bluntly, Scripture scholars believe that Paul actually wrote the letters

---

of the Theoretical, Practical, and Religious Fictions of Mankind, trans. C. K. Ogden, 2nd ed., International Library of Psychology, Philosophy, and Scientific Method (London: Routledge and Kegan Paul, 1935).

13. See Chapter 2, p. 65.

to the Galatians and to the Corinthians; he may or may not have given a speech at the Areopagus during his visit to Athens. The speech may be Luke's way of illustrating how Paul approached his mission to the gentiles, and to the philosophers of Athens in particular.[14] Despite this question mark regarding its historical authenticity, Paul's speech at the Areopagus represents a remarkable episode in the "great world-historical drama" in the course of which Jerusalem encountered Athens.[15]

Paul's reaction, upon entering Athens, is very "Jewish": he is shocked at the pervasiveness of idols: "his spirit was stirred within him, seeing the city wholly given to idolatry" (Acts 17:16). His missionary work takes him first to the synagogue, but this is mentioned only in passing: the focus of this episode lies elsewhere, namely, in the marketplace, the ἀγορά, where Paul, we are told, "disputed" "every day with them that were there" (v. 17). The description of the scene, together with the use of the words ἀγορά and διαλέγεσθαι ("to dispute"), evokes neither an Old Testament prophet nor Jesus, but rather a famous Greek philosopher: "Both verb and noun recall," C. K. Barrett comments, "the archetypal philosophical figure of Socrates, who was always available for discussion in the public places of Athens."[16] In philosophy, the verb δια-λέγεσθαι, which connotes a careful going "through" the λόγος, designated the activity of philosophical "dialectic," the investigation of truth through discussion.

The story moves fast, as the next verse already introduces those with whom Paul disputed every day in the *agora*: these people were none other than representatives of the two leading philosophical currents of the day, namely, Epicureanism and Stoicism. These philosophers were, it seems, almost as superficial as the Corinthians; an aside in verse 21 informs us that "all the Athenians, and strangers that were there, employed themselves in nothing else, but either in telling or in hearing some new thing." Thus the novelty of Paul's message ("he preached to them Jesus and the resurrection"; v. 18) on the one hand piqued the curiosity of the philosophers in the *agora*: "May we know what this new doctrine is, which thou speakest of?" (v. 19). On the other hand, it presented a real danger to the Apostle, who

14. For a good introduction to Acts, see Robert W. Wall, "The Acts of the Apostles," in *The New Interpreter's Bible*, 10:3–34.

15. That Paul's speech at the Areopagus represents "a scene, playing itself out on Athenian soil, of the great world-historical drama" is Eduard Norden's judgment; see *Agnostos Theos. Untersuchungen zur Formengeschichte religiöser Rede*, 5th ed. (Stuttgart: Teubner, 1971), 1.

16. C. K. Barrett, *A Critical and Exegetical Commentary on the Acts of the Apostles*, vol. 2 (Edinburgh: T. & T. Clark, 1998), 828.

was accused, just like Socrates, of introducing new gods to the city: "He seemeth to be a setter forth of new gods" (v. 18).

The beginning of verse 19 is ambiguous regarding the philosophers' reaction to Paul's new teachings: "And taking him, they brought him to the Areopagus . . ." "Taking" is ἐπιλαβόμενοι in the Greek text, whose meanings range from "an arrest, with or without violence," to "a well-intentioned attachment."[17] So Paul either got dragged to the Areopagus to defend himself before the council (Socrates-like), or he was given the opportunity to spread his message in a prominent place, the Areopagus hill (not a mountain, but still an elevated location perhaps recalling other such places in the Scriptures). Or is the reader meant to entertain both possibilities, as Barrett suggests?[18]

The speech that Paul now delivers is carefully crafted. As the famous classicist Eduard Norden demonstrated in his pioneering study *Agnostos Theos*, the writer uses the literary form of a traditional missionary speech to interweave biblical and Hellenistic elements.[19] Following in Norden's footsteps since *Agnostos Theos* first appeared in 1913, biblical scholars have identified several currents that flow together in Paul's speech.

1. The first current stems from the Jewish abhorrence of idols. Thus, when Paul rises to address the Athenian philosophers, his first impulse is to critique their idolatry: "Ye men of Athens, I perceive that in all things you are too superstitious. For passing by, and seeing your idols . . ." (vv. 22–23). But the interpretation of these verses is not straightforward. Instead of critiquing the Athenians for their idolatry, Paul could be praising them for their piety, in a *captatio benevolentiae*. This is because the phrase that Douay-Rheims has translated as "too superstitious" is ambiguous: ὡς δεισιδαιμονεστέρους ὑμᾶς θεωρῶ could mean "I perceive you as extremely superstitious," or "as extremely pious"! Barrett may have a solution to the dilemma when he draws attention to the particle ὡς, which of course means "as if." On Barrett's interpretation, Paul may be saying, "I perceive you as though [you were] extremely pious": so the Athenians live in a world of "as if" piety.[20] What is the problem? Are they hypocrites?

2. As verse 23 shows, the problem is that the Athenians live a religion in which the reality of the divine remains vague and implicit: "For pass-

17. Barrett, *A Critical and Exegetical Commentary*, 831.

18. See Barrett, *A Critical and Exegetical Commentary*, 831.

19. Norden spoke of a "hellenische und jüdisch-christliche Missionspredikt" (*Agnostos Theos*, 125).

20. See Barrett, *A Critical and Exegetical Commentary*, 836.

ing by, and seeing your idols, I found an altar also, on which was written, *To the unknown God.* What therefore you worship, without knowing it, I preach to you." While archaeologists have not found a temple with such an inscription in ancient Athens, there is literary evidence that it existed—with one crucial difference (already reported by Saint Jerome): the dedication was not "to an unknown God" but rather "to the unknown gods." The Greeks were polytheists, after all. The idea—we came across it in discussing Corinth—was to ensure that no god who deserved worship was excluded, even foreign deities unknown in Athens. Norden conjectured that Paul (or, rather, the author of Paul's speech) changed the plural into a singular in order to emphasize the implicit presence of the one God in Greek religious practice.[21]

"What therefore you worship, without knowing, I preach to you": Paul's strategy here, in addressing the philosophers of Athens, very much resembles Jesus's approach to the law, as well as the Christian interpretation of the New Testament as a sublation of the Old. For Paul conceives of Greek religion as a prelude to Judaism and Christianity. The value of Greek polytheism, in the providential unfolding of history, consists in the fact that it foreshadows the fullness of religion in an implicit and inchoate way.[22] This fullness is what Paul now preaches, challenging the Athenian philosophers to overcome their ignorance: they worship what they do not know.[23]

3. The "powerful resonance" of the word "to preach" (καταγγέλλειν) will have eluded the Athenian philosophers; in the Gospels καταγγέλλειν

21. See Norden, *Agnostos Theos,* 121. In a sympathetic examination and critique of Norden's theses, Pieter W. van der Horst comes to the conclusion that there may well have been an altar with the singular inscription "To the unknown god" in Athens. But this is not certain. "*If* there was no altar with an inscription in the singular in Athens or *if* in a periegetic handbook Luke had only read about Athenian altars with dedications in the plural, he may have seen fit to bring about this adaptation in order to get a convenient point of departure for Paul's speech" ("The Altar of the 'Unknown God' in Athens (Acts 17:23) and the Cults of 'Unknown Gods' in the Greco-Roman World," in Pieter W. van der Horst, *Hellenism—Judaism—Christianity: Essays on Their Interaction,* 2nd ed., Contributions to Biblical Exegesis and Theology 8 [Louvain: Peeters, 1998], 187–220, at 217).

22. See Bultmann's commentary on this passage, in his *Theology of the New Testament,* vol. 2, trans. Kendrick Grobel (New York: Scribner's Sons, 1955), 117: "The author of Acts further classifies Christianity as a religion within world history by letting Paul in the Areopagus-discourse appeal to heathen piety by the reference to an inscription on an Athenian altar and to the Stoic belief in God (17:23, 28). This amounts," Bultmann continues, citing Philipp Vielhauer, "to acclaiming 'heathen history and culture and the heathen religious world as Christianity's pre-history.'"

23. This is well seen in Wall, "The Acts of the Apostles," 10:246.

is used "for the church's prophetic witness, when the good news is proclaimed for conversion."[24] Part of the brilliance of the speech is that it plays with the Athenians' ignorance of the "new doctrine" Paul announces. Thus, the address is full of allusions to the Old Testament, which however remain in the background as the Apostle foregrounds the congruence between his "new doctrine" and the philosophers' own teachings. The next verse is a good example: I preach to you, declares the Apostle, "God, who made the world, and all things therein; he, being Lord of heaven and earth, dwelleth not in temples made with hands" (v. 24). A Jewish/Christian listener hears Genesis 1 here, but the Epicureans could find in this verse confirmation for their critique of anthropomorphism. Similarly, a couple of verses later, Paul speaks of the single origin of the human race (v. 26), which could be read as an allusion either to the creation of all men in Adam or to the Stoic doctrine that the human race is one, stemming from a single origin.

Paul continues in this vein for several verses, quoting Greek poetry, for example, to focus on "what religious Athenians would find familiar."[25] Only at the very end does his speech take an unambiguously Christian turn, as he preaches penance, the final judgment, and the resurrection of the dead. At this point, the attention span of most of the audience in the Areopagus is exhausted: "And when they had heard of the resurrection of the dead, some indeed mocked, but others said: We will hear thee again concerning this matter" (v. 32). There are a few converts, however: "But certain men adhering to him, did believe; among them was also Dionysius, the Areopagite, and a woman named Damaris, and others with them" (v. 34). What an irony that Dionysius the Areopagite would return, a few centuries later, to preach the unknown God to the Christians.

The conclusion that emerges from our discussion of the meaning of the foolishness of the cross in First Corinthians, and of the Areopagus speech in Acts, is that there are similarities as well as differences in the relationship of Christianity to Judaism, on the one hand, and to the Greco-Roman culture, on the other. There is a similar movement toward "fulfillment" or sublation in both cases, Christianity conceiving of itself as bringing the other traditions to completion, that is to say, as absorbing them at a higher level and thus superseding them. The case of Judaism, however, is especially delicate because the Jews, unlike the Greeks and the Romans, had much more than a merely inchoate understanding of God: they had met

24. Wall, "The Acts of the Apostles," 10:246.
25. Barrett, *A Critical and Exegetical Commentary*, 839.

him! While Israel's covenant with the Lord bestows an enduring validity upon the law ("one jot, or one tittle shall not pass"; Matt. 5:18), the Jews' proximity to the Christian community—nay, the initial identity of the two groups—also caused the emerging church to reject its roots with particular force: Ἀνάθεμα ἔστω![26]

The gentiles were less close, although the Greco-Roman culture was also by no means foreign to Jesus and his followers. Jesus was born a Roman subject and died a Roman death; the canonical accounts of his life and that of the early church have come down to us in Greek. Yet the relationship was different from that with Judaism: the church arose *out of* Judaism, one could say, and *into* the Greco-Roman civilization. It is clear that Christianity could not reject the pagan culture of antiquity any more than it could ultimately eliminate Judaism from its identity.

On the face of it, Paul's word of the "foolishness of the cross" suggests a radical negation of Greek wisdom. As our reading of the passage has shown, however, the situation is more complex. Worldly wisdom is not so much negated as transcended by faith—faith in God's higher wisdom and in his greater power. Paul's call to live in a world of the "as if" puts the wisdom of the world in suspension: it is not so much annulled as rendered irrelevant. His speech at the Areopagus goes a step further in demonstrating that the "new doctrine" he is preaching can be couched in the language of Greek philosophy and poetry—before transcending them in the good news of the resurrection. This willingness to engage with the pagan world in a more positive way is due not least to the different historical contexts in which the Pauline epistles and the Acts of the Apostles were composed. As Bultmann has remarked, "while for Paul, Christ, being 'the end of the Law' (Rom. 10:4), is also the end of history, in the thought of Acts he becomes the beginning of a new history of salvation, the history of Christianity."[27] For the Paul of the epistles, the end is nigh, whereas the "Paul" who speaks at the Areopagus is looking toward a Christian future.

It is in this light that we now consider another strategy that the church employed during the first centuries of its encounter with Greece and Rome. This strategy will lead us back to the Old Testament—read not as the history of Israel, but as the future of the Christian church.

26. On the dynamics of the proximate in relation to a dominant identity, one may read with profit Jonathan Dollimore, *Sexual Dissidence: Augustine to Wilde, Freud to Foucault* (Oxford: Oxford University Press, 1991), 33.

27. Bultmann, *Theology of the New Testament*, 2:117.

The Spoils of Egypt

One of the Old Testament passages that have most embarrassed exegetes occurs in the book of Exodus, in the context of the final plague that the Lord visits upon the Egyptians to make possible the departure of the Israelites. After Pharaoh ignores Moses's entreaties as well as all the prior warnings that he was given through a succession of natural disasters, the Lord kills the firstborn of Egypt: "And it came to pass at midnight, the Lord slew every firstborn in the land of Egypt, from the firstborn of the Pharaoh, who sat on his throne, unto the firstborn of the captive woman that was in the prison, and all the firstborn of cattle" (Exod. 12:29). Horrified, the Egyptians let Moses's people go; in fact, they urge them to depart.

This action, however, is not what caused the exegetes' unease, for it only reestablished justice and order in God's realm. After all, Pharaoh had the male babies of the Israelites killed first (Exod. 1:22), directly transgressing the Lord's commandment to his people that they should "increase and multiply" (Gen. 1:28). Moreover, the struggle between Pharaoh and Moses revolved around whom the Israelites should serve: Pharaoh, who oppressed them through hard labor, or the Lord, who was entitled to their worship. Egypt's utter defeat, then, ensured the recognition of "God's absolute sovereignty," both by the Egyptians and by his own people.[28]

This is the background to Exodus 12:35–36, which narrates some of the circumstances that surrounded the exodus from Egypt: "And the children of Israel did as Moses had commanded: and they asked of the Egyptians vessels of silver and gold, and very much raiment. And the Lord gave favor to the people in the sight of the Egyptians, so that they lent unto them: and they stripped the Egyptians." These verses become even clearer when read in conjunction with two earlier Exodus passages in which the Lord respectively prophesies and orders these very events:

> And I will give favor to this people, in the sight of the Egyptians: and when you go forth, you shall not depart empty: But every woman shall ask of her neighbor, and of her that is in her house, vessels of silver and of gold, and raiment: and you shall put them on your sons and daughters, and shall spoil Egypt. (3:21–22)

---

28. I have been following the exegesis in Joel S. Allen, *The Despoliation of Egypt in Pre-Rabbinic, Rabbinic, and Patristic Traditions*, Supplements to Vigiliae Christianae 92 (Leiden: Brill, 2008). The quotation occurs on p. 9.

Therefore thou shalt tell all the people that every man ask of his friend, and every woman of her neighbor, vessels of silver, and of gold. And the Lord will give favor to his people in the sight of the Egyptians. (11:2–3)

So, as the Israelites leave Egypt, they ask their Egyptian neighbors to borrow valuable items—gold, silver, and precious clothing—which the Egyptians give them, under the Lord's providential guidance. However, as the texts make clear, there was no intention to return the borrowed goods: the Israelites "stripped" or "spoiled" (נצל, *nṣl*) their Egyptian neighbors.

Some modern interpreters see little difficulty in this course of events. Thus, Walter Brueggemann believes that the talk about "asking" the Egyptians for precious items is "likely ironic": "The language of 'favor from Yahweh' and 'asking' in fact disguises marauding and plundering, which the erstwhile slaves work against their deeply resented masters."[29] Given the dynamic of the narrative—the struggle of the Israelites against their Egyptian oppressors, and of the God of Israel against Pharaoh—the plundering does not trouble Brueggemann. It signifies the total victory of God's people and the downfall of an unjust regime: "oppressive regimes vanish in the twinkling of an eye and leave only stories told by those newly endowed with power."[30]

Earlier commentators did not find it so easy to account for the despoiling of the Egyptians, involving as it did deception of one's neighbors, as well as theft. Is there not a direct violation here of two commandments, "Thou shalt not steal" and "Thou shalt not covet thy neighbor's house . . . nor any thing that is his" (Exod. 20:15 and 17)? In addition to the inherent difficulty of the passage, it became a favorite anti-Judaic argument in polemical Greco-Roman literature that sought to depict the Hebrew Bible in a negative light. Thus, "textual therapies" had to be devised to address both internal Jewish questions and external criticism.[31]

The first strategy to defuse the passage took it quite literally, but added an explanation for the pillaging: all Moses's people did was claim their just

---

29. Walter Brueggemann, "The Book of Exodus," in *The New Interpreter's Bible* (Nashville: Abingdon, 1994), 1:781.

30. Brueggemann, "The Book of Exodus," 1:782.

31. "Textual therapies" is a felicitous expression from Joel S. Allen's article, "The Despoliation of Egypt: Origen and Augustine—from Stolen Treasures to Saved Texts," in *Israel's Exodus in Transdisciplinary Perspective: Text, Archaeology, Culture, and Geoscience*, ed. Thomas E. Levy, Thomas Schneider, and William H. C. Propp, Quantitative Methods in the Humanities and Social Sciences (Cham, Switzerland: Springer, 2015), 347–56, at 348.

wages for the long period of servitude and hard labor to which Pharaoh had subjected them. We find this approach reflected within Scripture itself, namely, in the book of Wisdom, which was composed—in Greek, as there is no evidence of a Hebrew original—in the Hellenistic Jewish circles of Alexandria, perhaps under Caligula's rule (AD 37–41). Wisdom alludes to the despoliation of Egypt in the following terms:[32]

> She [wisdom] entered into the soul of the servant of God, and stood against dreadful kings in wonders and signs. And she rendered to the just the wages of their labors, and conducted them in a wonderful way: and she was to them for a covert by day, and for the light of stars by night: And she brought them through the Red Sea, and carried them over through a great water (Wisd. of Sol. 10:16–18).[33]

Wisdom was neither the first nor the last commentary to explain the Exodus narrative in this manner; the "just wages" theory was common among both Jewish and Christian exegetes.[34] In another Jewish tradition that took the despoliation literally—represented by Flavius Josephus, for example—the claim was advanced that the Egyptians let the Israelites have precious items as a parting gift, out of feelings of neighborly affection.[35]

Philo of Alexandria was the first interpreter to understand the despoliation allegorically. For Philo (who does not make his remarks in the context of Exodus, but draws on Genesis 15:14, "But I shall judge the nation which they shall serve, and after this they shall come out with great substance"), the spoils of Egypt signify the viaticum that the Lord has given his people for their journey from enslavement to the passions toward the heavenly kingdom. What is the nature of this food for the road? Philo responds

32. For a full interpretation of Wisd. of Sol. 10, see Andrew T. Glicksman, *Wisdom of Solomon 10: A Jewish Hellenistic Reinterpretation of Early Israelite History through Sapiential Lenses*, Deuterocanonical and Cognate Literature Studies 9 (Berlin: de Gruyter, 2011).

33. For commentary on the awkward phrase "and she was to them for a covert by day, and for the light of stars by night," see the following chapter, pp. 125–26.

34. The most complete inventory of Christian interpretations of the despoiling of the Egyptians is the article by Georges Folliet, "La *spoliatio Aegyptiorum* (Exode 3:21–23; 11:2–3; 12:35–36). Les interprétations de cette image chez les Pères et autres écrivains écclésiastiques," *Traditio* 57 (2002): 1–48. The book already cited by Joel S. Allen, *The Despoliation of Egypt*, studies the interpretive history in a series of in-depth chapters on both Jewish and Christian writers and texts.

35. On Flavius Josephus's interpretation, and the particular circumstances that brought it about, one may read Allen, *The Despoliation of Egypt*, 119–36.

that the soul's journey back to its native land is sparked and sustained by education in the Greek "encyclical" disciplines—arithmetic, geometry, astronomy, and music—which instill a sense of the harmony of the universe. Joel S. Allen has found Philo's interpretation to be "completely unique in all its details"; nevertheless, Philo first saw the possibility of employing the despoliation motif to assign a role to secular education in the soul's spiritual growth. This connection "had a strong impact on the theology and praxis of the Christian world."[36]

We see evidence of this impact in Origen's famous letter to Gregory, which employs the Exodus narrative to develop a detailed allegory. The young Gregory (later bishop of Caesarea) is hesitating regarding his vocation. In his letter, Origen offers him advice. The young man's gifts, Origen remarks, are considerable, so that a career as a Roman lawyer would be just as possible as work in one of the famous Greek schools of philosophy. However, that is not what Origen urges Gregory to pursue: "But my desire for you has been that you should direct the whole force of your intelligence to Christianity as your end, and that in the way of production." Applying one's intelligence to Christianity of course means interpreting the Scriptures. This in turn requires philosophy:

> The children of the philosophers speak of geometry and music and grammar and rhetoric and astronomy as being ancillary to philosophy; and in the same way we might speak of philosophy itself as being ancillary to Christianity. It is something of this sort perhaps that is enigmatically indicated in the directions God is represented in the Book of Exodus as giving to the children of Israel. They are directed to beg from their neighbors and from those dwelling in their tents vessels of silver and gold, and raiment; thus they are to spoil the Egyptians, and to obtain materials for making the things they are told to provide in connection with the worship of God.[37]

36. Allen, *The Despoliation of Egypt*, 117.

37. "Letter of Origen to Gregory," trans. Allan Menzies, in *The Ante-Nicene Fathers: Translations of the Writings of the Fathers down to A.D. 325, Original Supplement to the American Edition*, ed. Allan Menzies, vol. 10 (Grand Rapids: Eerdmans, n.d.), 295–96, at 295. The Greek text is conveniently accessible in Sources chrétiennes; see Grégoire le Thaumaturge, *Remerciement à Origène, suivi de la lettre d'Origène à Grégoire*, ed. and trans. Henri Crouzel, Sources chrétiennes 148 (Paris: Cerf, 1969), 185–95. For commentary, see Allen, *The Despoliation of Egypt*, 211–33, as well as the classic study by R. P. C. Hanson, *Origen's Doctrine of Tradition* (London: SPCK, 1954), chap. 9: "Revelation outside the Bible" (157–73). Matthew J. Pereira's

Origen develops this allegory by elaborating on the scriptural text, adding details that, one may assume, he derived from haggadic sources. Thus, he explains that the Israelites took from Egypt gold of various degrees of quality, which they used to build the tabernacle: the finest gold was used for the ark of the covenant and the holy of holies; gold of lesser quality was wrought into the golden candlestick—and so forth, down to the precious garments, which embroiderers, "working with the wisdom of God" (μετὰ σοφίας θεοῦ),[38] made into curtains for the tabernacle. The implication for Origen's allegorical interpretation is that the Christian will find knowledge of various degrees of usefulness in Greek philosophy: some elements of pagan thought may indeed be suitable for the highest theological use; others may aid us in thinking through matters of lesser importance. Discernment is important here, is what Origen appears to be suggesting, as well as humble reliance upon God's graceful guidance: "The Egyptians had not made a proper use of them [i.e., the precious goods]; but the Hebrews used them, for the wisdom of God was with them (διὰ τὴν τοῦ θεοῦ σοφίαν), for religious purposes."[39]

What renders the plundering of the Egyptians legitimate, then, is the fact that they did not use their possessions properly, for the worship of God. The Israelites did not steal anything, but only returned the precious metals and garments to their rightful owner, who is ultimately God himself. The strategy behind these thoughts is ingenious, allowing for a Christian use of pagan philosophy because the Christian adaptation will allow the genuine wisdom that Greek philosophy contains to be connected with the Source of all wisdom. We are no doubt dealing with another case of fulfillment or sublation here: Christians are able to raise Greek wisdom to the theological level where it belongs, and to preserve it at that level, while the imperfect version that the pagans themselves possessed is canceled. Interestingly, the Christian tradition generally reserved the despoliation motif to conceive of its relationship to pagan thought; occasional voices,

---

piece, "From the Spoils of Egypt: An Analysis of Origen's *Letter to Gregory*" (in *Origeniana Decima: Origen as Writer*, ed. Sylwia Kaczmarek, Henryk Pietras, and Andrzej Dziadowiec, Bibliotheca Ephemeridum Theologicarum Lovaniensium 244 [Louvain: Peeters, 2011], 221–48), reads the letter in light of Michel Serres's concept of the "parasite." But Pereira never answers his central question, "Does Origen's appropriation of Hellenistic philosophy reveal the abuse parasitical relationship demonstrated in Serres' analysis of networks, or is there something more symbiotic occurring underneath the surface?" (237).

38. "Letter of Origen to Gregory," 295.

39. "Letter of Origen to Gregory," 295.

however, did notice the structural analogy to the way in which the gospel was thought to have sublated the law. Thus, Ambrose of Milan declared, commenting on Psalm 119:162 ("I will rejoice at thy words, as one that hath found great spoil"):

> *The law is spiritual* [Rom. 7:14]; the Jew who hears in a bodily manner does not hear it, but the one who hears in the spirit does. They have books, but they do not have the meaning of the books; they have prophets, but they do not have the one whom the books have prophesied. For how could they have the one whom they have not received? . . . The one who has the word of God has copious spoils: he has the resurrection, he has justice, virtue, and wisdom—he has everything, because *by him all things consist* [Col. 1:17]. The Hebrews plundered the Egyptians and carried off their vessels; the Christian people have the spoils of the Jews, and we have everything that they did not even know they had. They carried off material gold and silver, we have received gold of the mind, we have acquired the silver of heavenly speech.[40]

This passage from Ambrose throws into clear relief a problematic element in an otherwise brilliant hermeneutic strategy—whether this strategy is applied to the Hebrew Scriptures or to pagan philosophy. I mean the element of condescension inherent to a view according to which those who originally received God's revelations, or produced certain texts and ideas, did not understand them. The Jews and the Greeks may have had a lot of books, but we have had to wait for Christian eyes to read these books in the right spirit. There is not a little violence in such a view: it really is a plundering.

But let us return for a final thought regarding Origen's letter to Gregory. Origen's encouragement to study Greek philosophy ends on a cau-

---

40. Ambrose, *Expositio Pslami CXVIII*, ed. Michael Petschenig, Corpus Scriptorum Ecclesiasticorum Latinorum 62 (Vienna: F. Tempsky; Leipzig: G. Freytag, 1913), p. 490, ll. 9–21: "lex spiritalis est [Rom. 7:14]; non illam audit Iudaeus qui audit corporaliter, sed ille audit qui audit in spiritu. habent illi libros, sed sensum librorum non habent; habent prophetas, sed non habent quem illi prophetauerunt. quomodo enim habent quem non receperunt? . . . multa habet spolia qui habet dei uerbum; habet resurrectionem, habet iustitiam, uirtutem atque sapientiam, habet omnia, quia omnia in ipso constant [Col. 1:17]. Hebraei spoliauerunt Aegyptios et uasa eorum abstulerunt; Iudaeorum spolia habet populus christianus et totum habemus, quod illi habere se nesciebant. illi aurum et argentum materiale abstulerunt, nos aurum mentis accepimus, nos adquisiuimus caelestis sermonis argentum."

tionary note. Conflating two narratives from 1 Kings—the story of Hadad the Edomite (11:14–25) and that of Jeroboam, which follows immediately after the first (11:26–14:20)—Origen reminds Gregory that not every Israelite who spent time in Egypt returned with treasures to his native land. Indeed, Hadad/Jeroboam was drawn into idolatry, making his people worship golden calves. Interpreting this biblical narrative, Origen warns that there are many "who, founding on some piece of Greek learning, have brought forth heretical ideas, and have as it were made golden calves in Bethel, which is, being interpreted, the house of God."[41] What an irony that Origen himself was later found to belong in this category.

Augustine imported Origen's allegorical treatment of the despoliation narrative into the Latin West, albeit with some important nuances.[42] He knew the literal exegesis, which he employed (and elaborated upon) at several points in his oeuvre in order to respond to Manichaean criticisms of the Old Testament.[43] His allegorical interpretation in *De doctrina christiana*, however, became "the *locus classicus* to which medieval authors usually referred when addressing the problem of the relationship between pagan culture and Christian revelation."[44] Given Augustine's indebtedness to the tradition preceding him, many motifs from the following text are already familiar to us:

41. "Letter of Origen to Gregory," 296.

42. It is not clear how Augustine learned of Origen's interpretation, given the absence of a Latin translation. Allen, *The Despoliation of Egypt*, 258, believes that Origen's allegorical reading "was already deeply embedded in the interpretive tradition."

43. See Allen, *The Despoliation of Egypt*, 241–42.

44. Pier Franco Beatrice, "The Treasures of the Egyptians: A Chapter in the History of Patristic Exegesis and Late Antique Culture," in *Studia Patristica*, vol. 43, *Papers Presented at the Fourteenth International Conference on Patristic Studies Held in Oxford 2003*, ed. F. Young, M. Edwards, and P. Parvis (Louvain: Peeters, 2006), 150–83, at 179. Frederick Van Fleteren expresses a widely shared view when he writes that *De doctrina christiana* "may be justly reckoned the charter of the Christian intellectual"; see his article, "St. Augustine, Neoplatonism, and the Liberal Arts: The Background to *De doctrina christiana*," in *De doctrina christiana: A Classic of Western Culture*, ed. Duane W. H. Arnold and Pamela Bright, Christianity and Judaism in Antiquity 9 (Notre Dame: University of Notre Dame Press, 1995), 14–24 (at 14). In the same volume, Christoph Schäublin counters that "*De doctrina christiana* is composed from a narrowly utilitarian, extremely reductionist viewpoint. All that counts is the Bible and its message." It is true that Augustine centers all knowledge on Scripture, so that there is no autonomous value to secular branches of knowledge. But Schäublin lets himself be carried away when he claims that "Augustine would prefer simply to eliminate the arts and sciences altogether." See "*De doctrina christiana:* A Classic of Western Culture?" in Arnold and Bright, *De doctrina christiana: A Classic of Western Culture*, 47–67 (the quotations are both on p. 53).

Any statements by those who are called philosophers, especially the Platonists, which happen to be true and consistent with our faith should not cause alarm, but be claimed for our own use, as it were from owners who have no right to them (*tamquam ab iniustis possessoribus*). Like the treasures of the ancient Egyptians, who possessed not only idols and heavy burdens which the people of Israel hated and shunned but also vessels and ornaments of silver and gold, and clothes, which on leaving Egypt the people of Israel, in order to make better use of them, surreptitiously claimed for themselves (they did this not on their own authority but at God's command, and the Egyptians in their ignorance actually gave them the things of which they had made poor use)—similarly all the branches of pagan learning contain not only false and superstitious fantasies and burdensome studies that involve unnecessary effort, which each one of us must loathe and avoid as under Christ's guidance we abandon the company of pagans (*duce Christo de societate gentilium exiens*), but also studies for liberated minds which are more appropriate to the service of the truth, and some very useful moral instruction, as well as the various truths about monotheism to be found in their writers. These treasures—like the silver and gold, which they did not create but dug, as it were, from the mines of providence, which is everywhere (*de quibusdam quasi metallis divinae providentiae, quae ubique infusa est*)—which were used wickedly and harmfully in the service of demons must be removed by Christians, as they separate themselves in spirit from the wretched company of pagans (*cum ab eorum misera societate sese animo separat*), and applied to their true function (*ad usum iustum*), that of preaching the gospel. As for their clothing—which corresponds to human institutions, but those appropriate to human society, which in this life we cannot do without—this may be accepted and kept for conversion to Christian purposes. This is exactly what many good and faithful Christians have done. We can see, can we not, the amount of gold, silver, and clothing with which Cyprian, that most attractive writer and most blessed martyr, was laden when he left Egypt; is not the same true of Lactantius, and Victorinus, of Optatus, and Hilary, to say nothing of people still alive, and countless Greek scholars? This is what had been done earlier by Moses himself, that most faithful servant of God, of whom it is written that he was trained in "all the wisdom of the Egyptians" [Acts 7:22]. Pagan society, riddled with superstition, would never have given to all these men the arts which it considered useful—least of all at a time when it was trying to shake off the yoke of Christ and persecuting Christians—if it had suspected that they would be adapted to the purpose of worshipping the one true God, by whom the worship of idols would be eradicated. But they did give their gold and silver and clothing to God's people as it left Egypt, little knowing that the things they were giving away would be put back (*redderentur*) into the service of Christ. The event narrated in Exodus was certainly a figure, and this is what it foreshadowed. (I say this without prejudice to any other interpretation of equal or greater importance.)[45]

A few remarks are in order:

1. Augustine dispossesses pagan culture of its fruits, on the argument that the pagans are "owners who have no right to them" or, more literally, that they are "unjust possessors" (*iniusti possessores*). This pagan injustice has everything to do with their misdirected, idolatrous worship. All that Christians are doing, therefore, in appropriating elements of the heathens' culture, is to return (*reddere*) these elements to their "true function"— again more literally, their "just use" (*usus iustum*)—which is the service of the true God.

2. The aspect of deception that troubled other interpreters of the Exodus narrative does not bother Augustine here. On the contrary, he repeatedly emphasizes the need to adapt suitable elements of the pagan cultural world secretly and surreptitiously to Christian use, as the pagans would not knowingly let their achievements be repurposed in this manner. Augustine seems to be recommending a certain duplicitousness in the Christian intercourse with the non-Christian world.

3. Like Origen before him, Augustine strongly urges discernment: much that the Greco-Roman civilization has produced is worthless. There is no need to occupy oneself with "false and superstitious fantasies"; indeed, much in the pagan civilization is closely connected with thoroughly misguided religious beliefs and practices. Like Saint Paul, who saw poten-

---

45. Augustine, *De doctrina christiana*, ed. and trans. R. P. H. Green, Oxford Early Christian Texts (Oxford: Clarendon, 1995), 2.40.60–61, pp. 124–27. Another allegory that functioned in the same context was that of the beautiful captive woman in Deut. 21:10–14, where the Lord allows the Israelites to take beautiful women from conquered enemies as their wives. Henri de Lubac discusses the allegory in detail in *Medieval Exegesis*, vol. 1, *The Four Senses of Scripture*, trans. Marc Sebanc, Ressourcement: Retrieval and Renewal in Catholic Thought (Grand Rapids: Eerdmans; Edinburgh: T. & T. Clark, 1998), 211–24. There are connotations of rape or at least humiliation ("thou hast humbled her"; 21:14) in the Deuteronomy passage, which render it similar to the despoliation episode in Exodus.

tial in the Athenians' worship of the "unknown god" yet was appalled by their idolatry, Augustine judges the Roman world that surrounds him to be demonic in many ways—hence his strong emphasis on the importance of separating oneself from the "wretched company of pagans."

4. On the other hand, Augustine is able to envision a degree of institutional integration of Christians into society that earlier church fathers would have found difficult to imagine. Or is he talking about a kind of parallel Christian society—another "city"—that would accept and keep certain Roman institutions "for conversion to Christian purposes"? Be that as it may, Augustine's more positive view of Roman institutions reflects the improved status of Christians in the Roman Empire that followed the Edict of Milan (313) and especially the Edict of Thessalonica (380), which elevated Christianity to the Roman state religion. In these circumstances, it was possible to avoid the "wretched company of pagans" and yet be a Roman citizen.

5. Why is it even possible to find elements of truth in pagan civilization? The answer is that the "mines of divine providence"—the source of the precious metals of the Egyptians—occur everywhere. More literally Augustine says that the divine providence *ubique infusa est*: it has been poured out or spread everywhere. This is a biblical conviction, which we already discovered in Paul's references to the "unknown god,"[46] but it is also a view that Augustine would have encountered in Saint Justin Martyr's doctrine of the *logos spermatikos*, according to which God has implanted in all things a "seed" or trace of his own goodness.[47] This theory was widely held by the church fathers, for whom it provided a metaphysical basis for—in modern parlance—intercultural dialogue. If God has endowed all cultures with some spark of his presence, obnubilated as that spark may be by falsehoods and superstitions, then no one stands totally outside of God's revelation, and every civilization has a potential to contribute to humanity's quest for truth. Furthermore, the theory takes care of the problem of incommensurability: if we are all God's children, we should be able to talk to each other, even if sometimes with difficulty. This theory is still held by contemporary Christian thinkers.[48]

---

46. Rom. 2:15 is similar, speaking of the "work of the law written in their [i.e., the gentiles'] hearts."

47. On the sources and meaning of Justin Martyr's teaching regarding the *logos spermatikos*, one may read Ragnar Holte's carefully argued piece, "Logos Spermatikos: Christianity and Ancient Philosophy according to St. Justin's Apologies," trans. Tina Pierce, *Studia Theologica: Nordic Journal of Theology* 12 (1958): 109–68.

48. Josef Pieper articulates a contemporary version of the *logos spermatikos* theory in

Among all of Augustine's talk regarding the wretchedness of the heathens and their appalling idolatry, it is easy to forget one crucial presupposition of the Bishop of Hippo's interest in pagan thought and life—and not just interest, but intense commitment, in his own oeuvre, to create a Christian synthesis thoroughly informed by Greco-Roman learning. Augustine never spells out this assumption, which is that the Egyptians have a lot of gold, silver, and precious garments to offer! Christianity has a lot to learn from the Romans and Greeks. The gesture of condescension and domination that the allegory of the despoliation implies—one despoils a vanquished enemy—does not reflect the reality that the church fathers turned to Greco-Roman sources because they found there the means to think through and articulate the truths of biblical revelation.

6. Finally, Augustine is not a trailblazer in bringing Greco-Roman philosophy to bear on Christian revelation. The quotation from *De doctrina christiana* includes a list of ecclesiastical writers whom Augustine cites as evidence for the fruitfulness of "despoiling the Egyptians." The development of the tradition has already confirmed the validity of his approach.

---

his small book, *Tradition: Concept and Claim*, trans. E. Christian Kopff (South Bend, IN: St. Augustine's Press, 2010), 30, 50–57.

A First Summary

It is time for a first, preliminary summary of our findings. What is the role of difference and rupture in the constitution of the Christian tradition? Where are the elements of transgression that we can expect to find if we take seriously Foucault's claim according to which transgression "opens up the space where the divine functions"?[1] What are the limits that needed to be established for something like "Christianity" to emerge, and what are the boundaries over against which Christianity, once established, continued to define itself? Is it true that, at the threshold of the Christian era, we encounter a "tragic structure"?[2]

Christianity, of course, begins with Judaism: to *that* extent we can agree with Rémi Brague's thesis regarding the "eccentricity" of Christian civilization: it has its center, or at least its origin, outside of itself, in the covenant that God concluded with the people of Israel.[3] The founding act of this covenant occurred on Mount Sinai, where God revealed himself to Moses in a "powerful, disruptive, cataclysmic" theophany that was "never to be repeated" (W. Brueggemann).[4] The irruption of the divine was over-

---

1. Quoted in the introduction, p. 5 above.

2. For the phrase "a tragic structure at the threshold of time," see the introduction, p. 11 above.

3. See Rémi Brague, *Eccentric Culture: A Theory of Western Civilization*, trans. Samuel Lester (South Bend, IN: St. Augustine's Press, 2002). Brague's book is full of fascinating insights, but in the end he romanticizes the constitution of the Western Christian tradition. His omission of any discussion of the despoliation metaphor is characteristic in this regard, as is his claim that "Christianity . . . presupposes the acceptation of an inferiority complex in relation to Judaism, a true circumcision of the heart" (63–64).

4. Walter Brueggemann, "The Book of Exodus," in *The New Interpreter's Bible* (Nashville: Abingdon, 1994), 1:833.

powering even though the Lord always remained veiled: for seeing him face-to-face brings death to mortals. In Moses, even the mediated encounter at the summit wrought a terrifying change—he grew horns, according to the tradition that the Vulgate represents—so that he had to cover his face with a veil. Exodus speaks about this encounter repeatedly, as Moses keeps going up and down the mountain. It is as though human words tried over and over to capture the events that transpired. The language is raw and prerational, employing images of thunder, lightning, deafening trumpets, fire, and smoke to express the inexpressible theophany.[5] Perhaps it is appropriate to quote Foucault here, who saw at the origins of history "a muted noise" and an "obstinate murmuring" bearing witness to the fact that all history is founded in an absence of history, in an "initial decision" uttering itself in "words without language." If most historians do not believe it can be ascertained that Moses existed, this ambiguity does not in the least detract from the truth of the Exodus narrative, located as it is "beneath history."[6] The origins withdraw.

The Lord's appearance on Mount Sinai at once transgresses the boundary between the sacred and the profane, and establishes it. For the limits that Moses is asked to demarcate around the mountain—symbolizing a kind of primordial no—are mediated in the law, which establishes the fundamental rules for the relationship between God and man, and for life in the human community. In this manner, the sacred is brought into the profane without annihilating it.

The encounter between God and man that the gospel narrates is softer, weaker—it is a *kenosis*—but it is by no means less transgressive. For in Christ Jesus, God becomes man, overstepping for once, in that one person, decisively the boundary that separates God and human. In Jesus, God even becomes visible (not merely audible, as in the Old Testament); yet we have discussed in what sense his human nature still functions like a veil (which makes possible both misrecognition and faith). Jesus, who is born (almost) like a regular child, does not come into the world violently, but he leaves it in a spectacle of death: the crucifixion. This "foolishness of the cross" shocked both Jews and gentiles because of the total reversal that the cross entails for conceiving of divinity, of the sacred Other. Can God become ab-

5. To quote Brueggemann's excellent commentary again: "Theophany is by definition disruptive. As an alternative mode of discourse, it employs dramatic images in order to say what cannot be said and to witness what cannot be portrayed. This raw, pre-rational mode of discourse is crucial for what is uttered in Scripture" ("The Book of Exodus," 1:838).

6. For the Foucault quotations, see the introduction, p. 13.

ject? Can God be the object of horrific violence? One important difference between the Old Testament and the New is that the burden of violence has been displaced: in the gospel, God carries it for us, scandalously.

Boundaries have been displaced, as well. What counts now is no longer the difference between Jew and gentile, but that between believer and nonbeliever. Jesus, who knows that this new boundary creates conflicts, does not relieve his followers of their burden, despite the message of radical peace and love that he preaches in the Sermon on the Mount.

Is this burden too heavy to carry, especially in a situation in which world history stretches out for a longer period than the early church expected—and a situation, a few centuries after Christ's death and resurrection, in which a formerly marginalized Jewish sect finds itself elevated to the official religion of the Roman Empire? There are tendencies to blunt the transgressive nature of Jesus's teaching already in the Bible itself. We noticed in a small detail of the scriptural text how even first-century Christians must have been struggling with the Sermon on the Mount when they inserted the little word εἰκῇ, "without cause," into Matthew 5:22, where Jesus scolds those who are angry with their brothers: their heavenly judgment will await them! Yes, but what if my brother has done me serious wrong?

Jesus's prophetic message of a radicalized and fulfilled law is alienating, just as Moses's prophetic office alienated him from his fellow Israelites: it divides fathers and sons, mothers and daughters, brothers and sisters. This is perhaps why Saint Paul already moves into a more accommodative direction with his theology of the "as if." Awaiting the fullness of the kingdom, we are allowed to live in our families, earn money, experience the joys and sorrows of this life, as long as we treat these activities as if they do not matter. There is a certain forgetfulness here—a forgetfulness of Jesus's radical call—but it is one that makes life bearable.

The postponement of the second coming, then, creates a new dynamic in the young Christian community, and that is the need to enter into a closer relationship with the "world"—even the (initially) pagan world of the Roman Empire. In addition to the theology of the "as if," there were other strategies to render such intercourse possible. One of them we saw in Saint Paul's speech at the Areopagus, where the Apostle presents pagan religion as an inchoate version of the fullness of the faith. There is no irreconcilable opposition between Christians and gentiles because Christians already have what the gentiles are longing for, unbeknownst to themselves: the one and true God.

Boundaries are broken down here, but there is a price to this accommodative attitude, fruitful though it turned out to be in the development of the Christian tradition, which learned not to treat any culture as intrinsically hostile to God. This price is well illustrated in the allegory of the plundering of the Egyptians: the riches of other cultures are valued only to the extent that they can be used to build the tabernacle (if we want to follow Origen's version of the allegory for a moment). They do not possess any value in their own right; indeed, outside of their role to serve the true God, other cultures are superstitious, demonic even. This position certainly does not appear attractive in our contemporary world of "multiculturalism." But is there a logically coherent alternative, apart from relativism? This is a question that we will have to address in the next chapter.

Before we move on, however, a word about another boundary is necessary, namely, the boundary between Jews and Christians. This was a boundary that had to be built—unlike the boundary between Christians and gentiles, which needed to be rendered more permeable as the history of Christianity unfolded. The process in which this limit was established was painful, as we saw in the example of the incident at Antioch. We discovered in this process the quintessential example of Foucault's theory of the "limit-experience," through which a culture defines itself against another that used to be part of it. Just as Foucault suggested, the "hollowed-out void" of Judaism at the center of Christianity has continued to haunt us Christians. We have attempted to despoil the Jews of the Old Testament, by regarding it as sublated in the New: kept safe and maintained in its truth as revelation, but at a higher level, and thereby canceled if read as a self-contained document. It is only recently that the church has distanced itself from this approach, which may well constitute the founding tragedy of the Christian faith.

CHAPTER 4

The Unfolding of the Christian Tradition

We have been trying to understand what one could call the *a priori* structure of the Christian tradition: not its actual historical development, that is (which fills libraries), but rather the logic that rendered this historical development possible. Irruption of the divine, transgression, limit, fulfillment: these have turned out to be some of the central elements in this logic.

In the textual evidence that we have examined so far, we have concentrated on Scripture, and a few key texts from the first Christian centuries—like *The Mystical Theology* of Saint Paul's "disciple" Dionysius and Saint Augustine's treatise *De doctrina christiana*, that "charter of the Christian intellectual."[1] One later text caught our attention in connection with the uses of the Mount Sinai narrative, namely, the Pseudo-Peter of Poitiers gloss.[2] Composed in the second half of the twelfth century, this gloss on Peter Lombard was able to look back on the development of scriptural interpretation since the incarnation, and in so looking back to discern some structural features. Thus, the Pseudo-Poitiers gloss discovered a basic hierarchy—one could also speak of several layers in the unfolding of the Christian tradition. Let us recall: for the gloss, Scripture is—like Mount Sinai—the sacred locus where an encounter with God occurs. In Scripture, we do not have a record of God's self-revelation as a static product, without veil, for all to see. Rather, Scripture is profoundly obscure. Penetrating it requires an effort—or, to return to the Mount Sinai metaphor, an ascent—which is possible only by God's grace, that is to say, through inspiration.

1. This phrase by Frederick Van Fleteren was cited in Chapter 3, note 44.

2. What follows is a summary and further interpretation of our discussion from Chapter 1, pp. 42–50 above.

The Pseudo-Poitiers gloss names Paul and the apostles as being endowed with this grace. We noted the assumption implicit in this view, namely, that the Gospels constitute the core of the Scriptures, with the apostolic letters as a first layer of interpretation. (This is how the New Testament wants to be read, in the canonical arrangement of the books that has come down to us. Historically, we now know that the Pauline epistles predate the Gospels.) Another assumption is clearer now, after our discussion of the notion of fulfillment: the Old Testament seems to have been sublated so completely in the New that it has disappeared. Thus, it is not included in Pseudo-Peter of Poitiers's notion of Scripture.

According to his gloss, the church fathers had the function of demarcating the limits of interpretation, that is to say, the limits of orthodoxy. This suggests that the fathers acted by divine inspiration as well, just as Moses established the limits around Mount Sinai following the Lord's command. The Pseudo-Poitiers gloss emphasizes the role of the fathers so strongly that little room seems left for any substantial developments since patristic times: the "eager doctors" of whom the gloss speaks "ascend right to the limits." There are two elements here: the eager doctors ascend, that is to say, there is still a dynamism of revelation, not merely a passive reception of a ready-made meaning; yet the ascent follows a path already charted by the fathers. The ascent also does not lead to the summit of the mountain. Indeed, transgressing the limits amounts to heresy.

In sum, the Pseudo-Peter of Poitiers gloss distinguishes four types of readers of Scripture: Paul and the apostles, the fathers of the church, the scholastic doctors, and heretics. The first three categories are historical, designating layers in the tradition, whereas heretics exist at all stages of the tradition's unfolding.

Another Dionysius

The Pseudo-Peter of Poitiers gloss looks back, from the vantage point of the nascent scholastic age, at the development of the Christian tradition through the twelfth century. The vantage point in question is none other than Peter Lombard's *Book of Sentences*, whose success in subsequent centuries came precisely because it was considered to offer the best summary—the best *summa*, according to a thirteenth-century term—of scriptural interpretation since the fathers.

In the fifteenth century, the period of the great *summae* was draw-ing to a close. Building on the *Book of Sentences*, theologians working in the universities had both established the overall structure and content of Christian doctrine, and engaged in deep and frequently controversial examinations of specific questions within the theological field. Sometimes they left this field altogether, or at any rate focused on matters that used to be considered propaedeutic, by devoting large portions of their *Sentences* commentaries to issues pertaining to the logic and grammar of theolog-ical discourse. Thinkers in the fifteenth century felt that the scholastic movement had reached a certain conclusion, or had perhaps even strayed too far from the tradition. This caused a sense that it was harvest time.[3] Some of the most eminent late scholastics turned back, therefore, and once again tried to pull the strands together in a new synthesis. One of these harvesters was Denys the Carthusian.

On account of his frequent mystical experiences, Dionysius Cartu-sianus came to be called the "ecstatic doctor." He lived a life of outward stability, leaving the charter house at Roermond (Netherlands), which he joined at the age of twenty-one, on only two occasions over his long reli-gious life (he died in 1471, when he must have been almost seventy).[4] De-nys's spiritual and intellectual life, on the other hand, was intense. Striving to imitate Christ, Denys was drawn to the abject. As part of his monastic *kenosis*, he preferred to eat spoiled food, for example: "he was not put off his food by conditions, dwelt upon with some relish by his biographers, which would have ruined the appetite of others."[5] His mystical visions often lasted such a long time and were so overwhelming that he had dif-ficulty regaining consciousness or standing on his feet. Several of these visions were induced by sacred music.[6]

3. This is Heiko Oberman's argument in his classic work, *The Harvest of Medieval Theology: Gabriel Biel and Late Medieval Nominalism* (Cambridge, MA: Harvard University Press, 1963).

4. The most recent overview of Denys the Carthusian's life and work is Dirk Wasser-mann, *Dionysius der Kartäuser. Einführung in Werk und Gedankenwelt*, Analecta cartusiana 133 (Salzburg: Institut für Anglistik und Amerikanistik, 1996). The book—a doctoral disser-tation—is uneven. But the scholarly literature on Denys is surprisingly sparse; in our time Kent Emery Jr. has been singular in producing some very fine work. Several of his essays are collected in his *Monastic, Scholastic, and Mystical Theologies from the Later Middle Ages*, Var-iorum Collected Studies Series CS 561 (Aldershot, UK, and Brookfield, VT: Variorum, 1996).

5. Anselm Stoelen, OCart, "Denys the Carthusian," in *Spirituality through the Centuries: Ascetics and Mystics of the Western Church*, ed. James Walsh (New York: P. J. Kenedy, 1965), 220–32 (at 221).

6. See Stoelen, "Denys the Carthusian," 225.

Denys's literary oeuvre, too, exceeds normal measures. Putting him in the same quantitative category as some of the great scholastics like Bonaventure, Aquinas, Scotus, or Ockham, it fills forty-two large volumes in the complete edition that was launched toward the end of the nineteenth century.[7] As one would expect, many of the works of this ardent admirer of Pseudo-Dionysius the Areopagite were devoted to mystical topics; but Denys also contributed to scholastic theology, especially through a close commentary on Peter Lombard's *Book of Sentences*. The prologue, or *prooemium*, to this commentary is what interests us here, for it contains a detailed reflection on the development of the theological tradition, beginning with revelation itself. Here is an attempt to render Denys's beautiful Latin:

> Yet, although the deficiency, smallness, and paucity of the wisdom of the way are enormous by comparison with the wisdom of the fatherland, nonetheless the wisdom revealed at the time of the evangelical law is very splendid and great. [This wisdom was revealed] first by Christ, then by the mission and inspiration of the Holy Spirit, next by the glorious apostles and evangelists, then by the holy fathers, and finally by the Catholic and scholastic doctors, excellently learned not only in the divine Scriptures but also in all philosophy. [This wisdom] powerfully exceeds (*vehementer transcendens*) that of the philosophers, but also of the theologians of the Old Testament and of the natural law. For—as Gregory testifies—just as wisdom grew in the course of time (*per temporum processum crevit*) before the coming of the Savior, so it also does in the meantime [since his coming]. And most of all from the time when Master Peter Lombard, bishop of Paris, collected his *Book of Sentences*, wisdom appears to have received much and great elucidation, growth, and abundant increase. Which Isaiah once foresaw, saying, *the earth is filled with the knowledge of the Lord, as the covering waters of the sea* [Isa. 11:9], that is to say, very abundantly. And those things that were hidden have been brought forth into the light; the difficulties of the Scriptures have been unknotted; and points that can be objected to the Christian faith, and have been objected by the faithless, have been solved outstandingly. Indeed, the aforesaid Master and illustrious learned scholastics who have written famously on the *Book of Sentences*, have subtly

7. See Doctoris ecstatici D. Dionysii Cartusiani *Opera omnia*, 42 vols. (Montreuil, Tournai, and Parkminster: Typis Cartusiae S.M. de Pratis, 1896–1935).

discussed, magisterially made clear, and Catholically treated not only the more difficult places of Scripture, but also the words and writings of the holy fathers, who have written much that is difficult and obscure in their expositions of the Scriptures and other treatises.

Since it is known, however, that almost innumerable people have already written upon this *Book of Sentences*, and that moreover even today some are writing [on it]—perhaps even more than is expedient, as due to some less illustrious writings of recent people, the more illustrious writings of the older ones are less attended to, read, and investigated—hence it is my intention in this work to prepare a kind of collection of extracts from the commentaries and writings of the most authoritative, famous, and excellent doctors, and to bring the reflection of these doctors back into one volume (*in unum volumen redigere*). For just as the very text of the *Book of Sentences* is gathered from the words and testimonies of the holy fathers, so this work too is put together (*adunetur*) from the doctrines and writings of the aforesaid writers upon the *Book of Sentences*.[8]

Let us try to unpack this rich text step-by-step.

1. Denys immediately places the "wisdom of the way" (that is to say, of this life) in the higher perspective of the wisdom of the fatherland. What we are given in this life—even by revelation—is defective, small, and quantitatively little in relation to the vision of God in the hereafter. In the paragraph preceding this passage, Denys is more explicit: "by comparison with the beatific contemplation and the light of glory and perfection of the blessed, all wisdom of the present life, every light of knowledge of this life, every progress and splendor in the effort of those who are on the way are like ignorance, like a shadow, and like a complex deficiency—so much so that the most perfect cognition that we have of the highest God in this world is by negation and removal from him of absolutely everything, just as the divine Dionysius explains in the second chapter of the *Mystical Theology*."[9] Pseudo-Dionysius is the first nonbiblical authority that Denys quotes in the opening pages of his *Sentences* commentary. If we believe his biographers,

8. D. Dionysii Cartusiani, *Commentaria in primum librum Sententiarum*, Doctoris Ecstatici D. Dionysii Cartusiani *Opera Omnia* 19 (Tournai: Typis Cartusiae S. M. de Pratis, 1902), prooemium, 36. Because of the scarcity of this edition, which few libraries own, I have reproduced the Latin text in the appendix. A parallel passage is found in the prologue to the *Elementatio theologica*, Opera Omnia 33 (Tournai: Typis cartusiae S. M. de Pratis, 1907), 112.

9. D. Dionysii Cartusiani, *Commentaria in primum librum Sententiarum*, prooemium, 35.

Denys knew what he was talking about. In the language of transgression that we have been using, the Carthusian emphasizes that the step beyond this world—its negation—is the privileged path to the divine. Theological talk is nothing but the shadow of a real encounter with God.

2. "Nonetheless, the wisdom revealed at the time of the evangelical law is very splendid and great." The term rendered as "splendid" here is *praeclara*, which could also mean "beyond bright," "excessively bright." If this is what Denys intended, the term would convey that God's light exceeds the capacity of the human intellect even as he reveals himself to us in the incarnation and in Scripture. In other words, what is but a shadow in relation to the beatific vision and to mystical experience, is still more than we can grasp. In turn, the revelation that occurred at the time of the incarnation "powerfully exceeds" the wisdom conveyed in the Old Testament, in the philosophers, and in the natural law. Note how Denys places these three on the same level, as though they were of equal dignity from a Christian point of view. It is a bit strange. Even if we allow for the idea that we encountered in Augustine, that the "mines of providence" are everywhere, one would still expect the revelation that occurred in the Old Testament to hold a higher status than the obscure and implicit knowledge of God had by the philosophers and in the natural law. Denys must be speaking loosely here, although what he says demonstrates an attitude toward the old law with which we are already familiar: the New Testament "powerfully exceeds" or "transcends" (*vehementer transcendens*) the Old.

3. Next, Denys defines the hierarchy that characterizes the revelation of wisdom associated with the new law. Christ comes first, naturally, followed by the Holy Spirit, the apostles and evangelists, the church fathers, and finally the scholastic doctors. The connection of these persons with Scripture is clear, in that Christ is the subject matter of the Gospels; the Holy Spirit guides the church after his departure from this world; the apostles and evangelists were first to record, interpret, and spread the good news; and the fathers and scholastic doctors ensured the continued transmission of the gospel while deepening its interpretation. Denys's emphasis on the personal aspect of the revelation of wisdom is striking. There is no contradiction in the conception presented here between a static Scripture and a hypostatized Tradition of interpretations forming on its basis or around it; on the contrary, the process of revelation is personal through and through.[10]

---

10. It is this thoroughly personal dimension of tradition that Yves Congar endeavored to recover in his work on tradition. This idea is expressed in many different ways in his classic

At the heart of the revelation of wisdom in the new law stands the person of Christ.

Syntactically, the predicate "excellently learned not only in the divine Scriptures, but also in all philosophy" could have as its subject both the fathers and the scholastic doctors, although Denys has placed it closer to the latter. Either way, he has well seen the role that philosophy has played in the interpretation of Scripture and, more generally, in the constitution of the theological tradition.

4. We have pointed out repeatedly that the church fathers and medieval Christian thinkers saw revelation as a process, rather than as an isolated historical event resulting in a static product. Denys the Carthusian is no exception. In our passage, he discusses the growth of revealed wisdom both before and after the coming of the Savior, emphasizing the role that Peter Lombard played in this process.

For anyone unfamiliar with the history of scholasticism, the central role that Denys assigns to the author of a basic theology textbook may be surprising. We must not forget, however, that no work in Christian literature, with the exception only of Scripture itself, received more commentaries than the *Book of Sentences*. The *Sentences* provided the structure for the teaching of university theology over several centuries—in some parts of the world, through the seventeenth century.[11] Peter Lombard was, in Foucauldian terminology, a "founder of discursivity," that is to say, an author who did not merely make a contribution—even a crucial contribution—to a particular type of discourse, but one who established the rules of this discourse. Founders of discursivity, Foucault explains, "are unique in that they are not just the authors of their own works. They have produced something else: the possibilities and the rules for the formation of other texts."[12]

---

study, *Tradition and Traditions: An Historical and a Theological Essay*, trans. Michael Naseby and Thomas Rainborough (New York: Macmillan, 1966). One passage is worth quoting, at the beginning of chapter 4 of part 2: "Tradition implies the idea of entrusting something to someone. This idea of personal entrusting is not found in the same way in the written word, which in itself would seem to imply the possibility of wide publication. In addition, tradition contains the avowal or affirmation that what is thus handed on contains more than what is formally expressed in it. Tradition is a treasure, a deposit, which a text could never fully represent, and which can only be preserved in a living subject" (348).

11. I am referring to the Iberian Peninsula and its American colonies; for detailed documentation, see Lidia Lanza and Marco Toste, "The *Sentences* in Sixteenth-Century Iberian Scholasticism," in *Mediaeval Commentaries on the "Sentences" of Peter Lombard*, vol. 3, ed. Philipp W. Rosemann (Leiden and Boston: Brill, 2015), 416–503.

12. Michel Foucault, "What Is an Author?" trans. Josué V. Harari, in *Essential Works*

For this reason, these other texts do not refer back, beyond the founder of discursivity, as it were, to a larger discipline, but take the founding work to provide the "primary coordinates" for their discourse. The normative power of the initiator of discursivity is such that periodic "returns to the origin" will assure the discursive field that it is still in touch with its source. Furthermore, each of these returns will reshape the discursive field in light of newly discovered or rediscovered aspects of the origin.[13] This is almost exactly how the *Book of Sentences* functioned in the theology faculties of the late medieval and early modern period.[14]

In what ways precisely the commentaries on the *Sentences* led to "much and great elucidation, growth, and abundant increase" in wisdom is something that Denys—who loves his tripartite phrases, no doubt meant to mirror the Trinity—specifies in two long sentences. Progress has been made in that hitherto hidden theological truths have been brought to light, scriptural interpretation has "unknotted" many difficult passages, and objections from detractors of the faith have been addressed and refuted. But the *Book of Sentences* and its commentators have not only helped to penetrate and synthesize the faith by building upon and weighing up all the biblical passages relevant to a particular doctrinal issue; they have also carefully considered the writings of the fathers.

5. The final paragraph of our excerpt from Denys's proem offers an unexpected turn. After his paean to the achievements of the tradition of the *Sentences* in the preceding sentences, Denys now adverts to problems that the same tradition has caused. "Almost innumerable people" have written on the *Book of Sentences*, he says—indeed, "perhaps even more than is expedient." The problem is that the more recent layers of the tradition have overshadowed the earlier ones; not only that, but the earlier commentators on the *Sentences* (Denys means illustrious scholastics like

---

of Foucault, 1954–1984, ed. Paul Rabinow, vol. 2, *Aesthetics, Method, and Epistemology*, ed. James D. Faubion (New York: New Press, 1998), 205–22, at 217. Foucault claims that "founders of discursivity" appeared only since the nineteenth century, with Marx and Freud as the most important examples. His view is too narrow and too "modern" here.

13. The quoted phrases occur in Foucault, "What Is an Author?," 217.

14. One could argue that the *Book of Sentences* always functioned against the background of a larger Christian discourse informed by the Bible. Indeed, Denys the Carthusian himself stresses the contribution that the *Sentences* tradition has made to the understanding of Scripture. This is a valid point, but a similar observation applies to Marx and Freud, Foucault's prime examples of founders of discursivity: for Marx may have inaugurated historical materialism and Freud may have founded psychoanalytic discourse, yet both are also thinkers who belong in larger traditions like philosophy and psychology.

Saint Thomas Aquinas) were often more insightful than representatives of more recent tendencies (nominalism is what Denys has in mind here). In other words, the accumulation of commentaries has led the tradition to forget its most important fruits.

This sentiment was widely shared in the fifteenth century, so that there were attempts from different quarters (including nominalism) to return to some of the great authorities of the past—perhaps even to synthesize them.[15] This is also the goal of Denys's *Sentences* commentary: to "prepare a kind of collection of extracts from the commentaries and writings of the most authoritative, famous, and excellent doctors," rather than to advance the debate of the overly technical issues into which the commentary tradition tended to drift after the "golden age" of scholasticism. The language that Denys uses to describe his efforts to pull together what is most worthwhile in the tradition has a strongly Neoplatonic ring to it: he intends to "bring back" (*redigere*) the best of the doctors' thought "into one volume" (*in unum volumen*). His work is "put together"—more literally, it is "moved toward unity, made one" (*adunetur*)—from the doctrines and writings of a tradition that has become too dispersed and is in need of unification.

Given Dionysius the Carthusian's fervent commitment to the "other" Dionysius, the Pseudo-Areopagite, we are entitled to interpret these last few sentences in the sense of a Neoplatonic emanation and return. The tradition of the *Book of Sentences* started from its center, the work of the Master, who himself had done nothing other than to bring together the fruits of the tradition preceding him. From this center, it radiated into layers of commentaries by successive generations of scholastic theologians. Although this emanation spread, and even increased, the wisdom of the center, this was not able to occur without dispersal. Multiplicity is an expression of the One, but it cannot but hide the latter: hence the need for a return, a selective pulling back of the multiplicity of commentaries into a unified whole. This is what Denys hopes to accomplish in his own work.

As Denys hints, the tradition preceding the *Book of Sentences*, and culminating in it, was structured in the very same way. The "words and testimonies of the holy Fathers" built upon the center of revelation, Christ,

15. I have sketched these developments in *The Story of a Great Medieval Book: Peter Lombard's "Sentences,"* Rethinking the Middle Ages 2 (Toronto: University of Toronto Press, 2007), chap. 4: "The Long Fifteenth Century: Return to the Sources" (137–83). For a more in-depth treatment, one should consult the three volumes of *Mediaeval Commentaries on the "Sentences" of Peter Lombard*, ed. G. R. Evans and Philipp W. Rosemann (Leiden: Brill, 2002–2015).

whose gospel reached them—thanks to the Holy Spirit—through the historical layers of the apostles and evangelists. Denys does not say that the church fathers wrote "more than is expedient," but their teachings certainly became sufficiently varied and complex to require distillation. Such distillation was the achievement of Peter Lombard, who summed up the wisdom of the apostolic and patristic age for the schoolmen.

We have, here, a fairly sophisticated theory of the unfolding of the Christian theological tradition. The theory has one defect, however: it is too "smooth," failing to take into account the crises, the battles, the exclusions—the anathemas—that punctuated the development of Christian doctrine and life. Maybe tradition is not very good at remembering its others. To remedy this forgetfulness, we need to seek assistance in more contemporary thought.

Reading Denys the Carthusian with Alasdair MacIntyre

Medieval Christian Europe did not experience otherness as an existential challenge. There was an effective judicial apparatus to discern and judge heresies.[16] Jews lived in ghettos and were subject to periodic pogroms. The existence of the Muslim world was known, to be sure, but it was too remote to be viewed as a threat—except in Spain, where the prolonged interaction among Christian, Jewish, and Muslim communities produced a culture quite distinct from other parts of Europe. Knowledge of non-Abrahamic religions was even more limited. All this is only to point out the obvious: the medieval Western world was not faced with the challenges that characterize postmodern globalism, in which the heritage of the Enlightenment, waves of migration, easy communication and travel, and the coexistence of people from different cultural backgrounds in large urban centers have loosened traditional religious bonds and created confusion in the minds of many. Medieval Christians studying at the University of Paris did not see themselves confronted with the possibility of converting to Islam, or to Buddhism, or of rejecting religion altogether; for students enrolled at most colleges and universities in the United States today, these are real options, embraced by many professors and friends. We are therefore, not surprisingly, much more sensitive to difference than our premodern predecessors.

---

16. On this subject, see J. M. M. H. Thijssen, *Censure and Heresy at the University of Paris, 1200–1400*, Middle Ages Series (Philadelphia: University of Pennsylvania Press, 1998).

But what happens when different traditions meet? More specifically, what are the possibilities of a fruitful encounter, especially from a Christian perspective? Even if we embrace the metaphor of the despoliation of the Egyptians, disregarding its violent—postmoderns would say, "totalizing"— overtones, how can such "pillaging" be made to work? Are there mechanisms that would allow those engaged in such cultural appropriation to develop a coherent synthesis? Under what conditions does a tradition open itself up to the outside in the first place?

These are questions that Alasdair MacIntyre attempted to address in his book *Whose Justice? Which Rationality?*[17] MacIntyre took inspiration from John Henry Newman, whose *Essay on the Development of Christian Doctrine* rediscovered, for the modern age and using a different register, what pre-modern theologians like Denys the Carthusian had discussed under the rubric of the development of wisdom—namely, the fact that "doctrine" unfolds in time.[18] "Doctrine" has different connotations from "wisdom" and "revelation," however, implying magisterial teaching from above rather than the mystical growth of God's people in the truth. This is undoubtedly why MacIntyre diplomatically points out a certain distance between Newman's approach and his own: "But if one is to extend Newman's account from the particular tradition of Catholic Christianity to rational traditions in general, and to do so in a philosophical context very different from any envisaged by Newman, so much qualification and addition is needed that it seems better to proceed independently, having first acknowledged a massive debt."[19]

MacIntyre distinguishes several stages in the development of a tradition.

1. Traditions, he submits, begin in a situation of "pure historical contingency, from the beliefs, institutions, and practices of some particular community which constitute a given" (354). Traditions are, in other

17. See Alasdair MacIntyre, *Whose Justice? Which Rationality?* (Notre Dame: University of Notre Dame Press, 1988).

18. See John Henry Cardinal Newman, *An Essay on the Development of Christian Doctrine*, Notre Dame Series in the Great Books (Notre Dame: University of Notre Dame Press, 1989). Owen Chadwick concluded his important book, *From Bossuet to Newman: The Idea of Doctrinal Development* (Cambridge: Cambridge University Press, 1957), with the following question: "The question then for those who think Newman's theology is Catholic, is this: these new doctrines, of which the Church had a feeling or inkling but of which she was not conscious—in what meaningful sense may it be asserted that these new doctrines are not 'new revelation'?" (195). This question was answered, I believe, by Ratzinger's research on the premodern understanding of the notion of *revelatio*.

19. MacIntyre, *Whose Justice? Which Rationality?*, 353–54. Hereafter, page references from this work will be given in parentheses in the text.

words, irreducible. A tradition has no justification outside of itself. In our context, the Mount Sinai narrative in Exodus furnishes the best illustration of this claim. As the founding story of God's covenantal relationship with Israel, it is not open to repudiation, although one can interpret it in various ways. Thus, some may wish to maintain that the scriptural text narrates a historically verifiable event for whose reality archaeological evidence can be adduced; perhaps they will insist on Moses's authorship. Other interpreters will regard the Exodus narrative as a voice from an elusive past, speaking to us in an attempt to capture the truth of Israel's relationship with the Lord—but speaking without a speaker, as it were, since it may no longer be possible to associate the text with any one identifiable author or to pin down the location where the events occurred. It is possible to hold views within this spectrum in the tradition that the Mount Sinai narrative crucially helps to ground. It is not possible, however, to regard the narrative as superstitious nonsense, characteristic of a stage in the development of the human mind that the Enlightenment has definitively left behind. Someone holding this view would place himself or herself outside the tradition in question. This critic would not be able to participate in the tradition or contribute to it; adherents of the tradition would not recognize his or her arguments and positions as valid expressions of it.

2. Does this mean that traditions are self-perpetuating systems immune to critical reflection? No, but the critical questions have to be generated internally. This is what begins to happen in the second stage MacIntyre describes. At this point, members of the tradition encounter "stimuli toward the reformulation of their beliefs" (355). Authoritative texts in the tradition may have turned out to pose difficulties—by appearing incoherent, for example—or they may have received different interpretations; new situations may have arisen to which the community needs to respond; or two branches of the tradition—each with its distinct customs, beliefs, and identity—may have met, thus occasioning tensions.

3. The tradition must now find the resources to deal with these difficulties, and in many cases will have to become inventive. It must generate interpretive methods to synthesize divergent texts, identify principles behind its beliefs and coherently extend them to new situations, and clarify its identity, either by broadening it or by pronouncing exclusions. We have seen an example of such a situation in the incident at Antioch: after gentiles and Jews came together in the young community of followers of Jesus, the different backgrounds that they (quite literally) brought to the table

created a conflict. There were two rival interpretations of this situation, Paul's and James's, with two different strategies to resolve the tension: one, to broaden the community by loosening Jewish ritual laws; the other, to isolate or exclude the gentiles who were unwilling to follow these laws. Paul ultimately prevailed, as the growing Christian community abandoned much of the Jewish ritual.

In the course of its development, a tradition will undergo many challenges. Each time a tension is resolved and a difficulty overcome, the tradition will have proven its continued viability. Indeed, for MacIntyre a tradition is viable only to the extent that it remains open to practical and theoretical challenges, and remains confident in its ability to address them: "The test for truth in the present," MacIntyre explains, "is always to summon up as many questions and as many objections of the greatest strength possible; what can be justifiably claimed as true is what has sufficiently withstood such dialectical questioning and framing of objections" (358).

4. Once a tradition has managed to address challenges of the sort that we just described, it will develop a theory explicitly formulating and generalizing the methods of problem resolution that it has found to be successful. The incident at Antioch, for example, came to be interpreted as only one case in a larger conflict between the new, Christian spirit of love and the old, Jewish insistence on the law. The emerging Christian tradition adopted the view that it had fulfilled, sublated, or even superseded the old law. This theory served as a fundamental principle of scriptural interpretation throughout the patristic and medieval periods.

5. Up to this point, there is nothing in MacIntyre's theory that would allow him to deny that truth is always relative to a particular tradition. Traditions prove themselves if they are capable of growth and self-correction as they unfold in time; but there is no means ever to weigh the truth claims of one tradition over against those of another, because each of these traditions has its own, historically contingent grounding.

This is where MacIntyre introduces the notion of "epistemological crisis." An epistemological crisis is in many regards comparable with the regular challenges and difficulties that every tradition continuously faces and overcomes—with the crucial difference that it confronts a tradition with the limits of its problem-solving ability. Put differently, in an epistemological crisis a tradition encounters internal problems that it does not have the resources to resolve. In this kind of situation a tradition must open itself to another, rival tradition that may possess the concepts and intellectual strategies that it needs to overcome the epistemological crisis. The alternative to such "imaginative conceptual innovation" (362) is defeat and death.

Before the postmodern age, in which Christianity and Judaism, monotheism and polytheism, post-Enlightenment religion and fundamentalism, democracy and tyranny all share the same digital space, traditions could not encounter each other without having coexisted for some time in the real world. This is clear from an example of such an encounter that MacIntyre already found in Newman's work: "Newman's own central example was of the way in which in the fourth century the definition of the Catholic doctrine of the Trinity resolved the controversies arising out of competing interpretations of scripture by a use of philosophical and theological concepts whose understanding had itself issued from debates rationally unresolved up to that point" (362). Thus, to clarify and synthesize scriptural statements regarding the Father, Son, and Spirit that lacked the rigor of theological doctrine, the church employed nonscriptural notions derived from Greek philosophy—especially the notions of person (hypostasis) and substance (*ousia*). The possibility of such innovative use of philosophical terminology to resolve disputes within the Christian tradition stemmed from two factors: first, the long coexistence of Christianity and Greco-Roman civilization, on whose soil the Christian faith came into existence and grew; and second, the ability of Christian thinkers to speak what MacIntyre terms a "second first language" (364).

In this context, the word "language" designates a system of thought, a tradition, and not necessarily a particular tongue. The Eastern church fathers who employed the new term *homoousios* to define the identity of the Trinitarian persons spoke Greek, just like Aristotle and Plotinus; what they had to become fluent in was philosophy. Thus, they had to grasp with precision not only the epistemological crisis—the irresolvable question— that had arisen within their own tradition; they also had to have a nuanced understanding of central philosophical terms in their own context because, for a term to perform a particular function in a new context, it is first necessary to know exactly how it works in its original conceptual environment. Finally, they had to make an imaginative leap by transplanting some of these terms into the new soil of Christian doctrine. What in retrospect, after the epistemological crisis was resolved and incorporated into a narrative of doctrinal continuity, appears like an "obvious" solution, at the time required—to repeat—both fluency in two traditions and the courage of a certain disruption. (I mean here a disruption of the Christian narrative through the introduction of extrinsic philosophical terminology.) It turns out, then, that the "pillaging" that Origen and Augustine biblically imagined as an appropriate approach to the use of non-Christian cultures in reality necessitates the most sophisticated conceptual work.

What our unusual conjunction of Denys the Carthusian's theory of tradition with Alasdair MacIntyre's thoughts on the same subject has yielded so far is a more precise understanding of the unfolding of the Christian theological tradition. Looking back over the roughly fourteen hundred years preceding him, Denys describes a smooth process in which wisdom grows harmoniously, layer after layer. He touches only in passing the role that Christianity's Jewish roots and its repeated assimilation of non-Christian philosophies played in this growth, when he remarks that the wisdom of the new law "powerfully exceeds that of the philosophers, but also of the theologians of the Old Testament and of the natural law." There is no mention of internal struggles, nor of epistemological crises that the Christian tradition was able to master only by borrowing from foreign sources. The combination of Denys's theory with MacIntyre's reflections therefore paints a more complete and realistic picture.

MacIntyre's theory of tradition also allows us better to grasp the statement by the Pontifical Biblical Commission that was cited at the end of Chapter 2. Understandably, the Biblical Commission wants to break with the theological heritage of sublation that has viewed the Jewish tradition exclusively through a Christian lens: the old law is good precisely as a preparation for the gospel; reading it in itself bespeaks nothing but Jewish illiteracy and the obstinate refusal of conversion. The commission hints that this approach is not only theoretically inadequate but also may have contributed to the catastrophic culmination of Jewish-Christian relations in the twentieth century. It therefore affirms that "both readings [of the Jewish Scriptures] are bound up with the vision of their respective faiths, of which the readings are the result and expression," adding that "both are irreducible."[20] These sentences could come straight out of *Whose Justice? Which Rationality?* There is nothing internally incoherent in the Jewish interpretation of the Hebrew Bible—according to the commission's nuanced stance—so that one does not have to be "illiterate" to approach it as a self-contained piece of God's revelation. The Christian sublation makes sense only within the Christian tradition; more than that, it is an integral part

20. Chapter 2, p. 75 above.

of the Christian identity to claim that the Lord's covenant with his people finds its fulfillment in the gospel. Again, however, there is nothing in the Jewish tradition that would compel a Jew to adopt this view.

From Pillaging to Translation

Translation has always played a crucial role in the Christian tradition: consider only the various translations of the Bible, from the Septuagint version of the Old Testament to the many recent attempts to render God's Word in contemporary English and other vernaculars. The most influential of these translations defined entire cultures: God's Word functioned as *the* text around which all other texts revolved, so that the great translations set standards through new linguistic forms that they invented to render the target languages capable of conveying sacred speech. Thus, medieval Latin was suffused with the language of the Vulgate; the King James Bible helped to shape modern English; and Luther's version was instrumental in the creation of the modern high German language.[21]

The translations just mentioned made it possible for the biblical message to spread to cultures beyond those to whom the text was initially addressed; a different category of translations inversely enabled the Christian tradition to "pillage" intellectual resources from the outside. In this category, we most importantly find the Latin translations of ancient Greek texts that, in wave after wave, brought the Western church into contact with Greek thought. These translations were crucial in patristic times, when Augustine, for example, encountered Neoplatonism through the translations by Marius Victorinus. In the early Middle Ages, the translations of Hilduin and John Scottus Eriugena introduced the West to the mystical tradition of Pseudo-Dionysius the Areopagite. The thought of the high Middle Ages was shaken by the rediscovery of the Aristotelian heritage, initially transmitted through Jewish and Muslim channels. Without translators like Michael Scot and William of Moerbeke, who brought Aristotle and his commentators into the universities, the scholastic movement would have taken a completely different course. The Renaissance, finally,

---

21. On the *Lutherbibel*, Franz Rosenzweig's insightful essay remains worth reading: "Scripture and Luther," in Martin Buber and Franz Rosenzweig, *Scripture and Translation*, trans. Lawrence Rosenwald with Everett Fox, Indiana Studies in Biblical Literature (Bloomington and Indianapolis: Indiana University Press, 1994), 47–69.

saw the rebirth of the hitherto neglected literary tradition of Greco-Roman antiquity. Marsilio Ficino prepared the first complete translation of Plato's works, which had had to wait until the fifteenth century to become fully available in Latin.

But "translation" can also be understood in a broader and deeper sense—not just as the rendering of words from one language in another, but as every effort to transfer (the verb from which "translation" is derived) aspects of one tradition into another. In this sense, Augustine and Thomas Aquinas were translators, even though neither knew Greek (or Hebrew or Arabic). MacIntyre, who devotes an entire chapter to "tradition and translation," oscillates between the two senses, taking literal translation as paradigmatic for translation in the broader sense.[22]

The issue of translation is pivotal if we want to move beyond ultimately unverifiable theoretical claims on how traditions relate to each other. In the context of our earlier discussion, it would be helpful to know more about the mechanisms at work in the "despoliation" of other cultures. The metaphor suggests violence: Is this how cultural translation operates—through hermeneutic violence? In the context of MacIntyre's book and its critical reception, the question of translation figures prominently as well. MacIntyre maintains that traditions alien to each other are incommensurable, so that translation is impossible. He offers the example of two incompatible names for the same place—is it the "same" place?—in Northern Ireland. Those who call the old city on the west bank of the River Foyle "Derry" are situating themselves, and perhaps their audience, in the Irish (Catholic) community. A person, on the other hand, who chooses the term "Londonderry" to designate the same location speaks from, and possibly for, the perspective of (Protestant) unionists. These terms cannot be translated without a crucial loss of cultural meaning. If one tried to evade the controversy by saying, for example, that one visited the city with the geographic coordinates N 54°99′58″ W 7°30′74″, one would be speaking from the point of view of one of the "languages of internationalized modernity," which assume everything can be translated into an idiom of rootless abstraction.[23] The tradition-rooted viewpoints that "Derry" and "Londonderry" encapsulate would not have been understood. For some critics, MacIntyre's position suggests a relativism of traditions hermetically closed to each other. These

22. The chapter "Tradition and Translation" is no. 19 in *Whose Justice? Which Rationality?* (370–88).

23. MacIntyre, *Whose Justice? Which Rationality?*, 379.

critics overlook that, for MacIntyre, the possibility of genuine translation is not excluded.[24] Neither is it a given. It is a project possible only on the assumption that the other may have insights that transcend one's own, being as yet unintelligible. "It follows," MacIntyre sums up his position, "that the only rational way for the adherents of any tradition to approach intellectually, culturally, and linguistically alien rivals is one that allows for the possibility that in one or more areas the other may be rationally superior to it in respect precisely of that in the alien tradition which it cannot as yet comprehend."[25] The words "as yet" are important here.

The practice of Christian translators indicates that they approached other traditions with exactly this attitude, rather than as conquerors. Before it could turn to alien traditions, however, Christianity faced a translation challenge at its very roots: it had to translate Judaism into Christianity. This translation involved both the theological problem that crystallizes in Matthew 5:17, and the transference of the Hebrew words of the Old Testament into the Greek text of the New. (We know that the authors of the New Testament mostly quote from the Septuagint, rather than making their own translations of the Hebrew text.) Christianity, then, is essentially a translation project.

Translation did not occur only *in* Scripture; translation *of* Scripture was just as essential, in particular for the Western tradition, which developed in the medium of Latin rather than Hebrew or Greek. Since all words found their ultimate measure in the Word, the translation of Scripture, moreover, set the standards for translation generally. This is why, when Saint Jerome chose a literal method of translation for the Vulgate, his *verbum e verbo* approach became the model for translation into Latin throughout the patristic and medieval periods. This is, however, not what Saint Jerome intended. In his famous Letter 57 to Pammachius, he reserved the literal method explicitly for use in sacred texts. Jerome had incurred criticism for his translation of a letter by Pope Epiphanius to Bishop John of Jerusalem. Defending himself against the accusation, he explains:

> In the above remarks I have assumed that I have made alterations in the letter and that a simple translation (*simplex translatio*) may contain

24. One such critic is John Haldane, "MacIntyre's Thomist Revival: What Next?" in *After MacIntyre: Critical Perspectives on the Work of Alasdair MacIntyre*, ed. John Horton and Susan Mendus (Notre Dame: University of Notre Dame Press, 1994), 91–107. I wish to thank my colleague Lance Simmons for drawing my attention to John Haldane's piece.

25. MacIntyre, *Whose Justice? Which Rationality?*, 388.

errors though not willful ones. As, however, the letter itself shows that no changes have been made in the sense, that nothing has been added, and that no doctrine has been foisted into it, "obviously their object is understanding to understand nothing" [Terence, *Andria*]; and while they desire to arraign another's want of skill, they betray their own. For I myself not only admit but freely proclaim that in translating (*in interpretatione*) from the Greek (except in the case of the holy scriptures, where even the order of the words is a mystery) I render sense for sense and not word for word (*non uerbum e uerbo, sed sensum exprimere de sensu*). For this course I have the authority of Tully, who has so translated the Protagoras of Plato, the *Oeconomicus* of Xenophon, and the two beautiful orations which Aeschines and Demosthenes delivered one against the other. What omissions, additions, and alterations he has made substituting the idioms of his own for those of another tongue, this is not the time to say. I am satisfied to quote the authority of the translator (*translatoris auctoritas*), who has spoken as follows in a prologue prefixed to the orations.[26]

The distinction of the two methods of translation—*verbum e verbo* and *sensus de sensu*—was not Jerome's invention. Cicero, whose authority Jerome invokes, distinguished the *interpres*, who translates word for word or literally, from the *orator*, whose task it is to adapt the meaning of a foreign text idiomatically to the conventions of Latin, and in this manner to produce a rendering of literary (or oratorical) merit. It was generally understood in antiquity that the *verbum e verbo* method was best suited for documents of a legal nature, as well as for pedagogical uses. Thus, in the Greek half of the Roman Empire, translations of Vergil and Cicero circulated that juxtaposed the Latin original with a literal Greek version in facing columns. The task of translating Scripture subverted this neat distinction, however. When the Hebrew Bible was first rendered into Greek,

26. Jerome, "Letter LVII: To Pammachius on the Best Method of Translating," trans. W. H. Fremantle, G. Lewis, and W. G. Martley, in *Nicene and Post-Nicene Fathers*, ed. Philip Schaff and Henry Wace, 2nd ser., vol. 6 (Buffalo: Christian Literature Publishing Co., 1893), 112–19, at 113–14. I have modernized the spelling and corrected punctuation mistakes. The Latin text is critically edited in *Sancti Eusebii Hieronymi Epistulae*, pars 1, *Epistulae I–LXX*, ed. Isidor Hilberg, Corpus Scriptorum Ecclesiasticorum Latinorum 54.1 (Vienna: F. Tempsky; Leipzig: G. Freytag, 1910), 508. G. J. M. Bartelink reprints Hilberg's text with small emendations in *Hieronymus: Liber de optimo genere interpretandi (Epistula 57). Ein Kommentar*, Mnemosyne Supplementa 61 (Leiden: Brill, 1980), 13; for detailed commentary, see 43–53.

the translators hesitated between the two methods. In the end, however, the Septuagint came down on the literal side, because of the heavily legal emphasis of the Pentateuch.[27]

Jerome hints at another reason for translating Scripture literally: "even the order of words is a mystery," he says—not just the *sensus*, but the *verba* in their materiality may reveal something holy.[28] Indeed, the literal rendering may be the safer choice because the translator must not foreclose the infinite depth of God's Word by limiting its meaning to a single well-defined sense, but should rather bring the reader to the sacred text and let him or her wrestle with it, ever anew. As Augustine asks rhetorically in *De doctrina christiana*, "Could God have built into the divine eloquence a more generous or bountiful gift than the possibility of understanding the same words in several ways, all of them deriving confirmation from other no less divinely inspired passages?"[29] But, in the words of the Syriac scholar Sebastian Brock, "to translate an inspired text *sensus de sensu* would be to imply that the *sensus* of the impenetrable mysteries of scripture had been fully grasped by the translator."[30]

Translating *verbum e verbo*, then, was a methodological choice for Saint Jerome and other Christian translators, not the inevitable consequence of lacking linguistic skills. Brock enumerates four principal ways in which literal translators move their readers in the direction of the text.[31]

1. The first aspect of the *verbum e verbo* method involves copying the original's word order, even if this is not natural in the target language. This, for Brock, is "the most obvious mark of any literal translation."[32] Re-

27. See Sebastian P. Brock's classic piece, "Aspects of Translation Technique in Antiquity," *Greek, Roman, and Byzantine Studies* 20, no. 1 (1979): 69–87.

28. Franz Rosenzweig expresses this idea beautifully in his essay on Luther: "And if we believe that not only a passage called to our attention by a particular circumscribed doctrine but *any human utterance* may conceal the possibility that one day, in his time or in my time, God's word may be revealed in it, then in that case the translator must, so far as his language permits, follow the peculiar turns of that potentially revelation-bearing utterance, whether by direct reconstruction or by implication" ("Scripture and Luther," 64).

29. Augustine, *De doctrina christiana*, ed. and trans. R. P. H. Green, Oxford Early Christian Texts (Oxford: Clarendon, 1995), 3.27.38, pp. 168–71. On Augustine's method of biblical interpretation, see Thomas Williams's fine chapter, "Biblical Interpretation," in *The Cambridge Companion to Augustine*, ed. Norman Kretzmann and Eleonore Stump (Cambridge: Cambridge University Press, 2001), 59–70.

30. Brock, "Aspects of Translation Technique," 79.

31. See Brock, "Aspects of Translation Technique," 81–87.

32. Brock, "Aspects of Translation Technique," 81.

specting the word order of the original includes rendering it completely. A modern translator of the Hebrew Bible, for example, would drop the *w-* at the beginning of sentences, interpreting it as something like the Semitic equivalent of the period in modern English. The Septuagint renders it by "and" (καί). Similarly, sometimes Latin translators would try to find equivalents for the Greek articles ὁ, ἡ, τό, and this although there is no article in Latin.

2. On the lexical level, literal translations endeavor to capture the terminology of the original as closely as possible. When there is no semantic equivalent in the receptor language, the *interpres* attempts an etymological translation by coining a neologism, or he may give a transliteration. Luther coined many neologisms in his translation of the Bible, expanding the vocabulary of the German language by adding words such as *Lückenbüßer*, *Machtwort*, and *Herzenslust*, which are now found in any German dictionary (where they are rendered as "stopgap," "decisive word or speech," and "heart's desire," respectively).

3. The *interpres* will typically aim at regular lexical correspondence, translating a particular word in the source language consistently with the same word in the target language. Good translators did not apply this principle slavishly, however. In studying Jerome's translation of the Gospel according to Saint John, for example, Christophe Rico has found that, in one particular context (John 10:14–15), the learned translator from Bethlehem rendered one and the same Greek verb, γινώσκειν (roughly, "to know"), by means of three different Latin verbs, *cognoscere*, *noscere*, and *agnoscere*, to capture nuances in the Greek.[33] Again, we see that the literal method of translation was by no means the result of linguistic ineptitude.

4. Finally, to make the target language better reflect certain features of the source language, the translator can try to extend existing linguistic properties of the receptor language into new areas. Brock offers the example of the Syriac word for "spirit," *ruha*, which is of the feminine gender. Under pressure from the Greek πνεῦμα, which is neuter, the Syriac word began to be treated as masculine (Syriac not having the neuter).[34]

33. See Christophe Rico, "L'art de la traduction chez saint Jérôme. La Vulgate à l'aune de la Néovulgate: l'exemple du quatrième évangile," *Revue des études latines* 83 (2005): 194–218, esp. 212–13. On Jerome's translation of the Hebrew Bible, the most comprehensive treatment is still Benjamin Kedar-Kopfstein's unpublished dissertation, "The Vulgate as a Translation: Some Semantic and Syntactical Aspects of Jerome's Version of the Hebrew Bible" (PhD diss., Hebrew University of Jerusalem, 1968).

34. See Brock, "Aspects of Translation Technique," 87.

Some of the biblical quotations cited earlier in this book offer good illustrations of the *verbum e verbo* method, which the translators of the Douay-Rheims Bible followed, just as Saint Jerome did. Indeed, when the Rheims New Testament first appeared in 1582, its preface cited Jerome's letter to Pammachius in defending the "religious care and sinceritie observed in this translation."[35]

Consider, for example, this text from the book of Wisdom, which was quoted in the previous chapter:[36] "She [wisdom] entered into the soul of the servant of God, and stood against dreadful kings in wonders and signs. And she rendered to the just the wages of their labors, and conducted them in a wonderful way: and she was to them for a covert by day, and for the light of stars by night: And she brought them through the Red Sea, and carried them over through a great water" (Wisd. of Sol. 10:16–18). The last two lines of verse 17, "and she was to them for a covert by day, and for the light of stars by night," are barely intelligible because of the unidiomatic expression "to be to someone for something." Why would the Douay-Rheims translators have chosen this awkward rendering? A more recent translation into English is much clearer: "[Wisdom] became a shelter to them by day, / and a starry flame through the night" (10:17 NRSV).

A first explanation for the woodenness of Douay-Rheims comes from the Latin text of the Vulgate, which the sixteenth-century translators followed with "religious care and sinceritie"; for the Vulgate reads *et fuit illis in velamento diei / et in luce stellarum nocte,* "and [Wisdom] was to them in a cover by day / and in the light of the stars at night." With the exception of "in" instead of "for," this is exactly what Douay-Rheims translated—but the Latin text is hardly any clearer than its English version. The explanation, then, must lie in the original Greek text: "καὶ ἐγένετο αὐτοῖς εἰς

---

35. "Preface to the Rheims New Testament, 1582," in Hugh Pope, OP, *English Versions of the Bible,* rev. Sebastian Bullough, OP (Saint Louis and London: Herder, 1952), 600–650, at 618: "This we professe onely . . . that we have used no partialitie for the disadvantage of our adversaries, nor no more licence then is sufferable in translating of holy Scriptures: continually keeping ourselves as neere as is possible, to our text and to the very wordes and phrases which by long use are made venerable, though to some prophane or delicate eares they may seem more hard and barbarous, as the whole style of Scripture doth lightly to such at the beginning: acknowledging with St. Hierom, that in other writings it is ynough to give in translation, sense for sense, but that in Scriptures, lesse we misse the sense, we must keepe the very wordes. *Ad Pammach. Epistola* 101. *ca.* 2. *in princip.*" Pope notes that the preface may have been written by Richard Bristow, one of the collaborators of the original Douay-Rheims version, but he adds that "this can only be a hypothesis" (601n1).

36. See Chapter 3, p. 91.

σκέπην ἡμέρας / καὶ εἰς φλόγα ἄστρων τὴν νύκτα." In classical Greek, this idea would have been expressed through the verb γίγνομαι ("to become") with a predicate in the nominative, just as we say in English, "she became a great help." But in the Septuagint and in the New Testament, γίγνομαι is frequently construed with εἰς and a noun in the accusative, as in the English "she turned into a great help." We now see the reason behind the unidiomatic Vulgate text: in their attempt to render the Greek word for word, the translators (Jerome only revised the existing "Old Latin" version of the deuterocanonical portions of the Old Testament very lightly) did not want to drop the preposition εἰς.[37]

A less extreme example of a word-for-word translation occurs in a text we encountered in Chapter 1 of this book. The Lord, commanding Moses to draw a boundary around Mount Sinai, warns that no one must cross it, under penalty of death: "And thou shalt appoint certain limits to the people round about, and thou shalt say to them: Take heed you go not up into the mount, and that ye touch not the borders thereof: every one that touches the mount dying he shall die" (Exod. 19:12).[38] In this quotation, the phrase "dying he shall die" immediately stands out as un-idiomatic. In English, we do not say "running he will run" or "speaking he will speak." The New Revised Standard Version avoids this irruption of linguistic strangeness with a much smoother text: "You shall set limits for the people all around, saying, 'Be careful not to go up the mountain or to touch the edge of it. Any who touch the mountain shall be put to death.'" Once again, the Douay-Rheims version turns out to be a faithful rendering of the Vulgate, which gives the last sentence as *omnis qui tetigerit montem morte morietur*, "anyone who will have touched the mountain will die in a death." The repetition of the idea of death both in a verb and in a noun reflects a common Hebrew construction, which uses this device for em-phasis. (Even in English, "dying he shall die," though odd, sounds much stronger than "he shall die.") We find the same construction in Genesis 2:17, in a similar context:

> But of the tree of knowledge of good and evil, thou shalt not eat. For in what day soever thou shalt eat of it, thou shalt die the death. (Douay-Rheims)

37. I wish to thank my colleague Dr. Andrew Glicksman (Theology Department, University of Dallas) for a helpful conversation regarding the text of Wisd. of Sol. 10:17.
38. See Chapter 1, p. 28.

But of the tree of knowledge of good and evil you shall not eat, for in the day that you eat of it you shall die. (NRSV)

The New Revised Standard Version translates *sensus de sensu*, bringing the text to the reader in well-formed contemporary English. The Vulgate and the Douay-Rheims "give the Hebrew some room," to use a phrase by Luther, and consequently require an effort as they attempt to pull the reader into the original text, whose phrase מוֹת תָּמוּת (*môt tāmût*) is allowed to shine through the translation.[39]

Sometimes there is more than a "shining through" of the original when Scripture is rendered word for word. We already commented on the Aramaic word *raca* in Matthew 5:22, which the Greek text does not translate, but simply transliterates.[40] Since Jesus and his apostles spoke Aramaic, the pericope in question is an example of a word uttered by Jesus that made it untranslated through the layers of transmission. There are about a dozen such passages in the New Testament, most significantly the words the Lord spoke dying on the cross: "And about the ninth hour Jesus cried with a loud voice, saying: Eli, Eli, lamma sabacthani? that is, My God, my God, why hast thou forsaken me?" (Matt. 27:46). The transliteration is highly appropriate, as it allows us to hear more authentically Jesus's cry of suffering. Even the New Revised Standard Version, which buries *raca* in a flat paraphrase, reports the cry on the cross in transliteration.

Neither the transliterated insult *raca* nor the Aramaic cry on the cross has made it into everyday Christian language. This is different in the case of "amen," a Hebrew word that has become a common term shared by the Christian community worldwide, across history. (Indeed, "amen" is also used in Judaism and Islam, thus binding the Abrahamic faiths together.) In the New Testament, Jesus characteristically inserts "amen" at the beginning of important declarations, rather than at the end, to confirm a thought already uttered (as had been Old Testament practice). In this manner, Jesus conveys the authoritative, divine nature of his speech—the fact, in the words of one commentator, that he "knew himself . . . firmly to be the mouthpiece of God."[41] In this book, we encountered an instance of such a use of "amen" in Matthew 5:17–18:[42] "Do not think that I am come

---

39. Rosenzweig quotes Luther in his essay, "Scripture and Luther," 49. In the same essay, Rosenzweig explains the "exponential powers" of Hebrew roots that are doubled (see 64–65).

40. See Chapter 2, p. 60.

41. See J. M. Ross, "Amen," *Expository Times* 102 (1991): 166–71, at 167.

42. See Chapter 2, p. 62.

to destroy the law, or the prophets. I am not come to destroy, but to fulfill. For amen I say unto you, till heaven and earth pass, one jot, or one tittle shall not pass of the law, till all be fulfilled." In a pattern with which we are already familiar, the Douay-Rheims version has retained the transliterated "amen" from the Vulgate, whereas more modern versions consider such a semantically obscure term too onerous for the reader or listener. Thus, the New Revised Standard Version gives us "For truly I tell you" in lieu of "For amen I say unto you."

Under the heading "Certain wordes not English nor as yet familiar in the English tongue," the preface to the New Testament in the Douay-Rheims Bible devotes a long paragraph to justifying the transliteration of "amen":

> For example, we translate often thus, *Amen, amen, I say unto you*. Which as yet seemeth strange, but after a while it wil be as familiar as *Amen* in the end of al praiers and Psalmes, and even as when we end with *Amen*, it soundeth far better then *So be it*: so in the beginning *Amen Amen* must needes by use and custom sound far better than *Verily Verily*. Which in deede doth not expresse the asseveration and assurance signified in this Hebrue word; besides that is the solemne and usual word of our Saviour to expresse a vehement asseveration, and therfore is not changed, neither in the Syriake nor Greeke nor vulgar Latin Testament, but is preserved and used of the Evangelistes and Apostles them selves, even as Christ spake it, *proper sanctiorem authoritatem*, as S. Augustine saith of this and of Alleluia, *for the more holy and sacred authoritie thereof.* li. 2 doct. Christ. c. 11. [16.][43]

Amen remains untranslated "for the more holy and sacred authoritie thereof": it is a word that can, in this very form, be traced to the Lord himself. It has *antiquitas*, as Augustine puts it in the *De doctrina christiana* passage quoted in the preface.[44] Unlike Augustine, however, who felt that both *amen* and *alleluia* were not in principle untranslatable (thus differing from *raca*, which is too emotional to be captured in another tongue), the preface suggests that "the asseveration and assurance signified in this Hebrue word" would be difficult to render in English. Certainly, "verily, verily" does not do the job.

43. "Preface to the Rheims New Testament, 1582," 639–40.
44. Augustine, *De doctrina christiana* 2.11.16, in Green, ed. and trans., p. 72.

Linguistically, "amen" is an affirmative interjection, like "yes" or "okay" in English. Old Testament scholars have long speculated that it may have entered the Hebrew language from Egyptian, where the root *mn* conveys firmness and stability.[45] As already indicated, in the Old Testament, "amen" expresses that the speaker accepts and affirms a statement (or an order) that was addressed to him. This usage can be seen, for instance, in 1 Kings 1:36 ("And Banaias the son of Joiada answered the king, saying: Amen: so say the Lord the God of my lord the king") and in Jeremiah 28:6 ("And Jeremias the prophet said: Amen, the Lord do so: the Lord perform thy words"). In these cases (and other, similar ones), "amen" indicates more than a merely theoretical agreement; it indicates the firm conviction or wish that something will indeed come to pass—and not as a result of some fortuitous chain of events, but with God's assistance. In accord with this meaning, we find the liturgical use of "amen" to ratify prayers in the Psalms. It is only one step, albeit a significant one, from this use of "amen" to Jesus's way of speaking, where "amen" implies the divine "asseveration and assurance" that something is indeed the case or will happen: "And whosoever shall give to drink to one of these little ones a cup of cold water only in the name of a disciple, amen I say to you, he shall not lose his reward" (Matt. 10:42). Here, with God himself speaking, "amen" approaches a performative sense.[46] Mysteriously, God's speech has the force to make what it says. It is appropriate for this powerful word to remain untranslated. It is closely connected with God himself, who transcends our comprehension.

In patristic and medieval culture, as we noted, the translation of Scripture set the standards for translation in general. It will not surprise us, therefore, that the writings of Dionysius the Areopagite, a theologian of subapostolic authority, were rendered into Latin in painstaking *verbum e verbo* translations.[47] These culminated in the thirteenth-century versions by Bishop Robert Grosseteste, the most literal of all of Denys's translators,

---

45. For this hypothesis, see Klaus Seybold, "Zur Vorgeschichte der liturgischen Formel 'Amen,'" *Theologische Zeitschrift* 48 (1992): 109–17, esp. 110–11.

46. We discussed performative speech in Chapter 2, p. 59, in the context of the beatitudes.

47. The translation history of the *corpus dionysiacum* is documented in Philippe Chevallier's monumental work, *Dionysiaca: Recueil donnant l'ensemble des traductions latines des ouvrages attribués au Denys l'Aréopagite*, 2 vols. (Bruges: Desclée de Brouwer, 1937). The two quarto tomes present all the known texts by Pseudo-Dionysius in an interlinear format that allows the reader to compare the Greek text with every translation from Hilduin (ca. 832) to Dom Claude David (d. 1705).

who was not satisfied until he had tried to render the Greek article in Latin.[48] In such a case, it is easy to argue that the literal method of translation was chosen out of reverence for a sacred text. But what about the Latin translations of the scientific and philosophical literature in Arabic that started flowing into Europe in the twelfth century? Here we have more of a test case for the encounter of genuine cultural otherness. As Charles Burnett has shown, after some initial hesitation, these texts too were rendered *verbum e verbo*, despite the considerable difficulty of capturing the syntactic structure of Arabic in the Latin language. The translations resulting from this approach often resembled foreign languages that had to be learned to be understood, like second first languages.[49] Readers of Avicenna's *Metaphysics*, for example, must have been stunned when they read in a crucial passage devoted to God, that "the necessary being has no quiddity, except that it is necessary being, and that quiddity is *anitas*."[50] *Anitas* was the translator's attempt to render the Arabic *anniyya* (أنية), or "thatness," a technical term derived from the conjunction *an* or *anna*, "that."

Some of the twelfth- and thirteenth-century translators of non-Christian philosophical and scientific literature have left us explicit reflections on their method. Burnett extensively quotes Burgundio of Pisa, who was responsible for Latin versions of Saint John Chrysostom, but also of Aristotle and Galen. Burgundio explicitly invokes the Septuagint version of the Hebrew Bible as his model. Furthermore, he maintains that a trans-

48. I have described Grosseteste's translation method in the chapter "Robert Grosseteste" that appeared in *The Oxford History of Literary Translation in English*, ed. Roger Ellis (Oxford: Oxford University Press, 2008), 1:126–36.

49. See Charles S. F. Burnett, "Translating from Arabic into Latin in the Middle Ages: Theory, Practice, and Criticism," in *Éditer, traduire, interpréter. Essais de méthodologie philosophique*, ed. Steve G. Lofts and Philipp W. Rosemann, Philosophes médiévaux 36 (Louvain-la-Neuve: Éditions de l'Institut supérieur de philosophie; Louvain and Paris: Peeters, 1997), 55–78. On p. 70, Burnett writes: "The wonder is that the *verbum de verbo* style of translation was preferred by those who used the translations, and that the text was apparently understood.... But perhaps our views are anachronistic in assuming that translation involves interpretation, and one must take into account too the possibility that oral interpretation of the cryptic text may have been available and/or that it was possible to learn the peculiar language of the translations."

50. Avicenna, *Liber de philosophia prima sive scientia divina V–X*, ed. Simone Van Riet, Avicenna latinus (Louvain: Peeters; Leiden: Brill, 1980), book 8, chap. 4, p. 401, ll. 31–32: "Igitur necesse esse non habet quidditatem, nisi quod est necesse esse, et haec est anitas." For commentary, see Marie-Thérèse d'Alverny, "Anniyya—Anitas," in *Mélanges offerts à Étienne Gilson*, Études de philosophie médiévale, hors série (Toronto: Pontifical Institute of Mediaeval Studies; Paris: Vrin, 1959), 59–90.

lation that does not proceed *verbum e verbo* risks being presumptuous and disrespectful of the authority of the writer being translated:

> If (equivalent) words (*dictiones*) can be found, and the style (*ydioma*) of each language does not prevent it, and if one does not wish to establish one's own glory and to pretend that what belongs to others is one's own, the translation *de verbo ad verbum* should not be rejected by a diligent and completely faithful translator. For if you wish foreign material to be thought your own and in your control, you will not care to render word for word like a *fides interpres*; rather, taking the sense (*sententia*) of that matter, you will explain it by the combination of your own words, and so you will not be an interpreter but you will seem to have composed your own words from yourself, which is what both Cicero and Terence attest that they did.[51]

One is not going too far in claiming that, in this passage, the literal translation appears motivated by a moral obligation to let the other text be other, rather than subsuming it under one's control. "Alienam materiam tuam tuique iuris vis esse putari," is what the Latin text says: if you wish "foreign material to be believed to be your own and to belong to the force of your law," then you should translate loosely. Burgundio of Pisa is rejecting the idea of "pillaging" the works of anyone, including nonbelievers, by doing intellectual violence to them. In the unfolding Christian tradition, the practice of "despoliation," then, looked different from the theory Origen and Augustine formulated at an early stage.

There is clearly a tension here. Perhaps more adequately put, there are competing frameworks within the Christian tradition for encountering the other—competing models of sublation. One type of sublation takes from the other what does not properly belong to the other anyway, because of the other's blindness to the true faith. The Egyptians were using the gold for the worship of idols, after all, so that the Israelites were more than justified in taking the precious metal with them—even if this taking involved lies and theft—and to appropriate it for the construction of the tabernacle. The second model of sublation, the one we discovered in examining techniques of translation, has a different emphasis. Christian translators learned to listen carefully to the language of their source texts, even if that language happened to be spoken by Greek pagans or by Muslims. (Or by

51. Quoted in Burnett, "Translating from Arabic into Latin," 57.

Jews, as in the case of the Hebrew Bible.) This careful listening had a price, however, which was a constant challenging, and frequent transgressing, of the limits of the Latin language. Just as the Vulgate created Christian Latin out of classical Latin, so the Latin that was shaped by Aristotle, Maimonides, and Avicenna was no longer the Christian Latin of the Vulgate.

It is possible that the two models ultimately grow from the same root, namely, the belief that diverse cultures stem from, and therefore point to, the same God.[52] It is a matter of "reducing" them, in the Bonaventurian sense, to the one Source of all.[53] It is not a medieval author, however, who has (at least to my knowledge) most beautifully expressed the possibility that, ultimately, there may be only one language. One finds this idea in the works of Franz Rosenzweig, who, in collaboration with Martin Buber, created a controversially literal and linguistically eccentric German version of the Hebrew Bible. Rosenzweig felt that making the Hebrew Bible audible, in its words and in its rhythm, through the text of a German translation, was by no means tantamount to a violation of the German language. Rather, the literal rendering only helped to bring out the Hebrew potential already inherent in the German tongue. As Klaus Reichert summarizes Rosenzweig's views, "what may first sound like alienation, an estrangement of one's own language, is fundamentally held to be a renewal of that language out of its own virtuality, which had been fully unfolded in another language. To make Hebrew audible in German at once marks the distance between translated text and original and shows how it may be sublated by listening to the other voice underneath or above one's own breath."[54] Rosenzweig and Buber's work on the German Hebrew Bible was interrupted by German anti-Semitism and the Holocaust, but Buber decided to bring the project to completion in the 1950s, after his emigration to Israel.

---

52. On the doctrine of the *logos spermatikos*, see Chapter 3, p. 98.

53. I am thinking, of course, of Bonaventure's treatise *De reductione artium ad theologiam*, "On the 'Reduction' of the Arts to Theology."

54. Klaus Reichert, "'It Is Time': The Buber-Rosenzweig Bible Translation in Context," in *The Translatability of Cultures: Figurations of the Space Between*, ed. Sanford Budick and Wolfgang Iser, Irvine Studies in the Humanities (Stanford: Stanford University Press, 1996), 169–85, at 174. For an in-depth exploration of Rosenzweig's philosophy of language and translation, see Barbara Ellen Gaddi, *Franz Rosenzweig and Jehuda Halevi: Translating, Translations, and Translators* (Montreal and Kingston, ON: McGill-Queen's University Press, 1995).

CHAPTER 5

Folding Back the Tradition

"Since it is known, however, that almost innumerable people have already written upon this *Book of Sentences*, and that moreover even today some are writing [on it]—perhaps even more than is expedient, as due to some less illustrious writings of recent people, the more illustrious writings of the older ones are less attended to, read, and investigated—hence it is my intention in this work to prepare a kind of collection of extracts from the commentaries and writings of the most authoritative, famous, and excellent doctors, and to bring the reflection of these doctors back into one volume." In this sentence, which we quoted in the previous chapter, Denys the Carthusian points to an important aspect in the development of traditions: as traditions unfold, earlier stages in their development risk being overshadowed by more recent ones. This will happen, not necessarily because the earlier stages have been rendered redundant by progress, but simply as a result of a certain quantitative overload: who can read—we hear Denys exclaim—all the material that "almost innumerable people" have contributed to the tradition of the *Sentences*! The contemporary theologian Joseph Mueller has spoken of a "homeostatic forgetting" that is integral to the very continuity of tradition as it must "slough off" aspects of the past in order to remain viable in the present.[1] With his emphasis on the necessary role of forgetting in history, Mueller has taken up an idea that Nietzsche already formulated in his *Advantages and Disadvantages of History for Life*: too much history will kill life in the present.[2]

1. Joseph G. Mueller, "Forgetting as a Principle of Continuity in Tradition," *Theological Studies* 70 (2009): 751–81, at 766.
2. For a good selection of passages from Nietzsche on this topic, with commentary, see Sybe Schaap, *Die Unfähigkeit zu vergessen. Nietzsches Umwertung der Wahrheitsfrage,*

Mueller illustrates his point with a case that the Russian psychologist Aleksandr Luria related in one of his books. A patient of Luria's, a certain Solomon Veniaminovich Sheresheveskii, suffered from the inability to forget even small details of his everyday life, such as the position of the hands on a clock at a particular time. Sheresheveskii's mind lacked a principle to discern between aspects of his experience that were of enduring relevance to his life in the present, and other details that needed to be filtered out lest they crowd out the relevant ones. As Sheresheveskii's memories accumulated—some of them since infancy—he became incapable of functioning in society and professionally, so that he sadly ended up as a kind of circus attraction: having lost all his other jobs, he was able to make a living only as a mnemonist. Mueller concludes: "In order to equip people for the tasks of living, human memory must be able to forget."[3]

As Denys the Carthusian already knew, however, the necessity of forgetting has a downside: as a tradition decides what it needs for its present tasks, it relegates to the deeper recesses of memory aspects of the past that it judges to be irrelevant. Such aspects are then confined to unread manuscripts, unopened books, dusty archives, and rarely visited storerooms. Furthermore, this concealing part of tradition is rarely remembered, despite the surprising ambiguity of the word "tradition" itself. In Latin, *traditio* and the verb from which it is derived, *tradere*, in their basic meaning designate respectively an act and the activity of handing over (*trans-dare*, "to give" something "across" a certain distance). But the handing over thus designated can involve knowledge or learning, just as, for example, a city that is defending itself against enemy forces: the city is "handed over," that is, betrayed, to the enemy. Quintus Curtius Rufus, the historian of Alexander the Great, uses the verb *tradere* in this sense to describe a kingdom about to be betrayed to its enemies: *regnum hostibus traditurum* (*Historiae Alexandri Magni* 3.8.18). And in Livy's *History of Rome*, *traditio* designates surrender, as in *haec traditio Gomphorum ingentem terrorem Thessalis intulit*, "this surrender of Gomphi instilled

---

trans. [from Dutch] Monique J. and Gershom M. H. Ratheiser-van der Velde (Würzburg: Königshausen & Neumann, 2002), esp. chap. 7 ("Vergessen und Versprechen"), 219–58. Schaap is the rare example of a philosopher-politician. Representing the *Volkspartij voor Vrijheid en Democratie* ("Popular Party for Freedom and Democracy") in the Dutch Senate, Schaap has published several widely discussed books on the contemporary political situation in the Netherlands.

3. Mueller, "Forgetting as a Principle," 768.

extreme fear in the Thessalians" (*Ab urbe condita* 32.14.3).[4] Mirroring the ambiguity of *traditio*, "tradition" in English can take on a sense of betrayal or surrender. Thus, the word has become a technical term in the context of the history of the early church, as exemplified in these sentences penned by the nineteenth-century English divine Henry Hart Milman: "The consecration of a bishop guilty of tradition was the principal ground on which his election was annulled," or "Both denounced their adversaries as guilty of the crime of tradition."[5] Here "tradition" means the betrayal of the Christian community during the period of persecution under Diocletian, when certain bishops handed over sacred books and liturgical vessels to save their own lives. Ecclesiastic historians still employ the word in this sense.[6]

Tradition betrays certain aspects of the past by surrendering them to oblivion. It does so not accidentally but necessarily, because tradition needs forgetting to function. What is forgotten can be lost entirely (like many works by premodern authors), although if it is lost completely without trace, it cannot even be remembered *as* forgotten. But what is forgotten can also be held in storage, where it is ready for a potential rediscovery. This is the situation that Denys the Carthusian has in mind in discussing the need to attend once more to the "more illustrious writings" of the older authors whose works have been forgotten amidst more recent compositions on the *Book of Sentences*. These older writings still exist, on the shelves of libraries, for example; they just need to be rediscovered. There has to be a *ressourcement*, a return to the sources.

Tradition is constituted, then, in a complex interplay of memory, forgetting, and recalling (as bringing back to memory). To better understand this interplay, we turn once again to Saint Augustine.

---

4. The examples are found in Charlton T. Lewis and Charles Short, *A Latin Dictionary* (Oxford: Clarendon, 1879), s.v. "trado" and "traditio."

5. Henry Hart Milman, *The History of Christianity, from the Birth of Christ to the Abolition of Paganism in the Roman Empire*, vol. 2 (London: John Murray, 1840), 369 and 371.

6. The *Oxford English Dictionary*, 2nd ed. (Oxford: Oxford University Press, 1989), s.v. "tradition" (II.4.b.), documents a 1989 use in an essay by the English church historian W. H. C. Frend.

The Lord of Song

Imagine the world is a psalm:

> Suppose I am about to recite a psalm which I know. Before I begin, my
> expectation is directed towards the whole. But when I have begun, the
> verses from it which I take into the past become the object of my mem-
> ory. The life of this act of mine is stretched (*distenditur*) two ways, into
> my memory because of the words I have already said and into my ex-
> pectation because of those which I am about to say. But my attention is
> on what is present: by that the future is transferred to become the past.
> As the action advances further and further, the shorter the expectation
> and the longer the memory, until all expectation is consumed, the entire
> action is finished, and it has passed into the memory. What occurs in the
> psalm as a whole occurs in its particular pieces and its individual syl-
> lables. The same is true of a longer action in which perhaps that psalm
> is a part. It is also valid of the entire life of an individual person, where
> all actions are parts of a whole, and of the total history of "the sons of
> men" (Ps. 30:20) where all human lives are but parts.[7]

An individual human life is like a story "distended" in two directions: the
words that have already been said, and the words that are as yet unspoken.
The two dimensions meet in the present of the speaker, who continually
transfers future into past, until the end is reached, and the whole story told.

In the *Confessions*, Augustine demonstrates how a human life—and
that is a life remembered, not a life just lived half-consciously—is a life put
into words, and through the words assimilated into memory. Yet Augustine
was not dead when he composed the *Confessions*, so how could he look
back on his life as a whole (as the quotation above suggests)? The answer is
that, in a significant sense, Augustine was in fact dead when he wrote the
Confessions: he had died to his old self. In book 9—before he starts thinking
about memory, time, and creation—we are told that he suffers chest pains
so severe that they force him to resign his position as a teacher of rhetoric
in Milan. The physical unease is providential, however, because it furnishes
him with a convenient excuse to leave behind his profession, which he

---

7. Saint Augustine, *Confessions*, trans. Henry Chadwick (Oxford: Oxford University
Press, 1991), 11.28.38, p. 243. For the Latin text, see Augustine, *Confessions*, ed. James J. O'Donnell, 3 vols. (Oxford: Clarendon, 1992), 1:163.

now judges to be dishonest and full of pride. Augustine is baptized, and in short order experiences a mystical vision with Monica, his mother, just before she dies. In passing, book 9 already mentions the untimely death of Augustine's son Adeodatus, which was to occur about two years later. With the ties to his profession and his family cut, and a foretaste of the life to come granted in the vision, Augustine is now free to open a new chapter—to use a tired metaphor that is unusually apposite in our context. But the new chapter already lies outside the pages of the *Confessions*. Looking back on his old life (and its death), Augustine is able to pull its different strands—the questions, the struggles, the temptations—into a memory unified by the knowledge that God's providence was at work behind it all, secretly giving a meaning to the ups and downs when there seemed to be only confusion.

All of us do what Augustine does in the *Confessions* (albeit not quite at the same literary and theological level, alas): we tell stories about ourselves to each other. A friendship or relationship can be thought of as a sharing, and perhaps merging, of the stories of the partners involved. A death of a loved one causes grief because, suddenly, the shared story needs to be rewritten from the point of view of the remaining half. A story never gains its full meaning before it is over. That is why there used to be the literary genre of the *ars moriendi*, a kind of handbook on how to die well, lest one's story be marred by a bad ending.[8]

It is more difficult to understand how Augustine's image of the psalm "is also valid . . . of the total history of 'the sons of men' (Ps. 30:20) where all human lives are but parts." Who would be in a position to tell the complete story of the entire human race? Who indeed, if not God, who has already written this story in Scripture. All we need to do is read his words correctly. This is why Augustine's autobiography culminates in three books that are devoted to biblical interpretation. Just as the task of writing the story of an individual life consists in finding its center in God's providential guidance, so the story of the sons of men as a whole turns out to be salvation history, that is to say, the path of God's people as the Bible relates it from creation to the last things. And just as with an individual life, finding its meaning requires pulling its distension together in one memory, so Scripture is interpreted correctly once its unifying principle is discovered in the Word.

8. For an overview, see Mary Catherine O'Connor, *The Art of Dying Well: The Development of the* Ars Moriendi, Columbia University Studies in English and Comparative Literature 156 (New York: Columbia University Press, 1942).

This "pulling together" is not simply a hermeneutic task, involving the question of how to read correctly the life of a man, or the life of mankind; it is a moral task at the same time, because sin is nothing but dispersal:

> I intend to remind myself [Augustine writes at the beginning of book 2] of my past foulness and carnal corruptions, not because I love them but so that I may love you, my God. It is from love of your love that I make the act of recollection. The recalling of my wicked ways is bitter in my memory, but I do it so that you may be sweet to me, a sweetness touched by no deception, a sweetness serene and content. You gathered me together from the state of disintegration (*conligens me a dispersione*) in which I had been fruitlessly divided. I turned from unity in you to be lost in multiplicity (*ab uno te aversus in multa evanui*).[9]

Augustine reminds himself of his sins in order not to rejoice in them, but to overcome them. Thus, the goal of Augustine's recollection is not to anchor his life of dispersal more firmly in the memory, but rather to restructure his memory by deepening it. This involves a dialectic of recollecting and forgetting: having forgotten the God who made the memory his dwelling place,[10] Augustine needs to remember the unifying root of his existence. This involves recalling his past dispersal in sin so as to relegate it, once and for all, to oblivion:

> "Because your mercy is more than lives" (Ps. 62:4), see how my life is a distension in several directions (*ecce distentio est vita mea*). "Your right hand upheld me" (Ps. 17:36; 62:9) in my Lord, the Son of man who is mediator between you the One and us the many, who live in a multiplicity of distractions by many things; so "I might apprehend him in whom also I am apprehended," and leaving behind the old days I might be gathered to follow the One, "forgetting the past" (*praeterita oblitus*) and moving not towards those future things which are transitory but to "the things which are before" me, not stretched out in distraction but extended in reach, not by being pulled apart but by concentration (Phil. 3:12–14).[11]

9. Augustine, *Confessions* 2.1.1, p. 24 (Latin, 1:16).

10. See Augustine, *Confessions* 10.25.36, p. 200 (Latin, 1:133): "But where in my consciousness (*memoria mea*), Lord, do you dwell? Where in it do you make your home? What resting-place have you made for yourself? What kind of sanctuary have you built for yourself? You conferred this honor on my memory (*memoriae meae*) that you should dwell in it."

11. Augustine, *Confessions* 11.29.39, pp. 243–44 (Latin, 1:163). I have moved the reference

The last sentence is so dense that it is best to read it in Latin. Augustine is talking about the invention of a new future (and a new past) after his perspective on himself has changed. Apprehending himself in God—rather than in and through the multiplicity of worldly things into which sin dispersed him—Augustine forgets the past (the "old" old days, those lived in sin, not the "new" old days in which he is able to read God's guiding hand amidst all the dispersal), in order to move "non in ea quae futura et transitura sunt, sed in ea quae ante sunt non distentus sed extentus, non secundum distentionem sed secundum intentionem": that is, in order to move not toward those things that lie in a transitory, merely human future, but toward those realities that lie before him in eschatological perspective. This new future allows Augustine to live not a "distended" existence but an "extended" one, and to do so, again, not according to "distension" but rather according to "intension." In other words, his new life is possessed of a religious intensity such that its extension into different areas no longer causes dispersal.

Augustine's conversion is due to the fact that he has discovered God at the center of his life, in his memory. What of God does he remember? At this point the Bishop of Hippo becomes tentative. What all human beings remember, he suggests, is a happiness that is beyond reach in this life while nonetheless attracting us with its promise of blessedness:

> How then am I to seek for you, Lord? When I seek for you, my God, my quest is for the happy life. . . . Is not the happy life that which all desire, which indeed no one fails to desire? But what have they known about it so as to want it? Where did they see it to love it? . . . My inquiry is whether this knowing is in the memory because, if it is there, we had happiness once. I do not now ask whether we were all happy individually or only corporately in that man who first sinned, in whom we all died [Adam, 1 Cor. 15:22] and from whom we were all born into a condition of misery. My question is whether the happy life is in the memory.[12]

Non quaero nunc, "I do not now ask": that is how Augustine introduces the idea according to which we may all remember the happiness that Adam

---

to Philippians to the very end of the quotation because the entire final sentence (starting with "so I might apprehend") echoes the Pauline epistle.

12. Augustine, *Confessions* 10.20.29, pp. 196–97 (Latin, 1:130–31). The square brackets are Chadwick's; he sometimes uses them to indicate translator's additions (in most cases, however, these appear in parentheses). Where Latin words and phrases appear in parentheses, the additions are mine.

and Eve enjoyed when they lived in paradise, in familiarity and intimacy with their Maker. Having just barely touched upon this hypothesis, Augustine moves on—not providing answers, but several more pages of insistent questions.

One commentator on book 10 of the *Confessions*, Johann Kreuzer, has well summarized the aporia at the heart of Augustine's quest for God: "God is found," Kreuzer explains, "as the unforgotten. Unforgotten is that which always needs to be remembered anew. . . . It is in the memory as that which withdraws, that which transcends every remembering."[13] Augustine cannot do more than gesture toward God's presence at the heart of human memory because the divine presence is a transcendent presence. It withdraws when one attempts to circumscribe it. This is how Moses encountered God on Mount Sinai: the Lord showed himself not showing himself, always remaining veiled. "Thou canst not see my face: for man shall not see me and live" (Exod. 33:20). If this is how God reveals himself—concealingly—then it is quite possible to forget him. Yet the forgetting, rather than creating a pure absence, will open a nagging empty space that will continue to remind us of its presence. This empty space will attract memories around it. In this way, the forgotten becomes an organizing principle of memories.[14]

God reveals himself to us as Word. Is this not how Moses first encounters the Lord, as a Speaker hiding in a cloud (or, even before that, in a burning bush)? Genesis introduces God as the one who speaks reality into existence in a performative speech act of transcendent power: "And

13. Johann Kreuzer, "Der Abgrund des Bewußtseins. Erinnerung und Selbsterkenntnis im zehnten Buch," in *Die Confessiones des Augustinus von Hippo. Einführung und Interpretationen zu den dreizehn Büchern*, ed. Norbert Fischer and Cornelius Mayer, Forschungen zur europäischen Geistesgeschichte 1 (Freiburg im Breisgau: Herder, 1998), 445–87, at 470: "Gefunden wird Gott als das Unvergessene. Unvergessen ist das, was immer von neuem erinnert werden will. . . . Als Sich-Entziehendes, jedes Erinnern Transzendierendes ist es in der Erinnerung."

14. The Swiss philosopher Christine Abbt offers an analysis of the dialectics of memory and forgetting that is inspired by both Augustine and Freud. In his essay "On the Psychic Mechanism of Forgetfulness," Freud describes how his inability to recall the name of a particular artist—Signorelli—tormented him as he recalled many details associated with this individual and his work, but could not come up with the name. Abbt concludes: "As such, as forgotten, the forgotten has become even more important" ("Das Vergessene ist so—als Vergessenes—noch wichtiger geworden"); quoted from Christine Abbt, *"Ich vergesse." Über Möglichkeiten und Grenzen des Denkens aus philosophischer Perspektive* (Frankfurt and New York: Campus, 2016), 45.

God said: Be light made. And light was made" (Gen. 1:3). Jesus is the Word made flesh. As Augustine embarks upon his interpretation of Scripture in book 11 of the *Confessions*, he begins at the beginning, with the creation narrative of Genesis 1: "May I hear and understand how in the beginning you made heaven and earth." Quickly, the question becomes, "But how did you speak?"[15] The answer, given after many pages famously devoted to the nature of time, comes in a further elaboration of the image of the psalm with which we opened this section:

> Lord my God, how deep is your profound mystery, and how far away from it have I been thrust by the consequences of my sins. Heal my eyes and let me rejoice with your light. Certainly if there were a mind endowed with such great knowledge and prescience that all things past and future could be known in the way I know a very familiar psalm, this mind would be utterly miraculous and amazing to the point of inducing awe (*ad horrorem stupendus*). From such a mind nothing of the past would be hidden, nor anything of what remaining ages have in store, just as I have full knowledge of that psalm I sing. I know by heart what and how much of it has passed since the beginning, and what and how much remains until the end. But far be it from you, Creator of the universe, creator of souls and bodies, far be it from you to know all future and past events in this kind of sense. You know them in a much more wonderful and much more mysterious way. A person singing or listening to a song he knows well suffers a distension or stretching (*distenditur*) in feeling and in sense-perception from the expectation of future sounds and the memory of past sound. With you it is otherwise. You are unchangeably eternal, that is the truly eternal Creator of minds.[16]

Augustine is contemplating the possibility that God could be like an infinitely condensed psalm: all the words of the psalm are in his Word, but not distended into the dimensions of time. To use an analogy from the big bang theory, we can imagine the linguistic equivalent of all the energy of the universe concentrated in an infinitesimally small yet infinitely dense point. Creation, then, would be the expansion, the spelling out, of this original psalm. Augustine expresses *horror*, deep religious awe, at this miracu-

---

15. Augustine, *Confessions* 11.3.5, p. 223 (Latin, 1:149), and 11.6.8, p. 225 (1:150).
16. Augustine, *Confessions* 11.31.41, p. 245 (Latin, 1:164).

lous and mysterious possibility: contemplation of the Word has revealed to him the *mysterium tremendum* that is God.[17]

On this account, the world would be psalm not only after the fact, that is to say, insofar as the words of Scripture tell "the total history of the sons of men." Rather, the world would be words in a much more radical sense: every created thing would, in its essence, be nothing but a signifier pointing to the Lord who uttered it. For God speaks things, not words. The world is his prose.[18] Augustine himself makes this very clear in *De doctrina christiana.*[19]

The difference—the only difference?—between God's psalm and ours is that the latter is distended, stretched out in time. A question that Augustine does not answer concerns the agent of this distension. Is it God himself who, by speaking reality into being, distends it temporally? Or is the distension a consequence of the constitution of the human mind? The latter possibility is certainly suggested by Augustine's well-known theory according to which time is a distension of the mind: "That is why I have come to think that time is simply a distension. But of what is it a distension? I do not know, but it would be surprising if it is not that of the mind itself."[20] If this is Augustine's theory, then distension would be the result of a human mind hearing God's words, and hearing them in the only way humanly possible: a distended way. A further dimension is opened up by the moral sense of the word "distension": Do we hear God's words in this way only because of sin? Was life in paradise not distended, neither morally nor temporally? Plotinus's theory of *tolma* ascribes an ontological role to

17. On the *mysterium tremendum*, see already Chapter 2, p. 55.

18. "Prose of the world" is of course an allusion to the title of chapter 2 in Foucault's *The Order of Things: An Archaeology of the Human Sciences*, trans. Alan Sheridan (New York: Vintage Books, 1994), 17.

19. Especially in book 1, in the discussion of things and signs.

20. Augustine, *Confessions* 11.26.33, p. 240 (Latin, 1:161). Pierre Lachièze-Rey, a Catholic expert on Kant, saw in Augustine's conception of time a precursor of the Kantian theory according to which it is the human mind that constructs the unity of the experienced world; hence the title of his contribution to the Augustinian congress of 1954: "Saint Augustin précurseur de Kant dans la théorie de la perception," in *Augustinus Magister. Congrès international augustinien, Paris 21–24 septembre 1954*, 3 vols. (Paris: Études augustiniennes, 1954), 1:425–28. Unfortunately, in the four pages of his article Lachièze-Rey is not able to do much more than juxtapose a few quotations. For further literature on Augustine's theory of time, see the excellent bibliography in Norbert Fischer, "'Distentio animi'. Symbol der Entflüchtigung des Zeitlichen," in Fischer and Mayer, *Die Confessiones des Augustinus von Hippo*, 490–552, at 549–52.

the Fall—a view in which he was followed by Christian thinkers like John Scottus Eriugena.[21] On this Neoplatonic view, all of reality is what it is— fallen, distended—only because we have forgotten the Father.[22]

Tradition between Memory and Forgetting

If we read what we have learned about the dynamics of tradition against the background of Augustine's theory of memory and forgetting, a deeper, more nuanced picture emerges. At the center of tradition stands the Word, who has made himself known in the performative speech act of creation, in revealing himself to prophets like Moses (who received the mediating law), in becoming flesh, by inspiring the authors of Scripture, and in guiding the church in its increasing understanding of wisdom. None of these theophanies, however, renders God accessible in unmediated presence. The Lord's presence is always veiled, a re-presentation, a memory at risk of slipping away. It is appropriate, therefore, that we do not know where exactly the biblical Mount Sinai was located or who composed many books of the Old and New Testaments. It is appropriate, as well, that we do not know what Jesus said in the Sermon on the Mount, except through the memory of others and in the medium of a language that was not his. (He did say "amen" and "Eli, Eli, lamma sabacthani," perhaps "raca" as well.)

The Christian tradition unfolds around powerful, awesome irruptions of the divine whose agent keeps withdrawing. Its root is charred. In its most basic sense, the Christian tradition is an effort to remember what happened, handing it down from generation to generation. However, as we know from Denys the Carthusian and from Alasdair MacIntyre, a tradition does not simply hand down what it received; it develops the deposit dy-

21. I have explored the ontological significance of the fall according to Eriugena in *Omne agens agit sibi simile: A "Repetition" of Scholastic Metaphysics*, Louvain Philosophical Studies 12 (Louvain: Leuven University Press, 1996), 128–34.

22. Norbert Fischer strongly denies that Augustine makes a connection between the fall and time: "Since Augustine does not assume that the soul has 'temporalized' itself through the fall from a better condition, its goal is not a 'de-temporalization' in the sense of a return to the One" ("Weil Augustinus nicht annimmt, daß die Seele sich selbst durch den Abfall von einem besseren Zustand 'verzeitlicht' hat, ist ihr Ziel auch keine 'Entzeitlichung' im Sinne einer Rückkehr zum Einen"); quoted from Fischer, "Distentio animi," 512. Fischer's interpretation, however, pays no attention to the moral dimension of the term *distentio*, and it struggles in its attempt to "rescue the extra-mental being of the temporal" ("das extramentale Sein des Zeitlichen zu retten," 522).

namically in response to varying circumstances. Tensions in the fledgling community of followers of Jesus led to theological clarifications, forcing Christianity to define itself over against its Jewish roots. This was not just a theoretical matter, but one of practice, as we saw in the example of the table fellowship at Antioch. Theory is always a reflection of and on practice, and practice expresses—often implicitly and inchoately—theoretical convictions. Continuing dialogue with the Greco-Roman civilization into which Christianity was born challenged it to answer critical questions about the "foolishness" in which Christians believed, and in so doing gave it the conceptual means to articulate the faith theologically. Councils, fathers, and later doctors of the church brought out implicit aspects of the faith, defined views incompatible with it, and refuted objections from outside the Christian community.

Within the concentric circles in which the tradition unfolded around the Word, various secondary centers developed, spawning derivative traditions. Thus, there is a Greek theological tradition, a Syriac one, and a Latin one; there is a Dionysian tradition and an Augustinian tradition; there is, finally, the tradition of the *Book of Sentences*, in which scholastic thought culminated—at least according to Denys the Carthusian. But perhaps it is better not to imagine these secondary traditions as existing outside the center of "the" tradition, for in the end, they are all but attempts to remember—rearticulate and reincarnate—the center.

These efforts to remember the Wisdom of the center reflect a basic reality of the human condition, namely, its distension in time, which is in turn an expression of human fallenness and finitude. It is unlikely that there would have been history in the garden of Eden. While the theological distension of Wisdom, of the divine irruption, functions as an authentic theophany, distension is closely connected with the risk of dispersal: the Word becomes concealed behind words that cover it up, rather than letting it speak. Thus, the danger arises that tradition may turn into an idol, a vehicle of forgetting.

To this danger, there is a remedy: the return to unity. Remembering the authentic past may require that the members of the tradition first die to the immediate present. Take the case of Denys the Carthusian. Rather than presuming to add insights of his own to the tradition, he dies to that ambition, contenting himself with the task of collecting the best of the past. At the critical juncture in which Denys finds himself, the way forward is the way backward. Therefore, the remembering that Denys attempts to bring about in his monumental commentary on the *Sentences* necessitates a forgetting, both of Denys's theological self and of more recent layers of the tradition that have concealed more of Wisdom than they have revealed of it.

This is the structure of the Christian theological tradition that our reading and interpretation of certain key sources have brought to light. We can imagine it as a kind of breathing movement around the sacred center, a movement that distends the scope of the tradition in speaking of its ineffable origin, only to contract in the realization that it has said too much.

The Remedy for Forgetting: Destruction

Denys the Carthusian's project was aimed at the recovery of the "golden age" of scholasticism that, Denys felt, had been overshadowed by more recent developments. As we indicated in introducing Denys, his unease about the direction of academic theology was widely shared in the fifteenth century.[23] Christian thinkers were trying to fold back a tradition whose connection with the center had become tenuous. In the fourteenth century, it was common for masters of theology, who had to lecture on Peter Lombard's *Sentences*, the standard textbook, to concentrate on a few areas of greatest interest to them, treating all the rest cursorily. Furthermore, oftentimes the areas focused on were philosophical rather than theological. There are some stunning examples of this tendency. The English Franciscan Roger Roseth, who lectured in the early fourteenth century, covered only five questions in his entire course, in which his students apparently learned little or nothing about creation, redemption, the sacraments, and many other essential Christian doctrines. There are only a handful of references to Scripture in the whole work. In studying Roseth's lectures, the Finnish scholar Olli Hallamaa reached the impression that they "epitomized the latest trends in Oxford theology. The tools of new logic and physics offered Roseth and his colleagues new perspectives on theological problems, keeping them close to the cutting edge of academic research. In Roseth's writing this approach was taken to the utmost limits, apparently, at the expense of theological substance."[24]

---

23. See Chapter 4, p. 106.

24. Olli Hallamaa, "On the Limits of the Genre: Roger Roseth as a Reader of the *Sentences*," in *Mediaeval Commentaries on the "Sentences" of Peter Lombard*, vol. 2, ed. Philipp W. Rosemann (Leiden: Brill, 2010), 369–404, at 403–4.

It is no wonder that fifteenth-century thinkers felt the need to arrest the centrifugal forces that threatened to tear apart the coherence and integrity of academic theology. A consensus built that a return was necessary to the "great texts"—whether one considered these to be represented by Thomas Aquinas (whose study John Capreolus sought to revive) or by William of Ockham (who served as Gabriel Biel's lodestar), or if one wished to give thirteenth-century scholasticism a mystical bent (as was the case with Denys the Carthusian).[25] However, the movement toward a recovery of the past extended well beyond the tradition of the *Book of Sentences* and academic theology. The humanists of the fifteenth century—men like Lorenzo Valla, Erasmus, and Lefèvre d'Étaples—reached back further: to Scripture, the classical languages, and the Greco-Roman literary and intellectual heritage, thus replacing Christianity within the context of ancient civilization. Concerning the broader religious culture, a series of councils, from Constance (1414) to the Fifth Council of the Lateran (1512–1517), attempted institutional and moral reforms of the inner life of the church. While the Council of Constance was able to end the schism that the wrangling for power had produced among three competing popes, in other respects the proposed reforms were much less successful.[26]

It is against this general background of reform and attempted reform that we have to read the Reformation. Although it cannot be reduced to its historical forerunners, the Reformation grew out of a common soil shared with other late medieval movements that diagnosed profound problems in the Christian tradition, endeavoring to remedy them.[27]

In Martin Luther, this remedy took the form of a radical "destruction." As Benjamin Crowe has shown, this is a term around which Martin Luther frequently framed his calls for reform.[28] His choice of words was inspired

---

25. On the return to the sources in fifteenth-century commentaries on the *Sentences*, one may read chapter 4 of my *Story of a Great Medieval Book: Peter Lombard's "Sentences,"* Rethinking the Middle Ages 2 (Toronto: University of Toronto Press, 2007), 137–83.

26. For an account of intellectual and religious life on the eve of the Reformation, see Steven Ozment, *The Age of Reform, 1250–1550: An Intellectual and Religious History of Late Medieval and Reformation Europe* (New Haven: Yale University Press, 1980).

27. Heiko Oberman chose the term "forerunners" for the title of his book, *Forerunners of the Reformation: The Shape of Late Medieval Thought, Illustrated by Key Documents* (New York: Holt, Rinehart and Winston, 1966). In chapter 1, Oberman argues in favor of a balanced historical approach that, by recognizing the "*many* levels of continuity" (37) between the late Middle Ages and the Reformation, makes it possible to set into relief the "*structure of the change*" (39).

28. See the detailed discussion in Benjamin D. Crowe, *Heidegger's Religious Origins:*

by scriptural passages like 1 Corinthians 1, on the foolishness of the cross: "And the base things of the world, and the things that are contemptible, hath God chosen, and things that are not, that he might bring to naught things that are (*ut ea quae sunt destrueret*)" (1 Cor. 1:28). Luther's critique was directed against what he called the *theologia gloriae*, which prevailed in the theory and practice of the contemporary church: God was discovered only through his greatness and glory. Theologians in the scholastic tradition were busy discussing God's being, infinity, goodness, and justice; this approach, in turn, was reflected in the self-image (and in the comportment) of a church full of pride, asserting its dominion over all realms of life.[29] Against these tendencies, Luther espoused a *theologia crucis*, which emphasized the brokenness of the crucified Lord—his abjection, we could say, in our earlier terminology. In his *Heidelberg Disputation* from 1518, Luther explained important aspects of the difference between the two theologies:

20. **He deserves to be called a theologian, however, who comprehends the visible things of God and his back (*visibilia et posterioria Dei*) as seen through suffering and the cross**. The back and visible things of God (*Posterioria et visibilia Dei*)[30] are placed in opposition to the invisible, namely, his human nature, weakness, foolishness. The Apostle in 1 Cor. 1[:25] calls them the weakness and folly of God. Because

Destruction and Authenticity, Indiana Series in the Philosophy of Religion (Bloomington and Indianapolis: Indiana University Press, 2006), chap. 2, 44–66. In 1994, John van Buren had already drawn attention to the Lutheran background of the early Heidegger's thought, adducing many pertinent references from both Luther and Heidegger; see John van Buren, *The Young Heidegger: Rumors of the Hidden King*, Studies in Continental Thought (Bloomington and Indianapolis: Indiana University Press, 1994), esp. chap. 8, 157–202. Van Buren's recent essay, "Aristotle Luther Heidegger: Travelling a Forgotten Path of Thought," *Existentia: An International Journal of Philosophy* 26 (2016): 257–74, is strange in that it fails to acknowledge any of the literature that has appeared on the topic since the author's book-length study.

29. Van Buren, *The Young Heidegger*, 161, writes: "The word 'glory' in the young Luther's *Heidelberg Disputation* is nothing less than his appellation for how, in Greek metaphysics and in Christian theology, the being of the divine appears as the speculative kingdom of an exalted radiant presence that is 'enjoyed' by quietistic, ocular-aesthetic contemplation.... For Luther, this *theologia gloriae* suffers from presumption (*praesumptio*) and *superbia*, the pride that willfully and hyperbolically oversteps its limits, elevates itself to the Beyond (*super*) of its speculative visions, and thereby seeks to satisfy its desire for dominion (*dominium*), power (*potestas*), empire (*imperium*)."

30. The word *posterioria* (God's "back") is an allusion to Exod. 33:23, where Moses is allowed to see only God's back (see Chapter 1, p. 27).

men misused the knowledge of God through works, God wished again to be recognized in suffering, and to condemn wisdom concerning invisible things by means of wisdom concerning visible things, so that those who did not honor God as manifested in his works should honor him as he is hidden in his suffering (*absconditum in passionibus*). As the Apostle says in 1 Cor. 1[:21], "For since, in the wisdom of God, the world did not know God through wisdom, it pleased God through the folly of what we preach to save those who believe." Now it is not sufficient for anyone, and it does him no good to recognize God in his glory and majesty, unless he recognizes him in the humility and shame of the cross. Thus God destroys (*perdit*) the wisdom of the wise, as Isa. [45:15] says, "Truly, thou art a God who hidest thyself." . . .

21. **A theologian of glory calls evil good and good evil. A theologian of the cross calls the thing what it actually is.** This is clear: He who does not know Christ does not know God hidden in suffering (*absconditum in passionibus*). Therefore he prefers works to suffering, glory to the cross, strength to weakness, wisdom to folly, and, in general, good to evil. These are the people whom the Apostle calls "enemies of the cross of Christ" [Phil. 3:18], for they hate the cross and suffering and love works and the glory of works. . . . Therefore the friends of the cross say that the cross is good and works are evil, for through the cross works are destroyed (*destruuntur*) and the old Adam, who is especially edified (*aedificatur*) by works, is crucified. It is impossible for a person not to be puffed up by his good works unless he has first been emptied (*exinanitus*) and destroyed (*destructus*) by suffering and evil until he knows that he is nothing (*sciat seipsum esse nihil*) and that his works are not his but God's.[31]

According to Luther, the recovery of the hidden center of the tradition requires a twofold work of destruction. God is the primary "destroyer," in that his suffering on the cross "unbuilds" and humbles the Christian who has prematurely been "built up" by his good works, convinced of his own crucial role in salvation. To be "destroyed," the believer must die with Christ on the cross to be brought face-to-face with his utter finitude, his nothingness, before being resurrected and justified through God's grace

---

31. *Luther's Works*, vol. 31, *Career of the Reformer I*, ed. Harold T. Grimm (Philadelphia: Fortress, 1957), 52–53. I have amended the translation in light of the Latin text: *D. Martin Luthers Werke. Kritische Gesammtausgabe*, vol. 1 (Weimar: Hermann Böhlau, 1883), 362.

alone.[32] This is what theses 20 and 21 above focus on.[33] Theology complements God's work through a sort of second-order destruction, namely, by reflecting critically on the theology of glory and thus contributing to its "unbuilding."

Luther's theses in the *Heidelberg Disputation* were meant to help "destruct" and destabilize a tradition that he believed had forgotten its center: the crucified Christ. Yet, although provocative, Luther was still careful not to be completely one-sided. If in theses 20 and 21 he vituperates against the "wisdom" of the *theologia gloriae* and against its emphasis on good works as a means for salvation, in thesis 24 Luther hastens to add a qualification: **"Yet that wisdom is not of itself evil, nor is the law to be evaded; but without the theology of the cross man misuses the best in the worst manner.** Indeed the law is holy [Rom. 7:12], every gift of God good [1 Tim. 4:4], and everything that is created exceedingly good, as in Gen. 1[:31]. But, as stated above, he who has not been destroyed (*destructus*), reduced to nothing (*ad nihilum redactus*) through the cross and suffering, takes credit for works and wisdom and does not give credit to God."[34]

Given what we have discovered in this book about the logic of tradition, we can assert that a radical folding back of the tradition to its center—a "destruction"—must periodically occur to counterbalance the forgetting that is an inescapable part of the tradition's unfolding. We can even say that this destruction will necessarily take on transgressive traits, as it challenges the boundaries of the tradition as commonly understood at the

32. Luther brings this point out in thesis 24: "He, however, who has been emptied [cf. Phil. 2:7] through suffering no longer does works but knows that God works and does all things in him. For this reason, whether God does works or not, it is all the same to him. He neither boasts if he does good works, nor is he disturbed if God does not do good works in him. He knows that it is sufficient if he suffers and is destroyed (*destruitur*) by the cross in order to be annihilated all the more. It is this that Christ says in John 3[:7], 'You must be born anew.' To be born anew, one must consequently first die and then be raised up with the Son of Man. To die, I say, means to feel death at hand" (*Luther's Works*, 31:55; amended in light of *D. Martin Luthers Werke*, 1:363). Luther calls the annihilation and subsequent rebirth of the Christian the *opus alienum* and *opus proprium* of God, respectively. For commentary on thesis 24, see Christian Sommer, *Heidegger, Aristote, Luther. Les sources aristotéliciennes et néo-testamentaires d'Être et temps*, Épiméthée (Paris: Presses universitaires de France, 2006), 47–52.

33. For detailed commentary on theses 20 and 21 from a Heideggerian perspective, see Sommer, *Heidegger, Aristote, Luther*, 38–44.

34. *Luther's Works*, 31:55 (Latin: *D. Martin Luthers Werke*, 1:363). I have adjusted the capitalization of some words.

time of the destruction. What, then, is the difference between one form of destruction that will help the tradition rediscover forgotten aspects of its center, and another form that will lead to a betrayal, destabilizing the tradition and dispersing it? We are asking here a version of Yves Congar's question regarding the difference between "true and false reform in the church."[35]

Without pretending to have grasped all the complexities that are at stake in Luther's Reformation, I find his extreme anti-Judaism—ultimately motivated by his criticism of good works and the law[36]—to be a worrying sign. To be sure, Christianity has had significant difficulties in defining the precise meaning of the "fulfillment" of Judaism that Christ asserts he has brought about.[37] Could one perhaps even say that, in one sense, Christianity is nothing other than this question? As its Jewish roots continue to haunt the identity of the Christian faith—remember what Foucault says about the formative presence of the excluded Outside at the center of a culture—there is a range of possible positions that one can embrace. The incident at Antioch remains paradigmatic in disclosing the options. One apostle, Paul, is less concerned about the continuity of the emerging Christian community with its Jewish origins, whereas another, James, representing "Jerusalem," insists on the continuing need to observe the law. There is one position, however, that it seems impossible to take, from the point of view of the very nature of Christianity, and that is advocating the eradication of Judaism. Unfortunately, this is exactly the perspective Luther adopted. Even before he became the Reformer, Luther delivered lectures on the Psalms at the University of Wittenberg in which he startlingly argued that, not only was the allegorical meaning of the Hebrew Scriptures to be sought in a foreshadowing of the gospel; no, even literally the Psalms were about the suffering of Christ. In this manner, Luther attempted to eliminate the Jews from salvation history. Only one role was left for them, as David Nirenberg explains, "a purely persecutory one: whenever the voice

---

35. See Yves Congar, *True and False Reform in the Church*, trans. Paul Philibert (Collegeville, MN: Liturgical Press, 2011).

36. Thus, Thomas Kaufmann is right in declaring Luther's anti-Judaism "no unimportant side note in his theology" (*A Short Life of Martin Luther*, trans. Peter D. S. Krey and James D. Bratt, Reformation Resources, 1517–2017 [Grand Rapids: Eerdmans, 2016], 105).

37. For a lucid statement of the problem (and a tentative solution), see Bruce Marshall, "Christ and Israel: An Unsolved Problem in Catholic Theology," in *The Call of Abraham: Essays on the Election of Israel in Honor of Jon D. Levenson*, ed. Gary A. Anderson and Joel S. Kaminsky (Notre Dame: University of Notre Dame Press, 2013), 330–50.

of the psalmist cries out, it is the voice of Jesus crying out against his tormentors, the Jews."[38]

Luther's extreme theoretical position did not remain without practical consequences, especially as he resented the quite predictable Jewish rejection of his biblical hermeneutic.[39] Even amidst the virulent anti-Judaism that was common in his day, the intensity of his hatred and the fanaticism of his proposed actions stand out.[40] Luther authored several anti-Jewish treatises, culminating in one entitled *On the Jews and Their Lies* (1543). "Even contemporary Protestants were shocked by these writings," according to Mark Edwards.[41] Abandoning the traditional Augustinian position according to which Jews ought to be tolerated in Christian lands—a toleration that came to be enshrined in papal bulls, starting with *Sicut Iudaeis*, issued in 1120 by Pope Callixtus II[42]—he demanded the suppression of the Jewish faith and the merciless expulsion of the Jewish population from Germany. His words fell onto receptive ears, reinforcing and even directly causing anti-Jewish violence.[43] By the end of the sixteenth century, most Jewish communities had disappeared from Germany. The Berlin synagogue had been destroyed. "The handful that remained in German lands," Nir-

---

38. David Nirenberg, *Anti-Judaism: The Western Tradition* (New York: Norton, 2013), 253.

39. As Thomas Kaufmann writes, "The weightiest theological motive for his bitter tirades against the Jews ... was probably grounded in their negation of Luther's biblical hermeneutic, which regarded the Old Testament essentially as a witness to Christ" (*Short Life*, 61).

40. To do justice to Luther, one has to see him in the context of his time, which is the objective of Heiko Oberman's book, *The Roots of Anti-Semitism in the Age of Renaissance and Reformation*, trans. James I. Porter (Philadelphia: Fortress, 1984). Yet even Oberman, who paints a very nuanced picture, must admit that Luther's anti-Jewish works were "written with a vehemence rivaled only by Johannes Eck's" (46).

41. Mark U. Edwards Jr., *Luther's Last Battles: Politics and Polemics, 1531–46* (Ithaca, NY: Cornell University Press, 1983), 3. Edwards emphasizes the eschatological expectations of the old Luther, whose positions became increasingly extreme as he considered himself living in the end-times in which the church was faced with the Antichrist.

42. The bull *Sicut Iudaeis* itself has not survived and is known only from later quotations; see Shlomo Simonsohn, *The Apostolic See and the Jews: Documents, 492–1404*, Studies and Texts 94 (Toronto: Pontifical Institute of Mediaeval Studies, 1988), #44, p. 44. For a comprehensive history of papal protection of the Jews, see Shlomo Simonsohn, *The Apostolic See and the Jews: History*, Studies and Texts 109 (Toronto: Pontifical Institute of Mediaeval Studies, 1991).

43. Mark Edwards writes (*Luther's Last Battles*, 135): "Fortunately, no Protestant prince attempted to put all Luther's recommendations into practice. Several did, however, take some measures against the Jews as a result of Luther's writings."

Title page of Luther's treatise *Von den Jüden und Iren Lügen* (*On the Jews and Their Lies*). Note the horned Jew at the bottom. (From the holdings of the Universitäts- und Landesbibliothek Sachsen-Anhalt, call number Ung I D 14(2).)

enberg comments, "were confined to the Catholic ecclesiastical states, governed by bishops under the protection of the Holy Roman emperor."[44]

Some four hundred years later in Germany, the so-called *Reichskristall-nacht*—a pogrom foreshadowing the Holocaust in which thousands of Jewish people were deported to concentration camps, Jewish-owned stores were shattered, synagogues destroyed, cemeteries desecrated, and hundreds killed or driven into suicide—began on November 9, 1938, the eve of Luther's birthday.

From *Destructio* to *Destruktion*

The formative role that Luther's thought played in Heidegger's early years is well documented.[45]

On January 9, 1919, Heidegger addressed a letter to his friend Father Engelbert Krebs in which he announced his conversion to Protestantism. In the following years, he immersed himself in the study of Luther's works, collaborated intensively with Rudolf Bultmann at Marburg, lectured on the Reformer, and even took over the seminar of a Protestant theologian who had taken ill. Indeed, Heidegger developed the reputation of being a Luther expert.[46] He commented on the *Heidelberg Disputation* on two separate occasions in the early 1920s, namely, in a lecture course and in a paper that he contributed to a seminar taught by Bultmann.[47]

44. Nirenberg, *Anti-Judaism*, 262.

45. In addition to the books already cited by van Buren, Crowe, and Sommer, one should mention the study by S. J. McGrath, *The Early Heidegger and Medieval Philosophy: Phenomenology for the Godforsaken* (Washington, DC: Catholic University of America Press, 2006). McGrath argues that "Heidegger has deliberately designed a philosophy symbiotic with Lutheran theology" (168). The consequence of Heidegger's option for Luther (and against the scholastic tradition) is a dangerous "agnostic piety" (223). I would now modify the critique of McGrath's book that I formulated in "The Lutheran Heidegger: Reflections on S. J. McGrath, *The Early Heidegger and Medieval Philosophy*," *Philotheos: International Journal for Philosophy and Theology* 7 (2007): 327–32; reprinted in *Analecta Hermeneutica* 1 (2009): 343–50. Finally, the German research on the topic is well represented in the essay by Karl Lehmann, "'Sagen, was Sache ist': Der Blick auf die Wahrheit der Existenz. Heideggers Beziehung zu Luther," in *Heidegger und die christliche Tradition*, ed. Norbert Fischer and Friedrich-Wilhelm von Herrmann (Hamburg: Meiner, 2007), 149–66.

46. See van Buren, *The Young Heidegger*, 149–50.

47. For references, see Sommer, *Heidegger, Aristote, Luther*, 36–38. In note 1 on p. 35, Sommer has compiled a list of references to Luther throughout Heidegger's oeuvre.

Heidegger's use of the term *Destruktion* in *Being and Time* can be properly understood, therefore, only against the background of his assimilation of Lutheran theology. This does not mean that there are not also other sources, since *Being and Time* is a brilliant confluence, synthesis, and transformation of much of the Western philosophical tradition. Particularly relevant in this context is the fact that Heidegger's teacher Husserl employed the German word *Abbau*—literally, "de-building" or "un-building"—to address the problem of what he termed "sedimentation and traditionalization" (*Sedimentierung bzw. Traditionalisierung*). As once groundbreaking insights that placed an entire branch of knowledge on a new footing come to be taken for granted, their presuppositions are forgotten. In this way, the grounds of knowledge become the sediment upon which further layers of a tradition of inquiry are built, such that these layers hide the basic strata on which they rest. Husserl illustrates what he means by citing the example of Galileo:

> *Galileo*, the discoverer ... of physics, or physical nature, is at once a *discovering and a concealing genius*. He discovers mathematical nature, the methodical idea, he blazes the trail for the infinite number of physical discoveries and discoverers. By contrast to the *universal causality of the intuitively given world* (as its invariant form), he discovers what has since been called simply the *law of causality*, the "a priori form" of the "true" (idealized and mathematized) world, the "law of exact lawfulness" according to which *every occurrence* in "nature" must come under *exact laws*. All this is discovery-concealment, and to the present day we accept it as straightforward truth.[48]

"All this is discovery-concealment" (*Das alles ist Entdeckung-Verdeckung*), Husserl declares about the way in which the tradition takes for granted the "garb of ideas" (*Ideenkleid*), the "so-called objective scientific truths" in which modern science has clad the intuitively given world.[49] Such taking for granted of a scientific construct, such sedimentation, has caused the

48. Edmund Husserl, *The Crisis of European Sciences and Transcendental Phenomenology: An Introduction to Phenomenological Philosophy*, trans. David Carr (Evanston, IL: Northwestern University Press, 1970), 52–53; German: *Die Krisis der europäischen Wissenschaften und die transzendentale Phänomenologie. Eine Einleitung in die phänomenologische Philosophie*, ed. Walter Biemel, 2nd ed., Husserliana 6 (The Hague: Martinus Nijhoff, 1962), 53; emphasis in original.

49. Husserl, *Crisis of European Sciences*, 51 (German, 51).

world of everyday life to be forgotten. This *Lebenswelt*, Husserl believes, must be the starting point of phenomenological inquiry. But how is one to get to this fresh beginning, given the massive concealment that has overshadowed the originally given world? Husserl calls for a systematic critique of tradition, for which he uses the term *Abbau*.[50]

It is significant that in *Being and Time* Heidegger decided to speak of *Destruktion* rather than *Abbau*, a term with which he was well familiar.[51] Anyone who knows *Sein und Zeit* realizes that the argument frequently turns upon careful attention to the etymology of German terms. In opting for *Destruktion* where *Abbau* would have been the natural German synonym (even mirroring, as it does, the etymology of the Latin word), Heidegger incorporated a Lutheran echo into his work that he could easily have avoided. Perhaps he just did not want to avoid it, despite the footnotes assuring the reader of the non-Christian character of the book. This is what Derrida seems to suspect, in a passage where he emphasizes—and distances himself from—the Christian ancestry of Heidegger's "destruction":

> Let us never forget the Christian, in fact, Lutheran, memory of Heideggerian deconstruction (*Destruktion* was first *destructio* by Luther, anxious to reactivate the originary sense of the Gospels by deconstructing theological sediments). Let us never forget this, lest one mix up all the "deconstructions" of this time. And of the world. But in truth, one can never forget this Christian (Lutheran, Pascalian, Hegelian, Kierkegaardian, Marxian, and so forth) memory when one reads Heidegger, when one also questions his denials. A "deconstruction of Christianity," if it is ever possible, should therefore begin by untying itself from a Christian tradition of *destructio*.[52]

For the project of the present book, of course, the residually Christian character of Heidegger's notion of "destruction" is particularly relevant, and

50. See J. Claude Evans, "Phenomenological Deconstruction: Husserl's Method of *Abbau*," *Journal of the British Society for Phenomenology* 21, no. 1 (1990): 14–25.

51. Heidegger employed the term *Abbau* in the lecture course *Die Grundprobleme der Phänomenologie*, which dates from 1927, the year in which *Being and Time* appeared. See *Die Grundprobleme der Phänomenologie*, ed. Friedrich-Wilhelm von Hermann, Gesamtausgabe 24 (Frankfurt am Main: Klostermann, 1975), 31.

52. Jacques Derrida, *On Touching—Jean-Luc Nancy*, trans. Christine Irizarry, Meridian: Crossing Aesthetics (Stanford: Stanford University Press, 2005), 60.

we can leave Derrida's "deconstruction" to one side.[53] But what, exactly, is "destruction"?

In section 6 of *Being and Time*, Heidegger introduces *Destruktion* as a crucial element in the task of renewing the ontological tradition. His philosophy of tradition is radical, in that for him tradition is fundamentally rooted in the historical constitution of Dasein. In other words, tradition is not something we can be "for" or "against." Rather, because Dasein "'is' its past, whether explicitly or not," tradition pervades our being. Or, to be more precise, tradition pervades our choices: the future that we create for ourselves through our projects stems from the manner in which we take up our past. Heidegger writes:

> Dasein "is" its past in the way of *its* own Being, which, to put it roughly, "historicizes" out of its future on each occasion. Whatever the way of being it may have at the time, and thus with whatever understanding of Being it may possess, Dasein has grown up both into and in a traditional (*überkommene*) way of interpreting itself: in terms of this it understands itself proximally and, within a certain range, constantly. By this understanding, the possibilities of its Being are disclosed and regulated. Its own past—and this always means the past of its "generation"—is not something which *follows along after* Dasein, but something which already goes ahead of it.[54]

Against this background, it is clear that for Dasein to achieve some degree of transparency regarding its own choices, and to be able to make these choices deliberately, it needs to examine its own tradition: "This elemental historicality of Dasein may remain hidden from Dasein itself. But there is a certain way in which it can be discovered and be properly cultivated.

53. Derrida was right in distinguishing his form of deconstruction from Heidegger's. Gadamer brings out the difference very clearly in his essay "Destruktion und Dekonstruktion," in *Gesammelte Werke*, vol. 2, *Hermeneutik II* (Tübingen: J. C. B. Mohr/Paul Siebeck, 1993), 361–72. Jeff Mitscherling comments usefully on Gadamer's distinction in "Deconstruction, *Destruktion*, and Dialogue," *Analecta Hermeneutica* 6 (2014): 1–8.

54. Martin Heidegger, *Being and Time*, trans. John Macquarrie and Edward Robinson (San Francisco: Harper and Row, 1962), 41. For the German text, see *Sein und Zeit*, Gesamtausgabe 2 (Frankfurt am Main: Klostermann, 1977), 27. I have occasionally amended the Macquarrie/Robinson translation in light of the German text as well as the choices made by Joan Stambaugh in her English version: *Being and Time*, trans. Joan Stambaugh, rev. Dennis J. Schmidt, SUNY Series in Contemporary Continental Philosophy (Albany: State University of New York Press, 2010).

Dasein can discover tradition (*Tradition*), preserve it, and pursue it explicitly. The discovery of tradition (*Tradition*) and the disclosure of what it 'transmits' and how this is transmitted, can be taken hold of as a task in its own right."[55] This discovery of tradition is all the more important since Dasein has a tendency to "fall": just as it takes an effort for it to question the opinions and attitudes of the They (*das Man*), which it unthinkingly adopts in its average everydayness, so Dasein tends to accept uncritically the guidance it receives from tradition:

> Our preparatory interpretation of the fundamental structures of Dasein with regard to the average kind of Being which is closest to it (a kind of Being in which it is therefore proximally historical as well), will make manifest, however, not only that Dasein is inclined to fall prey to its world (the world in which it is) and to interpret itself in terms of that world by its reflected light, but also that Dasein simultaneously falls prey to the tradition of which it has more or less explicitly taken hold. This tradition keeps it from providing its own guidance, whether in inquiring or in choosing.[56]

The last sentence sounds a little like Kant's call, in his Enlightenment essay, to shake off traditional tutelage and have the courage to know for oneself. However, we are not simply dealing with a question of self-transparency and self-determination here. Tradition, which allows Dasein access to the riches of its past by ensuring they are handed down from generation to generation, has the tendency of simultaneously obscuring what it transmits. This is Heidegger's way of describing what Husserl called "sedimentation":

> When tradition thus becomes master, it does so in such a way that what it "transmits" is made so inaccessible, proximally and for the most part, that it rather becomes concealed (*verdeckt*). Tradition takes what has come down to us and delivers it over to self-evidence (*Selbst-verständlichkeit*); it blocks our access to those primordial "sources" from which the categories and concepts handed down to us have been in part quite genuinely drawn. Indeed it makes us forget that they have had such an origin, and makes us suppose that the necessity

---

55. Heidegger, *Being and Time*, trans. Macquarrie/Robinson, 41 (German, 27–28).
56. Heidegger, *Being and Time*, trans. Macquarrie/Robinson, 42–43 (German, 28–29).

of going back to these sources is something which we need not even understand.[57]

In the context of *Being and Time*, the "sources" that Heidegger has in mind are sources of philosophical insight. In a different context—that of the more religious years preceding the publication of his chef-d'oeuvre—his remark could be read as a Lutheran critique of the Catholic tradition, which was believed to have concealed many truths of Scripture. The return to the sources would then mean a return to biblical thinking, which was made impossible by layers of scholastic theology.

In the passage on which we are commenting, the return to the sources has as its first purpose to overcome the *Selbstverständlichkeit* of traditional ideas. Macquarrie and Robinson translate *Selbstverständlichkeit* as "self-evidence," whereas Stambaugh chooses "obviousness." When traditional notions become self-evident and obvious, they are no longer subject to deep questioning. Instead, their truth is taken for granted, as something that needs no justification or further investigation. But what precisely are the "sources" from which these notions were originally derived—and derived (at least "in part") genuinely? Heidegger answers that the sources are "primordial experiences" that gave rise to structures of interpretation that, in turn, opened up certain well-delimited fields of investigation:

> If the question of Being is to have its own history made transparent, then this hardened tradition must be loosened up, and the concealments (*Verdeckungen*) which it has brought about must be detached.[58] We understand this task as one in which by taking *the question of Being as our clue*, we are to *destruct* the traditional content of ancient ontology until we arrive at those primordial experiences in which we achieved our first ways of determining the nature of Being—the ways which have guided us ever since.
>
> In thus demonstrating the origin of our basic ontological concepts by an investigation in which their "birth certificate" is displayed, we have

57. Heidegger, *Being and Time*, trans. Macquarrie/Robinson, 43 (German, 29).

58. Marquarrie/Robinson and Stambaugh translate "dissolved" and "dissolution," respectively. But the German reads, "... *bedarf es ... der Ablösung der durch sie gezeitigten Verdeckungen*," "a detachment of the concealments brought about by it [i.e., the tradition] is needful." *Ablösung* ("detachment") is not *Auflösung* ("dissolution"). What Heidegger seems to have in mind is the image of layers of sediment being detached from the lower strata that they hide.

nothing to do with a bad relativizing of ontological standpoints. But this destruction (*Destruktion*) is just as far from having the *negative* sense of shaking off the ontological tradition. We must, on the contrary, stake out the positive possibilities of that tradition, and this always means staking out its *limits* (*Grenzen*); these in turn are given factically in the way the question is formulated at the time, and in the way the possible field of investigation is then bounded off. The destruction (*Destruktion*) does not relate itself negatively towards the past; its criticism is aimed at "today" and at the prevalent way of treating the history of ontology, whether it is conceived in terms of doxography, intellectual history, or as a history of problems. But to bury the past in nullity is not the purpose of this destruction (*Destruktion*); its aim is *positive*; its negative function remains unexpressed and indirect.[59]

Macquarrie and Robinson's translation of Heidegger's phrase "Destruktion des überlieferten Bestandes der antiken Ontologie auf die ursprünglichen Erfahrungen" is quite good: "we are to destruct the traditional content of ancient ontology until we arrive at those primordial experiences," etc. *Destruktion auf* does not mean, as Stambaugh would have it, that "this destruction is based upon the original experiences."[60] Rather, the preposition *auf* indicates a direction, the direction of the destruction, which must proceed toward the original experiences, or must have as its goal to arrive at the latter, as Macquarrie and Robinson render the idea.

What is the content of the primordial experiences that it is the goal of destruction to recover? Heidegger is not explicit here, but we are not going to go wrong if we take his understanding from his definition of the phenomenological method in the immediately following section of *Being and Time*. There, in section 7, Heidegger offers a series of increasingly precise and technical definitions of the phenomenological approach. However, he begins with the simple maxim, "To the things themselves!"[61] The destruction, then, would be a way to rid ourselves of "all free-floating constructions and accidental findings"[62] and instead concentrate on the things that really showed themselves to a particular thinker, and that this thinker attempted to capture conceptually. Oftentimes, it may not be easy

---

59. Heidegger, *Being and Time*, trans. Macquarrie/Robinson, 44 (German, 30–31).
60. Heidegger, *Being and Time*, trans. Stambaugh, 21–22.
61. Heidegger, *Being and Time*, trans. Macquarrie/Robinson, 50 (German, 37).
62. Heidegger, *Being and Time*, trans. Macquarrie/Robinson, 50 (German, 37).

to wrest a thinker's genuine insights from the tradition of his interpreters, for whom everything he struggled to express has become obvious and self-evident—which explains the need for a certain degree of violence in the tasks of interpretation and destruction.[63] For example, simply to say that Thomas Aquinas made a "real distinction" between essence and existence in creatures while denying its applicability to God tells us very little about what Aquinas saw in God's nature. What did he want to express about God by claiming that he is the coincidence of Being and essence? This is what needs to be explained for the famous Thomistic distinction to be more than the relic of a moribund tradition.

But back to our Heideggerian passage, which in discussing the need to "stake out limits" (*Grenzen abstecken*) takes on a Kantian tone. The primordial experiences toward which the destruction is supposed to proceed by piercing through layers of traditional hardening and sedimentation have led to a certain way in which questions are formulated and approached. When such an approach arises, it creates a well-defined conceptual field in which future inquiries are made possible, but within whose limits they also remain confined. Tradition, then, sets up the conditions for the possibility of (philosophical) inquiry, and destruction has the purpose of uncovering these conditions—staking out these limits—in whose nature it lies to remain unexpressed "proximally and for the most part" (as Heidegger would say).

Is such a Kantian interpretation of the goals of destruction far-fetched? Not at all, because in section 7, from which we just quoted in order to clarify Heidegger's understanding of primordial experience, the phenomenological approach receives an explicitly and thoroughly Kantian definition: "If we keep within the horizon of the Kantian problematic, we can give an illustration of what is conceived phenomenologically as a phenomenon, with reservations as to other differences; for we may then say that that which already shows itself in the appearance as prior to the phenomenon as ordinarily understood and as accompanying it in every case, can, even though it thus shows itself unthematically, be brought thematically to show itself; and what thus shows itself in itself ('forms of the intuition') will be the phenomena of phenomenology."[64] Applied to destruction, the

63. On the need for hermeneutic violence, see John D. Caputo, *Radical Hermeneutics: Repetition, Deconstruction, and the Hermeneutic Project*, Studies in Phenomenology and Existential Philosophy (Bloomington and Indianapolis: Indiana University Press, 1987), 63–66. "'Destruction' is hermeneutic violence," Caputo writes (63).

64. Heidegger, *Being and Time*, trans. Macquarrie/Robinson, 54–55 (German, 42).

phenomenological method aims to uncover less the authentic historical positions of philosophers over against traditional misinterpretations (though this may well be part of the destructive project) than the implicit parameters that have defined and delimited philosophical thinking—one might even be tempted to use Foucault's term "historical *a priori*" here.[65] The aim of destruction, therefore, is to critique not the past but rather insufficient present appropriations of the past, such as doxography, intellectual history, and *Problemgeschichte*, which fail to take the tradition seriously as the framework whose scope and limits shape our possibilities.

According to Heidegger, however, destruction's return to the sources of particular ways to frame philosophical questions is not an end in itself. Its purpose does not exhaust itself in demonstrating, in a gesture of triumphant superiority, that the tradition is somehow lacking or limited.[66] Heidegger understands well that the limitations of tradition are ineluctable. As we have seen, he sometimes couches this insight in Kantian terms, although *Being and Time* is already moving toward the different, nontranscendental language that would be characteristic of Heidegger after the *Kehre*—namely, the language of *a-lētheia* as (un)concealment. In any case, destruction remains incomplete without a second, complementary movement. Once the limits have been thrown into relief, once the past has been reduced—in the sense of a medieval *reductio*—to its quasi-transcendental framework, the destruction turns into a construction. Heidegger prefers the term "repetition":

> *Repeating (Wiederholung) is handing down explicitly*—that is to say, going back into possibilities of the Dasein that has-been-there. The authentic repetition of a possibility of existence that has been—the possibility that Dasein may choose its hero—is grounded existentially in anticipatory resoluteness; for it is in resoluteness that one first chooses the choice which makes one free for the struggle of loyally following in the footsteps of that which can be repeated. But when one has, by repetition, handed down to oneself a possibility that has been, the Dasein

65. See the introduction, p. 7.
66. Thomas Arne Winter's critique of the Heideggerian conception of tradition and destruction is therefore one-sided when he imputes to Heidegger an understanding of tradition as nothing but a *Verdeckungsgeschichte*, a "history of concealment" (*Traditionstheorie*, Philosophische Untersuchungen 42 [Tübingen: Mohr Siebeck, 2017], 23, 42, 49–60, and elsewhere). Heidegger knows that tradition is what Winter himself calls "ambivalent" (153–54); even the few texts already cited from *Being and Time* make this quite clear.

that has-been-there is not disclosed in order to be actualized over again. The repeating of that which is possible does not bring again something that is "past," nor does it bind the "present" back to that which has already been "outstripped." Arising, as it does, from a resolute projection of oneself, repetition does not let itself be persuaded of something by what is "past," just in order that this, as something which was formerly actual, may recur. Rather, the repetition makes a *reciprocative rejoinder* (*erwidert*) to the possibility of that existence which has-been-there. But when such a rejoinder (*Erwiderung*) is made to this possibility in a resolution, it is made *in a moment of vision; and as such* it is at the same time a *disavowal* (*Widerruf*) of that which in the today is working itself out as the "past." Repetition does not abandon itself to that which is past, nor does it aim at progress. In the moment of vision authentic existence is indifferent to both these alternatives.[67]

Heidegger's explanation of *Wiederholung* makes us notice that the English term "repetition" is not an ideal translation, although *wiederholen* certainly means "to repeat." *Wiederholen*, however, can be pronounced in two ways: if the accent lies on the second syllable, it means "to repeat"; pronounced with the accent placed on the first syllable, "to bring back" captures its meaning. But then, Heidegger is not advocating a simple "bringing back" of past conceptions either, although the destruction certainly intends to bring us back to the sources of the tradition. In a footnote to his pioneering

---

67. *Being and Time*, trans. Macquarrie/Robinson, 437–38 (German, 509–10). The phrase in this quotation "handed down to oneself a possibility that has been" translates *das wiederholende Sichüberliefern einer gewesenen Möglichkeit*. Macquarrie and Robinson, as well as Stambaugh, interpret *Sichüberliefern* as an act of making available to oneself an aspect of the tradition. John Caputo, *Radical Hermeneutics*, 88, concurs, writing that "one's possibility is both inherited and chosen, which explains why Heidegger uses the active expression 'handing down to oneself' (*ein Sichüberliefern*)." Even Thomas Arne Winter (*Traditionstheorie*, 86) understands *Sichüberliefern* along these lines. What these scholars have overlooked is that the term *Sichüberliefern* is quite ambiguous—an ambiguity that Heidegger brings out starkly as his discussion of repetition continues: "Resoluteness implies handing oneself down by anticipation to the 'there' of the moment of vision; and this handing down we call 'fate'" (*Being and Time*, trans. Macquarrie/Robinson, 438 [German, 510]). What does it mean to "hand oneself down" to the particularity of a historical moment? Not much, I think. In the context of the sentence just quoted, *Sichüberliefern* must be rendered as "delivering oneself over." In retrieving or recovering the possibilities of the tradition, Dasein responds authentically to the historical constellation of ideas into which it has been thrown. Dasein is not willfully creating its possibilities out of an arbitrarily destructed and repeated tradition, but makes a rejoinder to that tradition out of its own historically contingent situation.

study of Heidegger's thought, William Richardson suggested "retrieval" as the most adequate English equivalent to Heidegger's *Wiederholung*, and John Caputo has more recently followed his example.[68]

The retrieval is characterized by great loyalty, being a struggle that defends one's hero as one follows in his footsteps (*kämpfende Nachfolge und Treue*). Nevertheless, nothing could be further from Heidegger's intentions than the idea that the retrieval amounts to a slavish regurgitation of the hero's thought. Rather, an *Erwiderung* takes place, a "reciprocative rejoinder," in which the hero's ideas may well be subject to significant change. For what is at stake in the retrieval is not that the "actual" may recur unchanged; repeating is, rather, a "going back into possibilities of the Dasein that has-been-there" (*der Rückgang in Möglichkeiten des dagewesenen Daseins*)—possibilities, not actuality. The "hero" may well not have chosen these possibilities; but they were there. Repeating the tradition means to embrace it in its contingency, in the multiple what-could-have-beens, the paths not taken, which have been concealed in "that which in the today is working itself out as the 'past.'" We could be different because the tradition could have been. Gadamer has well seen this dimension in Heidegger's conception of the retrieval. In a wonderfully lucid essay devoted to the difference between (Heideggerian) destruction and (Derridean) deconstruction, he wrote that "to come closer to the beginning always means to become aware, in retracing the path from whence one came, of other open possibilities. Whoever stands at the very beginning must choose his path. If one gets back to the beginning, one becomes aware of the fact that from that starting point one could have gone other ways."[69] Again, this means that the repetition or retrieval of an aspect of the tradition that destruction has laid bare by "unbuilding" the concealing layers covering it up is by no means slavish, but rather involves a dialogue with the past. Indeed, "dialogue" is not a sufficiently strong word for what Heidegger has in mind, for *Erwiderung* (paraphrased a bit clunkily but correctly by Macquarrie/

68. See William J. Richardson, SJ, *Heidegger: Through Phenomenology to Thought*, 4th ed. (New York: Fordham University Press, 2003), 89n181, and Caputo, *Radical Hermeneutics*, 60–61.

69. Hans-Georg Gadamer, "Destruktion und Dekonstruktion," in *Gesammelte Werke*, vol. 2, *Hermeneutik II* (Tübingen: J. C. B. Mohr/Paul Siebeck, 1993), 363. The English translation is quoted from "*Destruktion* and Deconstruction (1985)," trans. Jeff Waite and Richard Palmer, in *Dialogue and Deconstruction: The Gadamer-Derrida Encounter*, ed. Diane P. Michelfelder and Richard E. Palmer, SUNY Series in Contemporary Continental Philosophy (Albany: State University of New York Press, 1989), 102–13, at 106.

Robinson as "reciprocative rejoinder") entails an antagonistic element: *wider* means "against," so that an *Erwiderung* is literally an "againsting."

The retrieval that follows and complements the destruction, then, tests the limits of a tradition. Choosing certain possibilities while eschewing others, a foundational author, thinker, artist, or prophet set a tradition on a particular path, which, as a result of sedimentation, subsequently became *the* path. The destruction, retracing the steps to the moment in the past that gave rise to the present, uncovers the fateful place where the path forked—the forgotten, charred root of meaning. The repetition then enters into a dialogue over the wisdom of the choice that was made, bringing the past to life as relevant to the present. The outcome of this dialogue may well be a decision to explore the path not taken—despite the risks this poses, including the risk that such a path may turn out to be nothing more than a *Holzweg*. The plural form of this word is the title Heidegger gave to one of his essay collections, and it is almost impossible to translate.[70] Literally, a *Holzweg* is a "wood path," made by rangers and loggers to maintain the forest. These paths frequently lead nowhere, ending abruptly in the middle of the trees—hence the popular German idiom: *Da bist du aber auf dem Holzweg*, "you are on a wood path there," that is, you have erred in your judgment.

The *Holzweg*, then, is a dangerous and uncertain path. It transgresses the limits of a tradition in order to test the possibility of redefining them. The motivation for this perilous journey typically lies in the need to resolve an impasse in the present. Heidegger embarked on his destruction to explore the question regarding Being, which, he believed, the tradition of Western philosophy had forgotten from the very beginning—even necessarily so. Luther, for his part, was led into his destruction by the desperate conditions that afflicted the church of his day: the schisms, the corruption, the abuses, and the insufficient theological response to them. Again, there can be no question that such reforming transgressions can be necessary— but how much transgression, and what kind of transgression, is too much? This is the question for our next chapter.

---

70. See Martin Heidegger, *Holzwege* (Frankfurt am Main: Klostermann, 1950).

CHAPTER 6

A Genealogy of Transgression

In his early writings, Michel Foucault distinguishes two types of limits, and hence two types of transgressive relationships to the limit. In the Christian era, transgression was able to open up a "space where the divine functions," as Foucault puts it. As an encounter with the "limit of the Limitless" that was practiced by negative theologians like Pseudo-Dionysius, transgression constituted an attempt to think the Other—the Outside of human experience and subjectivity. After the "death of God," the nature of the limit has changed, and so has our relationship to it. In the era of the "limitless reign of the limit," crossing the limit has become an empty exercise, even though exploring the Outside remains a fundamental human quest. But that quest, tragically, has been "cast into an empty space where it encounters nothing but the meager form of the limit, and where it has no beyond, no prolongation, except in the frenzy that breaks it."[1]

Up to this point, this book has exclusively focused on the first, Christian type of transgression. Taking the Mount Sinai narrative as our point of departure, we have explored how the Christian tradition unfolds from the initial irruption of the divine—Moses's encounter with the Lord—that occurs on the mountain. It has become clear that a transgression of limits—and ultimately of the limit of the Limitless—constitutes a central component of the Christian tradition. Not all transgressions are equal, however: some may be necessary, others "destructive" in a way that decouples destruction from construction.

---

1. This paragraph summarizes some central points from the introduction. The final quotation was first cited on p. 17. In its original context, Foucault applied these words to sexuality, not the human quest for transcendence generally.

So we must investigate transgression further. In Scripture, there is a transgression that precedes (in what sense, we are going to see) the transgression at Mount Sinai: this ur-transgression is related in the story of the "fall." Immanuel Kant, who in Foucault's account plays a central role in the history of Western man's relationship to the limit, authored an essay in which he proposed a new, "enlightened" interpretation of the biblical narrative. Kant's view of the limit, and of the meaning of transgressing it, epitomizes a new understanding of humanity in relation to the divine. If we wanted to locate the "death of God"[2] in a particular historical moment, rather than viewing it as a process playing itself out over centuries, Kant's essay would be a good candidate.

The Genesis Narrative of the Ur-Transgression

Biblical scholars caution us to practice our own "destruction" in approaching Genesis 2:4 through 3:24, the verses that contain the narrative of the first overstepping of God's limits. In particular, if we approach the story with the expectation that it will provide an explanation of the fall and original sin, we are reading it through the eyes of the tradition. This is not an egregious mistake, since indeed the passage has played a crucial role in the formation of the Christian understanding of human nature, sin, and the saving work of Christ, the "second Adam." Paul's sublation of the passage in Romans 5:12–21 became the "normative exposition for much of

---

2. I am employing the term "death of God" here (as in the introduction) without wishing to suggest that the Godhead has in some sense passed away. Neither Nietzsche nor Foucault uses the term in this way. On Foucault, see the introduction, p. 17. For a nuanced interpretation of Nietzsche that highlights the ambiguities in his position, Eugen Biser's work remains inspiring: *"Gott ist tot". Nietzsches Destruktion des christlichen Bewußtseins* (Munich: Kösel, 1962). Biser takes "God is dead" to be both less and more than a denial of God's existence: the phrase encapsulates a "program for action" (*Aktionsprogramm*, on p. 117) through which Nietzsche aims to bring about a "destruction of Christian consciousness." In the context of my own argument, I follow Foucault's understanding, which is close to what Heidegger tried to think under the rubric of a "withdrawal of the divine" (*Entzug des Göttlichen*). On this notion, see Rainer Thurnher, "Heideggers Distanzierung von der metaphysisch geprägten Theologie und Gottesvorstellung," in *Die Gottesfrage im Denken Martin Heideggers*, ed. Norbert Fischer and Friedrich-Wilhelm von Herrmann, Blaue Reihe (Hamburg: Meiner, 2011), 175–94, esp. 182–92. How is such a withdrawal of the divine conceivable in a Christian manner? It cannot mean that God's offer of grace has become unavailable, but the question is too complex to be discussed here.

the church," in Walter Brueggemann's words.[3] And yet, it is constructive to bracket the traditional understanding in order to recapture the human experience of self and God, and of their relationship, which the author of the passage attempted to convey.[4]

Like the Exodus narrative that we studied in Chapter 1, the Genesis account of the first transgression has a complex literary history. The clearest indication that, in the final text as it has come down to us, the Yahwist author skillfully wove together at least two major narrative strands lies in the two trees that are placed at the center of the garden: the tree of life and the tree of the knowledge of good and evil. The body of the narrative ignores the distinction, dealing with one tree only, so that it is no longer possible to disentangle the two strands.[5] Thus, in its composition, the transgression narrative points to a past that remains elusive—again, just like the Mount Sinai narrative.

There is, however, an important difference, which Claus Westermann, among biblical scholars, has perhaps set in relief most sharply. The Mount Sinai episode occurred in a past that is, for us, remote and irrecoverable; yet the narrator depicts it as part of the history of Israel. The transgression story, on the other hand, understands itself as belonging in the genre of the fable. It was not meant to represent a historical event. The clue lies in the speaking snake, which engages Eve in conversation about God as though this were quite an ordinary occurrence. Eve, at any rate, is by no means taken aback by encountering a talking snake. "The animal that talks," Westermann explains, "is characteristic of the tale or fable. By resuming this fairy tale trait the narrator points the way into the realm of primeval event . . . i.e., an event on the other side of our historical experience."[6] Lying out-

3. Walter Brueggemann, *Genesis*, Interpretation: A Bible Commentary for Teaching and Preaching (Atlanta: John Knox, 1982), 42.

4. For a survey of interpretations of Gen. 2:4–3:24, with an emphasis on the twentieth century, see W. Sibley Towner, "Interpretations and Reinterpretations of the Fall," in *Modern Biblical Scholarship: Its Impact on Theology and Proclamation*, ed. Francis A. Eigo (Villanova, PA: Villanova University Press, 1984), 53–85.

5. See Claus Westermann, *Genesis 1–11: A Commentary*, trans. John J. Scullion (Minneapolis: Augsburg, 1984), 211–14. On the genesis and theological orientation of Westermann's monumental commentary, one may wish to read Rainer Albertz, "Das theologische Vermächtnis des Genesis-Kommentars von Claus Westermann," in *Claus Westermann: Leben—Werk—Wirkung*, ed. Manfred Oeming, Beiträge zum Verstehen der Bibel 2 (Münster: LIT-Verlag, 2003), 79–93.

6. Westermann, *Genesis 1–11: A Commentary*, 238 (first part of the quotation), 276 (after ellipses).

side of history as an *Urgeschehen*,[7] the transgression episode endeavors to convey, not the difference between a state before sin and a state after sin, but rather a structural characteristic of human beings in relation to their Maker. The chronological sequence of events in the story is the narrative means to that end.

To interpret the story, Westermann identifies what he calls a *Geschehensbogen*, an arc of events.[8] This begins with the Lord's planting of the garden, the "paradise of pleasure," in which he places Adam (Gen. 2:8). In 2:16–17, God specifies what man is permitted to eat in the garden, and what is forbidden: "Of every tree of paradise thou shalt eat: But of the tree of knowledge of good and evil, thou shalt not eat. For in what day soever thou shalt eat of it, thou shalt die the death."[9] The narrative moves toward its climax in the temptation scene, where the serpent talks Eve into eating of the forbidden tree (3:1–6). The consequences of the transgression follow swiftly (3:7–19): Adam's and Eve's eyes are opened, God discovers their misdeed and conducts a trial, and he determines the punishment for each of the transgressors—the snake, the woman, and the man. In its denouement, the story returns to its opening theme, the garden, from which God decides the disobedient humans need to be expelled (3:22–24). Let us comment on each of the major elements.

A **garden** lies somewhere between wilderness and a landscape-turned-resource—something unimaginable before the industrial age. To the human being, wilderness is threatening because it stands unmediated over against human needs, which it does not easily accommodate and may, in the worst case, even threaten. The landscape-turned-resource, by contrast, has lost its autonomy: it is there to serve *only* human needs. In an open-pit mine, for instance, the teleology of nature (that is, of the plants and animals that used to live where the open-pit mining is now occurring) has been canceled and replaced with the human goal to produce, say, coal or marble. The garden balances these extremes: it is a domesticated wilderness, in which nature is rendered serviceable to human ends while being

---

7. *Urgeschehen* is the term that the English translation renders as "primeval event." See Claus Westermann, *Genesis*, vol. 1, *Genesis 1–11*, 3rd ed., Biblischer Kommentar, Altes Testament I/1 (Neukirchen-Vluyn: Neukirchener Verlag, 1983), 324. *Urgeschehen* is a key term in Westermann's interpretation of Genesis, so much so that it appears in the title of a more accessible summary of his scholarly commentary: *Welt und Mensch im Urgeschehen. Die biblische Urgeschichte Genesis (1. Mose) 1–11* (Stuttgart: Deutsche Bibelgesellschaft, 1999).

8. See the translator's note, Westermann, *Genesis*, vol. 1, *Genesis 1–11*, 191.

9. On the phrase "die the death," see Chapter 4, pp. 126–27 above.

maintained, not canceled, in its own teleology. In this manner, the garden illustrates the kind of dominion over nature which the human race was created to exert (1:26 and 28). "It is an expression for a world that bears the imprint of the Spirit, for a world that came into existence in accordance with the will of the Creator."[10] This harmony and balance between human needs and natural teleology—between autonomy and heteronomy—is where our story begins.

Note that the human beings and God share the garden, where the Lord can be found wandering about casually on a pleasant afternoon (3:8). The relationship between God and man is therefore not characterized by the terror that is so much in evidence in the Mount Sinai narrative, where God appears (always veiled) on a mountaintop, and in a terrifying environment of thunder, lightning, and fire.

This does not mean, however, that there are no limits between creature and Creator. Adam is free to eat whatever he likes, with a single exception: God forbids him (and, by extension, Eve) to eat from the tree of knowledge of good and evil. The interpretation of this **prohibition** is complex. Biblical scholars point out, first of all, that the expression "good and evil" must not be construed in a narrow moral sense. Considering similar phrases in 1 Kings 3:9 and 2 Samuel 14:17, Terence Fretheim takes "good and evil" as an idiomatic expression that suggests discernment of what is in someone's best interests.[11] What is at stake in eating from the forbidden tree, then, is whether the humans dwelling in the garden are content to accept God's guidance for their lives, or whether they aspire to form their own judgments regarding what is good and bad for them. They opt in favor of autonomy, thereby ultimately rejecting their creaturely status. This is why both the serpent and God regard knowledge of good and evil as a divine attribute: "and you shall be as Gods, knowing good and evil," promises the snake (Gen. 3:5), a promise that God himself confirms: "Behold Adam is become as one of us, knowing good and evil" (3:22). One has to admit that becoming godlike is not altogether bad! The metaphor of the "fall," therefore, does not do justice to the consequences of the transgression: if there is a movement downward, toward a deteriorated form of human existence

10. Joseph Ratzinger, *"In the Beginning...": A Catholic Understanding of the Story of Creation and the Fall*, trans. Boniface Ramsey, Ressourcement: Retrieval and Renewal in Catholic Thought (Grand Rapids: Eerdmans, 1995), 64.

11. See Terence E. Fretheim, "The Book of Genesis," in *The New Interpreter's Bible* (Nashville: Abingdon, 1994), 1:350–51.

(and there certainly is), this is paralleled by a movement upward, toward divine autonomy.[12]

Why is the fruit so tempting? The biblical story assembles a mosaic of motivations; the hubris or Titanism that is involved in claiming godlike autonomy is only one of them. There is also the simple attractiveness of the fruit to the senses, as the text describes it as "good to eat and fair to the eyes" (3:6). Finally, and crucially, there is Eve's conversation with the **serpent.**

Biblical commentators agree that, in the story as told in Genesis, the serpent is not the incarnation of an evil principle. The figure of the snake may have its roots in an old Israeli cult (Num. 21 and 2 Kings 18:4 mention a brazen serpent made by Moses); it may hearken back even further, as Ratzinger believes, to an Eastern fertility cult that tempted Israel with the promise of a "fertility through which human beings plunge into the divine current of life and for a few moments experience themselves fused with the divine power."[13] This would make the serpent into a symbol of the Dionysian. Its function within the story, however, is different: it tempts Eve through probing questions. Brueggemann offers the most radical— radically Lutheran—interpretation of this conversation: the serpent is theology! He writes, "The serpent is the first in the Bible to seem knowing and critical about God and to practice *theology* in the place of *obedience*."[14] By asking the question *why*—"Why hath God commanded you, that you should not eat of every tree of paradise?" (Gen. 3:1)—the serpent invites Eve to opt for critical inquiry regarding God in lieu of simple trust. Succumbing to this temptation, Eve chooses wisdom rather than foolishness, Brueggemann diagnoses, making a connection with the language of First Corinthians. While Brueggemann's identification of the serpent with theology may be too extreme—man is a being of reason, with a vocation to think, even about God, and not *simply* to trust—a more nuanced version of what he argues appears convincing. The Genesis text, he explains, "probes the question: Are there modes of knowledge that come at too high a cost? ... It asks if there are boundaries before which one must bow, even if one could know more."[15]

It is difficult for human beings to accept such boundaries. We all know the effect of prohibitions: they kindle desire rather than thwarting

12. Fretheim makes this point: "The Book of Genesis," 1:367–68.
13. Ratzinger, *"In the Beginning...,"* 66.
14. Brueggemann, *Genesis*, 48.
15. Brueggemann, *Genesis*, 51.

it.[16] Westermann connects transgression with a desire for transcendence that is inherent in human nature: "With the greatest restraint and reserve J [the Yahwist narrator] is saying here that at bottom what entices a person to transgress a limit is not the sensual pleasure heightened even more by the prohibition, but the new possibilities of life that are apparently opened by the transgression. The narrator wants to point to the inscrutable riddle which is always part of human existence wherever and as long as it is lived, namely, that people have the urge to transcend themselves by overstepping the limits set for them."[17] Human nature, on this account, is conflicted; transgressive, it is also creaturely. Its desire for transcendence—for reaching beyond its limits—runs up against boundaries set by an Other, the Creator.

Eve and Adam's transgression produces a number of immediate **consequences**, even before God tries and punishes the transgressors: "And the eyes of them both were opened: and when they perceived themselves to be naked, they sewed together fig leaves, and made themselves aprons. And when they heard the voice of the Lord God walking in paradise at the afternoon air, Adam and his wife hid themselves from the face of the Lord God, amidst the trees of paradise" (3:7–8). A disruption has occurred in the relationship of the human couple with God, and this external disruption is paralleled by an internal one: they are no longer completely at one with their bodies. Before the temptation, they were unashamedly naked (2:25); now they are ashamed because of their nakedness, so that they try to hide it, and themselves, from God. Their transgression has exposed Adam and Eve in some way. Shame is a fundamental human emotion in reaction to such exposure. It does not necessarily entail a sense of guilt, which is located at a spiritual rather than at a bodily and emotional level. I will, for example, feel shame if a tear appears in my trousers, in a place that ought to be covered, but there is no guilt involved in such a wardrobe malfunctioning. To understand the image of nakedness, it is important to view it against the background of the cultural significance that clothes possessed in ancient Israel. Clothes were not a matter of individual preference, as they have become in the modern world, but indicated the place that a human being occupied in society: they bestowed a social persona. Moreover,

16. In the *History of Sexuality*, vol. 1, *An Introduction*, trans. Robert Hurley (New York: Vintage Books, 1990), 47, Foucault speaks of "spirals" in which power and pleasure amplify each other: whatever (sexual) conduct is singled out as illicit, by the very fact of the prohibition becomes all the more desirable.

17. Westermann, *Genesis 1–11: A Commentary*, 249.

clothes had a meaning beyond the merely human sphere: in Chapter 1, we saw that clean clothes signified ritual purity. Washed garments, in this context, indicated an inner disposition to encounter the Lord.[18] The Hebrew Scriptures, furthermore, contain many passages where clothes are associated with divine powers. Elias's cloak in 2 Kings is just one example (2 Kings 2:8–14; cf. 1 Kings 19:19). Nakedness, conversely, was tantamount to social annihilation, to an almost subhuman condition, which is why "to appear naked before God was an abomination for ancient Israel," as von Rad remarks in his commentary.[19] He cites Exodus 20:26: "Thou shalt not go up by steps unto my altar, lest thy nakedness be discovered."

Their nakedness thus exposes Adam and Eve—in the fundamental existential sense in which we speak of an exposed child who is left in the open to die. There is, however, an upside to this shameful and perilous condition, in that it prompts the human couple to fashion themselves basic garments out of fig leaves. Their loincloths are the first artifacts, products of human making that signify the rise of civilization. There is an interesting—Westermann says, a "deliberate"[20]—tension between Genesis 3:7 (". . . and made themselves aprons") and 3:21: "And the Lord made for Adam and his wife, garments of skins, and clothed them." The fig-leaf loincloths that Adam and Eve make for themselves are quite primitive; God's product is more sophisticated, hinting at a more advanced stage of civilization. More importantly, the text intimates that, even after man has claimed knowledge of what is best for him, civilization is not an autonomous human accomplishment but rather a divine gift, given as a remedy for the transgression.

The **trial** brings the human couple's sense of shame (and fear) to linguistic expression: "I heard thy voice; and I was afraid, because I was naked," says Adam in 3:10, in response to God's call. The ensuing questions and answers crystallize the shame as guilt. Moreover, the trial reveals

---

18. See Chapter 1, p. 28.

19. Gerhard von Rad, *Genesis: A Commentary*, trans. John H. Marks, Old Testament Library (Philadelphia: Westminster, 1961), 88. For a brief but helpful discussion of references to clothes in the Old Testament, see Johannes Schildenberger, "Kleidung. I. Biblisch," in *Lexikon für Theologie und Kirche*, 2nd ed., vol. 6 (Freiburg im Breisgau: Herder, 1961), cols. 324–25. The continuation of the entry (cols. 325–26), authored by Georg Teichtweier, offers a short theology of clothes and fashion. Claudia Bender studies the "language of textiles" in the Old Testament in fascinating detail: *Die Sprache des Textilen. Untersuchungen zu Kleidung und Textilien im Alten Testament*, Beiträge zur Wissenschaft vom Alten und Neuen Testament 177 (Stuttgart: Kohlhammer, 2008).

20. Westermann, *Genesis 1–11: A Commentary*, 269.

that the transgression has introduced fissures into the structure of God's good creation. To the Lord's question in the following verse—"And who hath told thee that thou wast naked, but that thou hast eaten of the tree whereof I commanded thee that thou shouldst not eat?"—Adam responds by blaming Eve and even God himself: it was the woman whom you gave me! When God then directs the question to Eve, she in turn uses the snake as an excuse.

God's **punishment** of the transgressors renders objective these fissures, which first arose in the humans' guilty conscience. It takes the form of a proliferation of limits, a cosmic alienation. Put differently, the couple's overstepping of the one boundary set by the Lord—"of the tree of knowledge of good and evil, thou shalt not eat"—leads to the appearance of subsidiary boundaries in all areas of life: the offspring of the cursed serpent will forever live in enmity with Eve's children; Eve will experience pain in childbirth, and therefore alienation from her own body (perhaps even from her children); there will be social disparity between Adam and his wife, whom he is assigned to dominate, even though God made her from Adam's own flesh and bones; finally, Adam's relationship to the earth will be disrupted, as he will have to toil amidst thorns and thistles to extract a livelihood from the soil. It is logical, then, that Adam will no longer be allowed to dwell in the beautiful garden of paradise, from which he is expelled "to till the earth from which he was taken" (3:23). The scriptural text does not spell out that this expulsion from paradise also removes the human couple from God's company.

Adam and Eve's transgression does not lead to death, despite the Lord's warning: "For in what day soever thou shalt eat of it, thou shalt die the death." Verse 22 has confused exegetes, in that it establishes, on the contrary, a connection between the transgression and the possibility of eternal life: "Behold," says God, "Adam is become one of us, knowing good and evil." The verse continues: "now, therefore, lest perhaps he put forth his hand, and take also of the tree of life, and eat, and live for ever," God decides to expel him from the garden. There had been no question earlier in the narrative of Adam and Eve reaching for eternal life. The only explanation is compositional: "One has the impression," writes Westermann, "that there have been gathered together in the conclusion all sorts of end pieces which happen to have been lying about and which could not be fully integrated."[21] Von Rad offers the following thought: "precisely because here and there

---

21. Westermann, *Genesis 1–11: A Commentary*, 267.

things do not fit and are not drawn together at the end, the narrative gains its unfathomable and inexhaustible character."[22] What von Rad means, I think, is this: the transgression story deals with some of the fundamental mysteries of human existence. Human beings have been created with an inexhaustible desire for transcendence, understood here as an overcoming of limits: transgression. There is nothing we cannot question, even God himself; nothing we will not attempt to do, even if it involves walking on the moon. At the same time, such transgression has the potential to produce disastrous results, that is to say, to wreak cosmic havoc. There is ultimately no satisfactory explanation for this paradox. This is why it is not unfitting that the biblical story unravels at the end.

To return to our question: Was God's threat that transgression would produce death an empty one? In truth, a thousand small deaths encroach every day on life outside paradise. Life is a struggle. There is no harmony in any aspect of human existence. Everywhere we are reminded of our finitude and brokenness, whether it is in human relationships, in the way our aging bodies remind us of the inescapable end, in the conflicts between advancing technology and the inevitable pushback of nature, and even in our spiritual quest, where the God we seek often cloaks himself in darkness. The first humans' transgression is the root of the structures of life as we know it; but the root is charred.

Kant's Transvaluation of the Ur-Transgression

In 1786, Immanuel Kant published his essay "Conjectural Beginning of Human History." In it the Königsberg philosopher offered an interpretation of Genesis 2–6. The status of this publication—along with other, similar ones—within the Kantian oeuvre is peculiar, in that it addresses questions that go decisively beyond the realm of human experience, outside of which there is, according to the principles of Kant's own critical philosophy, no possibility of certain knowledge. Kant is acutely aware of the difficulty, which he addresses in the opening paragraphs. What he tells us there is that he feels justified in embarking on what he calls a "pleasure trip" of the mind (hinting at a certain playfulness) as long as the resulting conjectures lay no claim to presenting a historical account; rather, the goal of these conjectures is to speculate how human history must have begun if the

22. Von Rad, *Genesis*, 97.

human condition "in its first beginning was not better or worse than what we encounter now."[23] In other words, assuming a stable human nature, how can the first human beings be thought to have stepped into history? Kant composed his essay in response to a series of publications on the same topic by his pupil Johann Gottfried Herder. Herder—no friend of the Enlightenment—had developed a fairly traditional understanding of the Genesis narrative, whose "poetic" form he took as an expression of truth that could not simply be absorbed into reason, or be transcended by it. Herder interpreted the Lord's prohibition in Genesis 2:16–17 as capturing the essential difference of human existence over against that of mere animals, whose behavior knows no moral limits. The assertion of rational autonomy over the prohibition, therefore, constitutes a distortion of human nature as made in God's image and likeness: "It is the snake," Herder writes, "that has raised man as an animal of reason; it is God who formed man as the image of God." On this account, the culture of the Enlightenment is nothing but a modern version of the expulsion from paradise. For man's true vocation does not lie in asserting the superiority of reason, but in retrieving his prelapsarian childhood through poetic language.[24]

Kant's approach differs from Herder's not only in the conclusions he reaches, but also in the status he assigns to the biblical narrative:

[S]ince I am here venturing on a mere pleasure trip (*Lustreise*), I hope I may ask the favor to be allowed to make use of a holy document as my

23. Immanuel Kant, "Conjectural Beginning of Human History," trans. Allen W. Wood, in Kant, *Anthropology, History, and Education*, ed. Günter Zöller and Robert B. Louden, Cambridge Edition of the Works of Immanuel Kant in Translation (Cambridge: Cambridge University Press, 2007), 8:109. I am referring to this essay according to the pagination of volume 8 of the *Akademie-Ausgabe*, as this pagination is conveniently noted in the margins of the Cambridge edition. For the German text, see *Kant's gesammelte Schriften*, ed. Preußische Akademie der Wissenschaften, Erste Abtheilung, vol. 8, *Abhandlungen nach 1781* (Berlin and Leipzig: de Gruyter, 1923), 107–23.

24. For a brief but penetrating account of Herder's views, see Wolfgang Düsing, "Die Interpretation des Sündenfalls bei Herder, Kant und Schiller," in *Bückeburger Gespräche über Johann Gottfried Herder 1988. Älteste Urkunde des Menschengeschlechts*, ed. Brigitte Poschmann, Schaumburger Gespräche 49 (Rinteln: Verlag C. Bösendahl, 1989), 227–44. The quotation from Herder appears on p. 232. For a full-length treatment of Herder's interpretation of Genesis, see Christoph Bultmann, *Die biblische Urgeschichte in der Aufklärung. Johann Gottfried Herders Interpretation der Genesis als Antwort auf die Religionskritik David Humes*, Beiträge zur historischen Theologie 110 (Tübingen: Mohr Siebeck, 1999). Bultmann's study focuses on the historical context of Herder's position.

map, and at the same time to imagine that my flight, which I make on the wings of the power of imagination, though not without a guiding thread attached by reason onto experience, might follow the same trajectory which that document contains in a historical sketch (*historisch vorgezeichnet*). The reader will open the pages of that document (*Genesis*, chapter 2 through chapter 6) and will check step by step whether the path that philosophy takes in accordance with concepts will join the one which the story provides.[25]

First, we note, once again, that reading the biblical story for Kant amounts to nothing more than a "pleasure trip." Furthermore, even though Scripture provides the map for this trip, philosophy is not ultimately bound to the path that the biblical narrative sketches out; rather, it finds its own way "in accordance with concepts." Concerning the relationship between the two paths, Kant is suggesting that they develop autonomously, each according to its own logic: the logic of concepts (*Begriffe*) and the logic of story (*Geschichte*), respectively. The reader is asked to verify, step-by-step, whether the conceptual logic and the narrative logic yield the same results. As we will quickly discover, however, Kant's hermeneutic practice leaves no room for the narrative logic to unfold independently of the philosophical conjectures. In the end, the biblical text will serve the sole purpose of illustrating claims reached by Kant's imaginative use of reason.

Kant's hermeneutic practice perfectly exemplifies the "eclipse of biblical narrative" that Hans Frei has diagnosed in the scriptural interpretation of the eighteenth and nineteenth centuries (while Herder's approach still largely conforms to an older way of reading Scripture).[26] Frei has a very precise definition—inspired by Erich Auerbach—of what the "eclipse of biblical narrative" amounts to: after the "great reversal" that his book chronicles, "interpretation was a matter of fitting the biblical story into another world with another story rather than incorporating that world into the biblical story."[27] This is what Kant does: he fits the biblical story into the world of his own philosophy, where the "story" is an

---

25. Kant, "Conjectural Beginning," 8:109–10. I have amended the translation in light of the German text. In particular, Wood's translation of *vorgezeichnet* as "prescribed" is too strong. Kant's meaning is that the biblical story contains a historical sketch (*Zeichnung*) that precedes (*vor-*) the philosophical reflection and so can provide a basic framework for it.

26. Hans W. Frei, *The Eclipse of Biblical Narrative: A Study in Eighteenth- and Nineteenth-Century Hermeneutics* (New Haven: Yale University Press, 1974).

27. Frei, *Eclipse of Biblical Narrative*, 130. Frei quotes Auerbach with the same idea on p. 3.

Enlightenment narrative of the triumph of autonomous reason. Read in a premodern way, however, Scripture does not have the purpose of illustrating, in an edifying manner, philosophical or theological claims arrived independently of it; neither is Scripture in need of being checked against the historical record for proof of its veracity. Rather, Scripture provides the master story that all other stories can only retell; thus, world history is salvation history, while the story of an individual life is nothing but the retelling of the sacred story of Jesus (or of one of his followers, such as an apostle or a saint). The story of Jesus, in turn, retells—by fulfilling it—the story of the Old Testament.

Let us turn to the content of Kant's interpretation. Although the first humans are already fully rational, capable as they are of speech and thought, during their stay in the garden they are initially guided by animal instinct. This is, in fact, what the voice of God signifies that utters the prohibition: "Instinct, that *voice of God* which all animals obey, must at first have guided the novice on its own."[28] Kant's identification of the voice of God with animal instinct sets the course for his entire interpretation of the garden narrative. The boundaries that in Scripture confront the human being as external law—that is to say, as limits set to human conduct by the limitless God, the all-powerful Creator—in Kant take on the role of an internal aspect of human nature: instinct directs the first humans toward edible fruit while turning them away from food that is unsuitable for human consumption. What is more, God's prohibition in Genesis 2 originates from above the human being, from his Maker, whereas instinct is located at an animal level that is not yet fully human. Consequently, in Kant's reading the whole story becomes one of a conflict between higher and lower elements within human nature. For reason challenges instinct: "Yet *reason* soon began to stir and sought through comparison of that which was consumed with that which was represented to him by another sense than the one to which instinct was bound, such as the sense of sight, as similar to what previously had been consumed, to extend his knowledge of the means of nourishment beyond the boundaries of instinct (*Genesis* 3:6)."[29] Kant has no place in his interpretation for the snake, a heteronomous element that would detract from his intramental reading of the conflict.

28. Kant, "Conjectural Beginning," 8:111; trans. amended. Wood does not translate *anfänglich* as "at first."

29. Kant, "Conjectural Beginning," 8:111; trans. amended. In particular, *genießen* in the context of food has the basic meaning of "to consume" (as in *ungenießbar*, "not suitable for consumption").

Now reason is capable not only of extending the range of human choices beyond items identified by instinct, but even of directing human action against instinct. Such a choice, Kant remarks, "probably did not turn out in conformity to expectation."[30] Kant imagines that the first humans might have seen another animal consume a certain type of fruit repellent to human instinct; tasting it could have led to unpleasant consequences. "Now the harm might have been as insignificant as you like, yet over this [experience] the human being's eyes were opened (*Genesis* 3:7). He discovered in himself a faculty of choosing for himself a way of living and not being bound to a single one, as other animals are."[31] With this discovery, Kant sees the human being standing on the brink of an abyss: exhilarated by the infinity of choices opened up by reason, he is simultaneously frightened by the overwhelming scope of objects rendered available for human use. But returning to the former condition of "servitude," the dominion of instinct, is impossible.

To any careful reader of the biblical narrative, it must be clear that the path of Kant's interpretation not only diverges from that taken by the scriptural story; the two in fact run counter to each other.[32] Thus, for example, Genesis represents the humans' life in paradise as a harmonious coexistence with God and nature, not as a condition of servitude. This harmony the transgression tragically disrupts, even if it leads Adam and Eve to godlike autonomy. Kant, by contrast, sees no cosmic alienation in the wake of the transgression. His evaluation of its consequences is mostly positive.

As a second consequence of the conflict between instinct and reason (after the opening of the humans' eyes), Kant mentions the fig leaves. In his reading, they signify reason's ability to humanize the sexual instinct by rendering it more mediate and stable, as well as sublimating it (as Freud would say). What in animals is but a periodic impulse to procreate—consider a bitch in heat—in humans becomes an enduring desire that is heightened by the imagination, whose activity the fig leaves serve to trigger. As

---

30. Kant, "Conjectural Beginning," 8:112.

31. Kant, "Conjectural Beginning," 8:112; trans. amended.

32. The divergences between the biblical narrative and Kant's interpretation are the focus of Elfriede Lämmerzahl's chapter on Kant in her booklet *Der Sündenfall in der Philosophie des deutschen Idealismus*, Neue Deutsche Forschungen, Abteilung Philosophie 3 (Berlin: Junker und Dünnhaupt, 1934), 9–53. Unfortunately, Lämmerzahl's own understanding of the scriptural text is rather naïve; sometimes it is highly questionable. She wants to deny, for example, that the serpent is one of God's creatures (as asserted in Gen. 3:1) and makes it into an autonomous principle of evil (53).

the object of sexual instinct is withdrawn from the senses, imagination prevents sexuality from becoming boring; reason elevates it further into the moral and aesthetic realms: "*Refusal* was the artifice for leading from merely sensed stimuli over to ideal ones, from merely animal desire gradually over to love, and with the latter from the feeling of the merely agreeable over to the taste for beauty, in the beginning only in human beings but then also in nature. Moreover, *propriety* . . . gave the first hint toward the formation of the human being as a moral creature."[33] Thus, the biblical sense of exposure disappears altogether from Kant's horizon, who views reason's transgression of the boundaries of instinct as a step into civilization; yet he forgets—and here lies the decisive difference over against the biblical story—the price that humanity has to pay for this step.

Kant interprets Genesis 3:13–19 as illustrating his claim that, as a third consequence of the conflict between instinct and reason, the human being discovers the future. In this context, Kant does advert to the downsides of the specifically human ability to look beyond the present moment, since the expectation of the future proves to be "the most inexhaustible source of cares and worries."[34] Most of all, the ability to think about the future brings an awareness of the inevitability of death, which in turn gives the humans a sense—unreasonable, Kant intimates—that their use of reason must have constituted a crime: "Both foresaw with fear that which, after a troubled life, lying in the background of the painting, befalls unavoidably all animals, to be sure, yet without worrying them—namely, death—and they seemed to reproach themselves and make into a crime the use of reason that causes them all these ills."[35] Yet the very same future that occasions endless worries also holds the remedy for these concerns, in that there is hope for progress. This is a crucial point on which Kant will dwell later on in the essay; we shall return to it.

In describing the fourth and final consequence of the transgression, Kant is particularly careless in his use of Scripture. He invokes Genesis 3:21: "And the Lord God made for Adam and his wife, garments of skins, and clothed them"—a verse that indicates that even after eating of the forbidden tree, Adam and Eve remain under God's care, who assists them in establishing human culture outside of the garden (the expulsion follows

---

33. Kant, "Conjectural Beginning," 8:113; trans. amended.

34. Kant, "Conjectural Beginning," 8:113.

35. Kant, "Conjectural Beginning," 8:113; trans. slightly amended (replaced comma after "death" with dash).

immediately in 3:22–24). In other words, the biblical narrative emphasizes the human beings' continuing heteronomy, their creaturely status, which the transgression has challenged but has not been able to shake off. This is not Kant's reading at all:

> The first time he said to the sheep: *Nature has given you the skin you wear not for you but for me*, then took it off the sheep and put it on himself (*Genesis* 3:21), he became aware of a prerogative that he had by his nature over all animals, which he now no longer regarded as his fellow creatures, but rather as means and instruments given over to his will for the attainment of his discretionary ends (*seinem Willen überlassene Mittel und Werkzeuge zu Erreichung seiner beliebigen Absichten*). This representation includes (albeit obscurely) the thought of the opposite: that he must not say something like this to any *human being*.... And thus the human being had entered into *an equality with all rational beings*, of whatever rank they might be (*Genesis* 3:22), namely, in regard to the claim of *being himself an end*.[36]

It is difficult to believe that Kant did not realize that he had imposed a meaning on the biblical text that runs directly counter to the sense of the narrative. Man's rule over his fellow creatures predates the transgression, being inscribed into the structure of the created order (1:26 and 1:28–31). The peaceful coexistence of all creatures with their Maker in paradise is therefore not incompatible with man's "dominion over the fishes of the sea, and the fowls of the air, and the beasts, and the whole earth, and every creeping creature that moveth upon the earth" (1:26; cf. 1:28). There is no question in Genesis of reducing all animals to tools given over to a tyrannical human will. That, however, is Kant's view of the order of ends, which moreover he has culminating in the human being rather than in God. This is a complete reversal of the biblical order.

The late German philosopher Odo Marquard coined a term to describe Kant's revaluation of biblical values: *Entübelung*. This neologism is odd even in German, but it does capture what Kant is doing: he "de-evils" what Genesis represents as evil and forbidden, namely, the human attempt to reach for godlike autonomy.[37] However, Kant's "de-eviling" is not yet quite

---

36. Kant, "Conjectural Beginning," 8:114; trans. amended.

37. See Odo Marquard, "Felix culpa?—Bemerkungen zu einem Applikationsschicksal von Genesis 3," in *Text und Applikation. Theologie, Jurispruden und Literaturwissenschaft im*

complete: he still has to find a way to deal with the general worries and the fear of death that result from reason's ability to open up the future. This way is progress through history.

While Kant interprets the transgression positively as the "transition from the crudity of a merely animal creature into humanity, from the baby walker of instinct to the direction of reason—in a word, from the guardianship of nature into the condition of freedom,"[38] he acknowledges, as we have seen, that it involves an alienation of instinct from reason. Another way to frame this alienation is to say that it opens a tension between the individual and the species: "Whether the human being has gained or lost through this alteration can no longer be the question, if one looks at the vocation of his species, which consists in nothing but a *progressing* toward perfection. . . . Nevertheless, this course, which for the species is a *progress* from worse toward better, is not the same for the individual."[39] The individual has to bear the brunt, as it were, of humanity's step into freedom, as the tension between man's animal side and his rationality plays itself out in the life of each person, who experiences the conflict as a moral "fall" expressing itself in terms of vices. For these, physical ills in turn serve as punishment. To couch the situation in religious language, on the side of the individual the choice for freedom comes to be associated with evil, for it can be conceived as a departure from the original goodness of nature: "the history of *nature* thus begins from good, for that is the *work of God*; the history of *freedom* from evil, for it is the *work of the human being*."[40] This conflict cannot be overcome as long as—and here Kant switches to Rousseauian terminology—nature and culture remain opposed: each individual's nature has to pay a price for the progress of culture, which belongs to the species.[41]

---

hermeneutischen Gespräch, ed. Manfred Fuhrmann, Hans Robert Jauß, and Wolfhart Pannenberg, Poetik und Hermeneutik 9 (Munich: Fink, 1981), 53–71, esp. (on Kant) 57–58, 64.

38. Kant, "Conjectural Beginning," 8:115; trans. amended. "Dominance" is too strong a translation for *Leitung*, which I have rendered as "direction." "Baby walker" renders *Gängelwagen*, for which Wood's translation has "go-cart."

39. Kant, "Conjectural Beginning," 8:115.

40. Kant, "Conjectural Beginning," 8:115.

41. One understands why Herder accused Kant of Averroism: in Averroës's philosophy, the individual human being is capable of rational thought only insofar as he or she participates in supra-individual material and agent intellects. Both Kant's practical and his theoretical philosophy exhibit Averroistic tendencies. I have examined the theoretical side in my article "Wandering in the Path of the Averroean System: Is Kant's Doctrine on the *Bewußtsein überhaupt* Averroistic?," *American Catholic Philosophical Quarterly* 73 (1999):

There is a resolution to this set of conflicts, which is the gradual assimilation of nature into culture. For the struggle between nature and culture remains irresolvable, Kant declares, "until perfect art again becomes nature (*bis vollkommene Kunst wieder Natur wird*), which is the ultimate goal of the moral vocation of the human species."[42] *Bis vollkommene Kunst wieder Natur wird*: we should understand this phrase as applying, first and foremost, to the inner moral formation of the human being, whose vocation Kant regards as lying in the reconciliation of animal instinct and reason. On the basis of this understanding, we can define the goal of progress as the full humanization of the human being, of man's complete arrival in himself as rational. It is this "step of the human being towards himself"[43] that in Kant takes the place salvation occupies in Scripture. For in Genesis, the cosmic alienation that Adam and Eve's disobedience unleashes can be remedied only through God's continuing offer of grace—culminating, in the Christian perspective, in the incarnation of the second Adam. The comparison shows that Kant's reinterpretation of Genesis amounts to a kind of "self-redemption"[44] of the human being. As progress replaces salvation history, God is no longer needed; he withdraws.

All this would be of only limited, theoretical interest if Kant's conception did not correspond so eerily to the structures of technological progress that we can observe in the contemporary world. Put differently, what we find in Kant is more than the abstract ruminations of an influential philosopher; in the structure of his thought we discover the intellectual foundations of the way in which our history has unfolded.

Bear in mind Kant's earlier claim according to which animals are mere "means and instruments" given over to the human will for the attainment of its discretionary ends. This means that, for Kant, the teleology of the subhuman world is canceled out and superseded by human ends. It means, to couch this point in Heideggerian language, that the world surrounding us is nothing but "resource": mountains are coal mines, trees IKEA tables, and pigs sources of protein. At the same time, while there is no longer any

---

187–230. Also see the more recent treatment of the question by Marco Sgarbi, "Immanuel Kant, Universal Understanding, and the Meaning of Averroism in the German Enlightenment," in *Renaissance Averroism and Its Aftermath: Arabic Philosophy in Early Modern Europe*, ed. Anna Akasoy and Guido Giglioni, International Archives of the History of Ideas 211 (Dordrecht: Springer, 2013), 255–69.

42. Kant, "Conjectural Beginning," 8:117–18.

43. Marquard, "Felix culpa?," 58: *Schritt des Menschen zu sich selbst*.

44. Marquard, "Felix culpa?," 57: *Selbsterlösung*.

realm of (semi) autonomous[45] ends left *beneath* the human being, there is also no goal *above* the human sphere: as we have just seen, the aim of progress is not some kind of ascent toward the divine, but rather the fully immanent realization and self-unification of human nature. In fact, Kant makes this idea explicit in his famous Enlightenment essay from 1784, where he boldly asserts: "One age cannot band together and conspire to put the following one into a condition in which it must become impossible for it to enlarge its cognitions . . . , to purify them of errors, and generally to progress further in enlightenment. This would be a crime against human nature, whose original vocation (*Bestimmung*) lies precisely in making such progress."[46] It would be a crime against human nature, says Kant—*ein Verbrechen wider die menschliche Natur*—to thwart the progress of enlightenment, since human nature has been appointed to pursue rational progress. Kant's term *Bestimmung* in the passage just quoted does not exactly (or at least etymologically) mean "vocation," which would be *Berufung*. The verb *bestimmen* could be translated as "to determine"; so it has been "determined" that the human being must pursue progress. If one were to ask about the agent of such determination, Kant would say that it originates in providence, that is, God.[47] Kant is certainly not an atheist, yet one can see that God withdraws in his conception of human reason: God releases man into autonomy, assuming the extrinsic role of the regulative idea.

Kant's statement in the Enlightenment essay confirms for the theoretical sphere what we discovered in "Conjectural Beginning" about the

45. I am saying "(semi) autonomous" because, even on the scriptural account, God appoints man as the ruler of the subhuman world. Ultimately, therefore, all of creation is made to serve the human being. But there are different types of rule. Tyrannical rule simply suppresses the teleology of creation (including, in the last analysis, the teleology of the human being himself). A more benevolent regime will let the created order come to itself even as it serves human needs. Think of the difference, for instance, between the pig that is allowed to roam and live a pig life before becoming meat for human consumption, and the pig that spends its entire existence in industrial livestock production.

46. Immanuel Kant, "An Answer to the Question: What Is Enlightenment?" in Kant, *Practical Philosophy*, trans. Mary J. Gregor, Cambridge Edition of the Works of Immanuel Kant (Cambridge: Cambridge University Press, 1996), 8:39; trans. amended. In particular, *sich verbünden* does not mean "to bind oneself," but "to band together" or "to conclude a treaty (*Bündnis*) together."

47. Providence plays a central role in the 1784 essay "Idea for a Universal History with a Cosmopolitan Aim," trans. Allen W. Wood, in Kant, *Anthropology, History, and Education*, 107–20. Ulrich L. Lehner has devoted a detailed study to the notion of providence in Kant's oeuvre: *Kants Vorsehungskonzept auf dem Hintergrund der deutschen Schulphilosophie und -theologie*, Brill's Studies in Intellectual History 149 (Leiden and Boston: Brill, 2007).

moral realm: human nature is teleologically self-reflexive; it has no end outside or beyond itself.[48] To realize this situation, and to free oneself from all manner of tutelage, is the purpose of the Enlightenment project. In the wake of this project, we have seen a veritable explosion of scientific and technological progress in the Industrial Revolution and beyond. While philosophy is only one factor in the complex web of social and historical forces that accounts for the direction of human development, it is obvious that the kind of progress which is typical of the industrial (and now, digital) world is quite incompatible with a traditional conception of teleology. As long as the world is viewed as creation, with determinate ends that are invariable, rather than being placed on the ever-receding horizon of progress, the spirit of constant (and constantly accelerating) overcoming of limits would be impossible. Challenging the idea of a natural end of life, medicine is wondering if aging cannot be "turned off" genetically; oblivious to the notion that there may be a level of consumption that destroys the happiness we all seek rather than furthering it, our economy is based on a paradigm that requires whipping "consumers" into ever new cycles of acquisitiveness; and while this happens, the natural environment is turned into a resource that both provides the material basis for consumption and serves as the dumping ground for the waste it produces. Even in the Catholic Church, the old notion that there could be a limit to the multiplication of the human race has been lost.[49]

48. Kant offered a second, tempered interpretation of the Genesis narrative in *Religion within the Boundaries of Mere Reason*, which appeared in 1793. This treatment differs from the one in "Conjectural Beginning" in a number of ways: for example, the serpent reappears, and Kant now associates the moral progress of the human race with the kingdom of God. He cautions the reader that he is not engaged in scriptural exegesis. There may be factors within Kant's oeuvre that explain the shift, as Andrew Edgar has claimed: "Kant's Two Interpretations of Genesis," *Journal of Literature & Theology* 6, no. 3 (1992): 280–90. On the other hand, the *Religion* book appeared after Kant had an encounter with Prussian censorship, precisely over his religious views; for a recent analysis of these events (and an account of the state of the question), one may read Ian Hunter, "Kant's *Religion* and Prussian Religious Policy," *Modern Intellectual History* 2, no. 1 (2005): 1–27. The classic treatment is by Wilhelm Dilthey, "Der Streit Kants mit der Zensur über das Recht freier Religionsforschung," in Dilthey, *Die Jugendgeschichte Hegels und andere Abhandlungen zur Geschichte des deutschen Idealismus*, Gesammelte Schriften 4, 2nd ed. (Stuttgart: Teubner; Göttingen: Vandenhoeck & Ruprecht, 1959), 285–309.

49. In the *Book of Sentences*, book IV, dist. 26, chap. 3, Peter Lombard had this to say about the biblical injunction to "increase and multiply": "And that which was said to the first human beings before sin: *Increase and multiply*, may certainly be understood as a precept. They were bound by this precept even after sin, until multiplication was achieved; afterwards

It is clear, then, that Kant's transvaluation of the ur-transgression from Genesis entails a radically new understanding of human limits, and hence of transgression. The limit is no longer associated with the divine and therefore regarded as sacred. Thus, overstepping the limit is viewed neither as producing cosmic cataclysms (as in Adam and Eve's case) nor as opening up a space for encountering the transcendent (as in the Mount Sinai narrative and the Dionysian mystical ascent). In other words, the limit has lost its numinous mystery. Transgression, as the counterpart of the limit, has become banal. Consider a couple of examples. Tattoos, which once marked the social outcast—the prisoner, the sailor, both unanchored in their different ways—are now omnipresent as signs of a new, ingenious form of consumption.[50] When the rapper releases his new CD protesting the conditions of life in the ghetto, its tracks immediately become available for download so that the suburban college kid can play it on his or her phone. As Hal Foster has remarked, "the (subcultural) other is at once controlled in its recognition and dispersed in its commodification."[51] Such mainstreaming of everything once regarded as transgressive deprives society of its Outside; or, rather, it forces society into a frenzied quest for an Outside that it will swallow as soon as it has generated it, and just as quickly as the horizon of progress recedes.[52]

To illustrate this dynamic in some detail, we turn to the example of contemporary art, contrasting it with premodern artistic practices.

---

marriage was contracted according to indulgence. In the same way, also after the Flood, by which almost all of humankind was annihilated, it was said according to precept to the children of Noah: *Increase and multiply*; but after human beings were multiplied, marriage was contracted *according to indulgence, not according to command*" (*The Sentences*, book 4, *On the Doctrine of Signs*, trans. Giulio Silano, Mediaeval Sources in Translation 48 [Toronto: Pontifical Institute of Mediaeval Studies, 2010], 158).

50. In 2001, a philosophical theoretician of tattoos declared that for her, "tattooed bodies evoke ambiguous feelings of fascination and fear" (Nikki Sullivan, *Tattooed Bodies: Subjectivity, Textuality, Ethics, and Pleasure* [Westport, CT: Praeger, 2001], 183). I doubt that the author would express the same sentiment now.

51. Hal Foster, "Readings in Cultural Resistance," in Foster, *Recodings: Art, Spectacle, Cultural Politics* (Seattle: Bay Press, 1985), 157–79, at 167.

52. Foster continues: "Difference is thus used productively; indeed, in a social order which seems to know no outside (and which must contrive its own transgressions to redefine its limits), difference is often fabricated in the interests of social control as well as of commodity innovation" ("Readings in Cultural Resistance," 167).

Transgressive Images, Medieval and Contemporary

In the 1980s, a photograph entitled *Piss Christ*, by the New York-based artist Andres Serrano, sparked national controversy. The outrage was such that discussion of the piece made it into the US Senate, where conservative senators signed a letter protesting the funding of Serrano's work through a grant of the National Endowment for the Arts.[53]

At first sight, the piece has nothing offensive about it. It shows a crucifix that appears "suspended in a hazy, golden substance," surrounded by small bubbles of air. The art critic Anthony Julius ascribed a "blurred, rather conventional beauty"[54] to the piece, pronouncing it to be on the slightly kitschy side of things. Maybe so, but then one reads the label associated with the photograph, which shockingly reads *Piss Christ*. The artist submerged the crucifix in urine and then photographed the installation.

It is not surprising that many who saw the piece or just heard of it were offended by the association of the crucifix, which depicts the Lord Jesus's torture and death, the highest and lowest point of salvation history, encapsulating all Christian hopes and fears—that many were offended to see the crucifix dragged down into piss. The artist seemed to be expressing a complete disrespect for all that is holy in the Christian faith. Clearly, a limit was being transgressed, and a taboo broken: desecration committed with taxpayers' funds.

This is not to say that the interpretation just suggested is the only possible way to approach *Piss Christ*. The Catholic philosopher Jorge J. E. Gracia proposed a distinction: it is true, he admitted, that the work can be viewed as hostile to everything that is dear to people of faith. But what if the work is read as an inner-Catholic critique? Then, Gracia explained, "the piece need not be interpreted as implying that the crucifix, Christ, or Christianity are being pissed on. The meaning of the work could be quite different. It could mean that Christ, and perhaps Christianity as a whole, is immersed in piss, which is something very different. Because then the work does not entail an insult to Christ or even Christianity, but a criticism of Christians, of the Christian community. The art work could then become a cry against those who have soiled the cross and the faith, not a soiling of

---

53. See *Congressional Record*, vol. 135, no. 64 (May 18, 1989): S5594–95.

54. The two quotations are both from Anthony Julius, *Transgressions: The Offences of Art* (Chicago: University of Chicago Press, 2002), 15.

the cross or the faith."[55] To elucidate his point further, Gracia referred to the endless scandals about sexual abuse by members of the clergy, or the Catholic hierarchy's support of dictators in Argentina and Chile. Could it be, then, that transgression is not an objective characteristic of a particular work of art, but is closely connected with the context in which such a work appears? So, for example, if the artist responsible for the piece belonged to the Catholic community, and if the work were displayed in a Catholic venue, *Piss Christ* might be perceived quite differently than it was in the context in which the public actually encountered it, namely, in avant-garde art galleries and museums.

Now consider a second transgressive image. We are looking at a Psalter that was produced in Ghent in the 1330s, for the use of Louis de Nevers, count of Flanders. Its pages are richly illuminated, as is to be expected in a devotional book intended for an aristocratic reader. Within the letter *Q* that forms the initial of Psalm 41:2, *Quemadmodum desiderat cervus ad fontes aquarum*, "As the hart panteth after the fountains of water," we discover the head of a monk, clearly recognizable by his tonsure.[56] Various other human faces pop up in the margins of the text, such as a lady's face to the right of the second line. There seems to be a little devil's visage to the right of lines 7 and 8; and to the left of the initial we have a man's head attached to the body of what may be a deer (given the mention of the hart in the psalm). Perhaps the hybrid gentleman depicted was one of the count's enemies, of whom the illuminator made fun for Louis's amusement. The margins outside the elaborate borders are further populated by a hare and a squirrel, beasts of the forest appropriate to the scene that the psalm evokes.

We can already see that there is something of a tension between the sacred text at the center of the page and the world conjured up in the margins. The latter is a secular world—indeed, more than that, it is at least in part a counterworld inhabited by strange creatures that are not exactly

55. Ilan Stavans and Jorge J. E. Gracia, "On Desecration: Andres Serrano, *Piss Christ*," in Stavans and Gracia, *Thirteen Ways of Looking at Latino Art* (Durham, NC: Duke University Press, 2014), 49–60, at 52. The book represents a series of conversations between the two authors.

56. MS. Oxford, Bodleian Library, Douce 5, fol. 117v. For a brief description of the page in question, see Frédéric Elsig, "La ridiculisation du système religieux," in Jean Wirth et al., *Les marges à drôleries des manuscrits gothiques (1250–1350)*, Matériaux pour l'histoire publiés par l'École des chartes 7 (Geneva: Droz, 2008), 276–326, at 304. MS. Douce 5–6 is featured prominently in this volume.

threatening, but do belong to a universe that is a little out of joint. The man-deer appears to have lost his fully human status. One wonders what transgression made him slip into animality.

So far, our page is amusing more than disquieting. But then, at the very bottom, we find an image that is outrageous. A bishop, fully vested and complete with miter and crozier, blesses a monkey who, sitting in front of him, is reading a book in which we discern both Latin and Hebrew characters. Could this be the Psalms? In this case, the monkey would signify a world gone crazy, in which animals can read and bishops bless them. The illustration would also be an auto-commentary on the work in which it is contained. Monkeys are frequent guests in the margins of Gothic manuscripts, where they signify the subhuman status that threatens the human being after the transgression in the garden.[57] Sin deprives man of his divine likeness.[58] Thus, in Daniel, God punishes the powerful King Nebuchadnezzar, ruler of the Babylonian Empire, for his pride by reducing him to animal life: "The same hour the word was fulfilled upon Nabuchodonosor, and he was driven away from among men, and did eat grass like an ox, and his body was wet with the dew of heaven: till his hairs grew like the feathers of eagles, and his nails like birds' claws" (Dan. 4:33). The ape offered itself as an illustration of this danger due to its similarity to the human being, especially because a folk etymology connected *simia* ("ape") with *similitudo* ("similarity").[59]

We have not yet touched on the most scandalous aspect of the monkey scene: the ape is depicted as defecating round objects that bear a cross. Is this money? It could be; but there were two types of objects in the Middle Ages that looked like the round pieces that emerge from the monkey's rectum: coins and the hosts that were employed in the celebration of the Eucharist. Indeed, the similarity was not accidental, since the Eucharist was

57. See the magisterial treatment by H. W. Janson, *Apes and Ape Lore in the Middle Ages and the Renaissance*, Studies of the Warburg Institute 20 (London: Warburg Institute, 1952). Chapter 6 is entitled "The Ape in Gothic Marginal Art" (163–98). Also see, more recently, the essay by Jean Wirth, "Les singes dans les marges à drôleries des manuscrits gothiques," *Micrologus* 8 (2000): 429–44.

58. On this topic, see the excellent reflections in Gil Batholeyns, Pierre-Olivier Dittmar, and Vincent Jolivet, *Image et transgression au moyen âge*, Lignes d'art (Paris: Presses universitaires de France, 2008), 21–33.

59. Isidore records this folk etymology, but dismisses it in his *Etymologies* 12.2.30 (see *The Etymologies of Isidore of Seville*, trans. Stephen A. Barney et al. [Cambridge: Cambridge University Press, 2006], 253).

Illuminated page from a Psalter for Louis de Nevers, count of Flanders, fourteenth century (MS. Oxford, Bodleian Library, Douce 5, fol. 117v).

often likened to a coin. In the twelfth century, Honorius of Autun coined a phrase according to which the Eucharistic bread was made *ad modum denarii*, "after the manner of a denarius." Honorius regarded this analogy as fitting because of the Gospel references to silver coins, or denarii, in the parable of the workers in the vineyard (Matt. 20:1–16), in the episode involving the coin with Caesar's image (Matt. 22:19–21), and in Judas's betrayal of Jesus for thirty silver coins (Matt. 26:15 and 27:3). Furthermore, in the Middle Ages hosts were manufactured much like coins, namely, by means of host presses.[60] The illuminator of our Psalms page is most likely playing on these connections. He may also have been aware—although we cannot, of course, be certain—of the scholastic discussions regarding the status of the consecrated host once it has entered the digestive system and has exited it, or is rejected from it.[61]

It is difficult to imagine a more irreverent depiction of the Eucharist. It is very unlikely, however, that the image is intended to mock the sacrament of the Eucharist as such, given its placement within a Psalter—that is to say, a devotional book meant for a pious reader. A clue for the correct interpretation of the monkey scene is that the book contains numerous illustrations mocking the clergy; only canons are excepted from the illuminator's dark and scathing humor.[62] Here, one must know that critique of the clergy is by no means rare in medieval art. In some scenes, groups of lost souls marching off to hell are often led by aristocrats, bishops, and monks. Thus, our monkey scene probably wants to convey derision for bishops who live as though the Eucharist were nothing but a piece of excrement, or, more broadly, clergy whose conduct desecrates the sacraments they are called to celebrate. Maybe the illuminator even had a particular bishop in mind. Undoubtedly canons are excluded because Louis de Nevers had a particular attachment to them; for instance, his confessor could have been a canon.

Finally, a word of caution is in order regarding the meaning of excrement in this particular illumination. For us, to associate someone or something with feces, in words or images, is tantamount to an expression of extreme disdain. Feces are the quintessential metaphor for a state of abjection. This is why, to understand the frequent scatological imagery in medieval art, we have to free ourselves from our own assumptions re-

60. On these points, one may read the fine essay by Aden Kumler, "The Multiplication of the Species: Eucharistic Morphology in the Middle Ages," *RES: Anthropology and Aesthetics* 59/60 (Spring/Autumn 2011): 179–91 (quotation from Honorius of Autun on p. 188). For further detail on the manufacture of the host and its broader implications for understanding medieval culture, see Kumler, "Manufacturing the Sacred in the Middle Ages: The Eucharist and Other Medieval Works of *Ars*," *English Language Notes* 53, no. 2 (Fall/Winter 2015): 9–43.

61. See Chapter 2, pp. 56–57 above.

62. See Elsig, "La ridiculisation," 304.

garding the meaning of bodily excretions. On this topic, the late Michael Camille remarked that "medieval people did not problematize fecal matter as 'dirt,' as Freud's 'matter out of place.' Shit had its proper place in the scheme of things. Not yet a secret secretion, it ran down the middle of the streets, its odors omnipresent. As manure it was part of the cycle of life, death and rebirth, and as everyday matter it found its way onto the pages of prayer-books."[63] We can no longer determine how transgressive exactly the monkey excreting coin-hosts was in the context of Louis de Nevers's Psalter. Still, art historians remind us to be aware of the "radical difference in the reception of the same image over time."[64]

Although the example from Louis de Nevers's Psalter is on the extreme side of things, illustrations mocking sacred realities are common in Gothic manuscripts—in particular in manuscripts of devotional literature. The association of transgression with devotion may seem paradoxical, but it testifies to the place that the margins played in medieval art (and, more generally, society) in relation to the normative center. Art historians who have studied this phenomenon emphasize the interplay of model and countermodel that in no way destabilized the social and religious order, but rather served to affirm it. To quote Michael Camille again, the center was "dependent upon the margins for its continued existence."[65] And we are not talking only about the margins of Gothic manuscripts. Medieval churches often featured carvings of an explicitly sexual nature that would make us blush.[66] Cathedrals held *festa stultorum*, "fools' feasts," that inverted the social and ecclesiastical order. During such occasions, bawdy performances by lower clergy took place both inside and outside the cathedral, and the events culminated in the election of a boy-bishop. This enactment, in which the "entire ecclesiastical establishment was turned upside-

63. Michael Camille, *Image on the Edge: The Margins of Medieval Art* (Cambridge, MA: Harvard University Press, 1992), 111. Further on scatological imagery in medieval art, see Karl P. Wentersdorf, "The Symbolic Significance of *Figurae Scatologicae* in Gothic Manuscripts," in *Word, Picture, and Spectacle*, ed. Clifford Davidson, Early Drama, Art, and Music Monograph Series 5 (Kalamazoo, MI: Medieval Institute Publications, 1984), 1–19.

64. Batholeyns, Dittmar, and Jolivet, *Image et transgression*, 110: ". . . différence radicale de réception de la même image dans le temps."

65. Camille, *Image on the Edge*, 10.

66. See Anthony Weir and James Jerman, *Images of Lust: Sexual Carvings on Medieval Churches* (London: B. T. Batsford, 1993). On the image of the anus in particular, see Michael Camille, "Dr. Witkowski's Anus: French Doctors, German Homosexuals and the Obscene in Medieval Church Art," in *Medieval Obscenities*, ed. Nicola McDonald (York, UK: York Medieval Press, 2006), 17–38.

down,"[67] found its justification in the Magnificat, one of the church's oldest prayers (with roots in Luke 1:46–55). The Magnificat echoes the themes of the foolishness of the cross and of the counterworld of the "as if" that God brings into existence by "calling those that are not as though they were" (Rom. 4:17).[68] One of its central lines reads, "He hath put down the mighty from their seat, and hath exalted the humble" (Luke 1:52). Thus, the election of a boy-bishop could appear at once as a subversion of the established ecclesiastical order and as a radical reaffirmation of the truth of the Christian message.

Not that the *festa stultorum* were uncontroversial in their own day! In a homily delivered on the feast of the circumcision, January 1, Richard of St. Victor complained:

> That which has been said by the Apostle, *And be renewed in the spirit of your mind* [Eph. 4:23], was said in former times by Jeremiah: *Be circumcised to the Lord, and take away the foreskins of your hearts, ye men of Juda, and ye inhabitants of Jerusalem* [Jer. 4:4]. For, that spiritual circumcision is the true renewal. Yet to the extent that the men of Israel were different, according to the letter, from the men of Juda (or the inhabitants of Jerusalem), so the former and the latter have to be understood differently according to the spiritual understanding. Consequently, the men of Israel are all carnal and carry themselves carnally, but the men of Juda (or the inhabitants of Jerusalem) are holy and spiritual, living spiritually. (Which we, brothers, must be to the highest degree, living as we do in a congregation, and having professed community, chastity, obedience, and the improvement of our morals.) And so the foreskins of the men of Israel are enormous and foul, for they are the works of the flesh: *which are fornication, uncleanness, immodesty, luxury, idolatry, witchcraft, enmities, contentions, wraths, quarrels, dissensions, sects, envies, murders, drunkenness, revellings, and such like. Of the which I foretell you, as I have foretold to you, that they who do such things shall not obtain the kingdom of God* [Gal. 5:19–21]. But on this day, which they call "New Year," the men of Israel have filthily come to be accustomed to the enormity of their foreskins. For today, they direct their attention to fortune-telling, divinations, untruths, and false insanities more than on other days of the year. Today, they outdo each other by observing vain and

---

67. Camille, "Dr. Witkowski's Anus," 25.
68. See Chapter 3, pp. 82–83 above.

superstitious activities. Today, seized by the furies of their Bacchic ravings and inflamed by fires of diabolical instigation, they flock together to the church and profane the house of God through vain and foolish speeches in which sin is not absent—nay, in which it is present, through impious rhythmic sayings, laughter, and jeers. And he who has said better that which is evil, that one is more *praised in the desires of his soul* [Ps. 9:24]. Today even some clerics, of whom it seems to have been written that their clerics do not profit them [cf. Isa. 44:9], prophesy in Baal [cf. Jer. 23:13], *and they foretell lies* [Ezek. 13:6], and quite a few of the priests clap their hands [cf. Ezek. 25:6], and the people love things of this sort.[69]

So here we have a firsthand account of some of the elements of a "feast of fools."[70] Furthermore, amidst the anti-Judaic ravings of this famous

69. Richard of St. Victor, *Sermo XLIX: In circumcisione Domini*, Patrologia Latina 177, cols. 1034–39, at col. 1036: "Quod autem per Apostolum dicitur: *Renovamini spiritu mentis vestrae*, hoc antiquitus per Jeremiam dictum est, ubi ait: *Circumcidimini Domino, et auferte praeputia cordium vestrorum, viri Juda, et habitatores Jerusalem.* Ipsa enim spiritualis circumcisio ipsa est vera renovatio. Sed quemadmodum alii erant viri Israel, alii viri Juda, sive habitatores Jerusalem, secundum litteram, sic intelligendum est alios istos, et alios illos, secundum spiritalem intelligentiam. Viri ergo Israel omnes carnales sunt et carnaliter se habentes, viri autem Juda sive habitatores Jerusalem sancti et spiritales sunt spiritaliter viventes. Quod nos, fratres, maxime esse debemus, qui in congregatione vivimus, et communionem, castitatem, obedientiam, et emendationem morum nostrorum professi sumus. Virorum itaque Israel praeputia valde turpia et enormia sunt, ipsa enim sunt opera carnis. *Quae sunt fornicatio, immunditia, impudicitia, luxuria, idolorum servitus, veneficia, inimicitiae, contentiones, aemulationes, irae, rixae, dissensiones, sectae, invidiae, homicidia, ebrietates, commessationes, et his similia, quae praedico vobis sicut praedixi, quoniam qui talia agunt, regnum Dei non consequentur.* Sed in hoc die, quem annum novum vocant, enormitatibus praeputiorum suorum viri Israel turpiter inveterascunt. Hodie namque sortilegiis et divinationibus, vanitatibus et insaniis falsis prae caeteris anni diebus intendunt. Hodie donis ad invicem vanae et superstitiosae intentionis observatione se praeveniunt; hodie debacchationis suae furiis rapti, et instigationis diabolicae flammis accensi ad ecclesiam convolant, et vaniloquiis ac stultiloquiis, quibus peccatum non deerit imo aderit, rhythmicis quoque dictis nefariis, risibus, et cachinnis domum Dei profanant. Et qui malum melius dixerit, ille plus laudatur in desideriis animae suae. Hodie etiam quidam clerici, de quibus scriptum esse videtur, quod clerici eorum non proderunt eis, prophetant in Baal, *et divinant mendacium*, et nonnuli sacerdotum plaudunt manu, et populus diligit talia." Jean Châtillon has established the attribution of the *Sermones centum* (among which this homily is found) to Richard of St. Victor in "Le contenu, l'authenticité et la date du *Liber exceptionum* et des *Sermones centum* de Richard de Saint-Victor," *Revue du moyen âge latin* 4 (1948): 23–52 and 343–66.

70. Further evidence comes from plastic art in medieval churches, which often incorporates motifs from the *festa stultorum*; see Reinhard Steiner, "'Deposuit potentes de sede': Das

Augustinian canon, addressing his community of brothers at the Abbey of St. Victor in Paris toward the middle of the twelfth century, suddenly Dionysus rears his head, in the form of his Roman equivalent, Bacchus. There was room in medieval Christianity for the Dionysian, which was not simply repressed or driven "into the depths of the sea," as Nietzsche said[71]—rather, it existed in full sight of the dominant culture, albeit in its margins. Admittedly, this balance did not last. It appeared at a particular point in the history of medieval Christianity, and existed as long as a shared public space permitted the center of society to contain the marginal transgressions. The rise of a large class of literate bourgeois, sufficiently wealthy to acquire manuscripts and read them in private, led to the gradual collapse of the transgressive margins.[72] In due course, the provocative carvings in churches disappeared as well, together with the *festa stultorum*. Michel Foucault himself chronicled the changed status of the fool at the dawn of modernity in his first major work, *History of Madness*.[73] There is only one, though greatly diminished, form in which the fool and his feast are still allowed to exist in modern societies: the *Fastnacht* or carnival.[74] Their connection with the faith has, however, become extremely loose; nowadays, they are regarded as purely secular celebrations that allow for some vague "fun."

If we now return to *Piss Christ* against the background of our reflections on Gothic art, it is clear how the transgression that occurs in Serrano's work differs from superficially similar medieval images. *Piss Christ* is not an expression of freedom in the margins of a dominant culture; it is not a playful rebellion which expresses the truth that whoever believes he possesses wisdom and power is but a fool in God's eyes—a rebellion that nonetheless recognizes that there is real wisdom, that there is legitimate power, and, above all, that there is a God, however ineffably transcendent.

'Narrenfest' in der Plastik des Hoch- und Spätmittelalters," in *Aufsätze zur Kunstgeschichte. Festschrift für Hermann Bauer zum 60. Geburtstag*, ed. Karl Mösender and Andreas Prater (Hildesheim: Olms, 1991), 92–108.

71. See the introduction, p. 8 above.

72. This is the hypothesis Batholeyns, Dittmar, and Jolivet offer in *Image et transgression*, 91–93. Also see Camille, *Image on the Edge*, chap. 6: "The End of the Edge" (153–60).

73. See Michel Foucault, *History of Madness*, ed. Jean Khalfa, trans. Jonathan Murphy and Jean Khalfa (London: Routledge, 2006).

74. For further literature on *festum stultorum* and *Fastnacht*, one may consult the relevant entries in *Lexikon des Mittelalters*, 9 vols. (Munich and Zurich: Artemis & Winkler/LexMA-Verlag, 1980–1999): Harry Kühnel, "Fastnacht," vol. 4, cols. 313–14, and Werner Mezger, "Narr, V. Brauchtum," vol. 6, cols. 1026–27.

Rather, Serrano's photograph runs up against limits that have already been subverted and become unstable, so that they must be defended vigorously and, perhaps, desperately. There could be no doubt about the faith of the irreverent illuminator of a medieval manuscript, or of the client who commissioned the work: the illuminator committed his carnivalesque transgressions from within the church. In his own practice, he affirmed what he mocked. Remember, Louis de Nevers would have seen the illustrations in his Psalter while saying his prayers, thus performatively negating any fundamental challenge to Christian truth.[75] The modern artist speaks from a very different place, and to a very different audience, like the museumgoer, or the customer of an avant-garde gallery. What values are affirmed in this type of context?

There is, first, a cult of originality. This stems in no small measure from the Enlightenment idea according to which there is no teleology to human reason higher than progress. In the wake of this idea, there developed a veritable cult of the transgressive. Hegel's world-historical individual helps to lift world history to a new level of consciousness and freedom by breaking the laws of an existing society, reshaping it completely. Nietzsche's overman, realizing the death of the Christian story, sets out to create an entirely new narrative to shape his existence. For modernity, to be human means to transgress existing limits, to expand the horizon of knowledge—or of artistic possibility, as the case may be. But these horizons keep receding: "the avant-garde enterprise," as Anthony Julius put it, "can no longer exceed the capacity of the art world to absorb it, nor can this subversive endeavor distinguish itself in a culture defined by subversiveness."[76] In an art world where every taboo has been broken—in a single public performance, the Viennese actionist Günter Brus once cut himself with a razor blade, drank his own urine, and smeared himself with excrement, before masturbating while singing the Austrian national anthem—the "transgressive aesthetic has exhausted its potential."[77] In the words of Arthur C. Danto, "artists

---

75. As Mikhail Bakhtin put it in the pages devoted to medieval parody in *Rabelais and His World*, trans. Hélène Iswolsky (Bloomington and Indianapolis: Indiana University Press, 1984), 95: "We know that men who composed the most unbridled parodies of sacred texts and cults often sincerely accepted and served religion."

76. Julius, *Transgressions*, 201.

77. Julius, *Transgressions*, 53. I have not made up the description of one of Günter Brus's performances. One may read about him in Cecilia Novero, "Painful Painting and Brutal Ecstasy: The Material Actions of Günter Brus and Otto Muehl," *Seminar: A Journal of Germanic Studies* 43, no. 4 (November 2007): 453–68.

pressed against boundary after boundary, and found that the boundaries all gave way."[78]

Neither the museum nor the art market can provide boundaries that do not give way. While the museum affords a space for the public, democratic viewing of art, "there is no a priori criterion as to what art must look like, and . . . no narrative into which the museum's contents must all fit."[79] The museum gives art a strange kind of context-less context, reflecting the fact that there no longer is a dominant narrative in contemporary society. To put this more precisely, following Danto's well-known argument, it is not so much that contemporary art has lost all context; rather, that role, which used to be fulfilled by rich life-worlds such as the agora, the church, or the guildhall, has been assumed by art theory.[80] No layperson would be able to tell that Andy Warhol's Brillo boxes represent avant-garde art. The theoretician of art, however, knows the place the Brillo boxes occupy in the matrix of artistic possibilities that constitutes the art world. Once again, though, that matrix is open-ended, such that those artists who expand it have the greatest claim to artistic creativity and originality.

The art market cannot function as a source of boundaries either. Money is nothing but an exchange function, devoid of substantive qualities. The unreality of money was masked as long as it took the form of gold and silver coins, or even impressive-looking banknotes; in the age of the Bitcoin, the character of money as pure function has been thrown in the highest relief.[81] When an art object gets dragged into the market, it therefore loses some of its distinctive characteristics as art: it becomes part of someone's investment portfolio, for example, alongside stocks, bonds, and real estate. Thus, money cannot bestow limits on art, in the sense of defining it as art. Every work will be good as long as its value appreciates, whether it is a Rembrandt or a Mapplethorpe. The process of commodification, then, dissolves whatever limits did remain even further, and it will do this while normalizing the artwork's transgressive aspects. Mapplethorpe's *Man in Polyester Suit* looked less like mere pornography after it fetched

---

78. Arthur C. Danto, *After the End of Art: Contemporary Art and the Pale of History*, A. W. Mellon Lectures in the Fine Arts, 1995/Bollingen Series xxxv, 44 (Princeton: Princeton University Press, 1997), 14.

79. Danto, *After the End of Art*, 5.

80. See Arthur C. Danto, "The Artworld," *Journal of Philosophy* 61 (1964): 571–84.

81. For penetrating analyses of the status of money and its role in Western society, see Georg Simmel, *The Philosophy of Money*, trans. Tom Bottomore and David Frisby, 3rd ed. (London: Routledge, 2004).

$500,000. This dynamic creates spirals of transgression and normalization, where each normalizing stage is followed by further transgression, which in turn is only waiting to be absorbed into the market: "Capitalism has at last dissolved the opposition between system and transgression."[82] It is not a coincidence that Andy Warhol's works account for a large percentage of today's art market: self-referential artworks that define their own boundaries as art enter a market driven by a desire for limitless profit. Warhol's *Silver Car Crash*, which depicts a mangled body in a wrecked silver car, painted multiple times on a canvas of 8 by 13 feet, was auctioned in 2013 for $105 million.[83]

Indeed, to repeat words by Michel Foucault that we first heard in the introduction, contemporary art seems to have been "cast into an empty space where it encounters nothing but the meager form of the limit, and where it has no beyond, no prolongation, except in the frenzy that breaks it."[84]

82. Julius, *Transgressions*, 201.

83. On Warhol's place in the contemporary art market: Bryan Appleyard, "A One-Man Market," *Intelligent Life*, November/December 2011, 78–89.

84. See the introduction, p. 17 above.

Conclusion

The conclusion of this book is very simple: tradition and transgression, far from excluding each other, are inextricably connected. While it is quite likely that this finding applies to traditions more generally—and pursuing such a hypothesis would surely be a worthwhile task for further inquiry—we have reached our conclusion by analyzing the constitution and historical unfolding of the Christian tradition.

The Christian tradition is often, and rightly, seen as a conservative force aimed at the transmission of the deposit of faith through time. Yet, despite this conservative impulse, the tradition could not exist without the transgressions that founded it, that is to say, without God's stepping over the limits of the profane world of everyday life to reveal himself. We have spoken of "irruptions" of the divine in this context. The prophetic human beings whom God chooses to hear his call are drawn into a corresponding transgressive movement beyond the normal boundaries of human society, toward the Lord. Moses's encounter with God on Mount Sinai exemplifies this structure paradigmatically. The incarnation possesses a similar dynamic: God suspends the boundary between the human and the divine in his Son, who unites the two natures in his person. Jesus is profoundly transgressive in other ways as well: Jewish, he challenges the traditions of Judaism, which he comes to radicalize and to "fulfill"; divine, he urges his human followers to a divine perfection that transcends the attachments and loyalties of ordinary life; broken on the cross, he undermines any simplistic conception of the glory of divinity with his abjection.

As the Christian tradition unfolded from its transgressive core, the image of the despoliation of the Egyptians became crucial for contact with the non-Christian world. This image is transgressive, too, as Jewish exegetes of the relevant Exodus passages clearly perceived when they tried to explain why the Lord permitted his people to deceive and to steal in their departure from Egypt. We have found, however, that in the practice of the Christian appropriation of other cultures, the violent connotations of pillaging were often counterbalanced by a different approach. Robbery is not a sufficiently sophisticated means of cultural encounter. For gold remains gold, whether it is in the possession of an Egyptian or an Israelite; but a concept or a theory cannot be appropriated without the painstaking work of translation. Translation is transgressive in a different sense than pillaging is. In translating from one language into another, it is oftentimes the receptor language that is violated and bent into the direction of its source. We saw the willingness to let a language be shaped by the Other to which (or to whom) it is listening paradigmatically exemplified in translations of Scripture. Saint Jerome, Luther, and the Douay-Rheims translators all knew that they could not simply impose existing structures of Latin, German, or English upon the scriptural texts that they endeavored to render. They knew that words have to become strange sometimes to accommodate the Word. Was Moses not changed after he sojourned with the Lord on Mount Sinai?

Yet another way in which tradition is linked to transgression is due to the inevitability of forgetting. Tradition, being human, is not capable of handing down the totality of its content. Thus, it sheds elements of its past as it grows—elements judged, implicitly or explicitly, to be dispensable in a particular situation. Standing at a crossroads, a tradition goes one way, forgetting that it could have taken the other path. When the path not taken is relegated to oblivion, the remaining one thus becomes *the* path, determining ways of thinking and avenues of inquiry to the exclusion of others. Sometimes, when the tradition runs into difficulties as a result of its choices, it may have to "unbuild," to destruct, layers of transmission in order to uncover some of these crossroads and reexamine seemingly past possibilities. Such destructions are transgressive insofar as they challenge the boundaries of the tradition, broadening the scope of what is possible to think or do traditionally. But destruction is also necessary periodically in order to lay bare the very foundations of the tradition, which the process of handing down cannot but obscure. This was, it seems, the basic impulse behind the Reformation: to remind Christians of the theology of the cross and to teach them to listen afresh to the words of Scripture, which scholasticism had unwittingly obscured in its very efforts to elucidate and systematize the irruption of Christ's message. Destruction is what drives negative theology as well: Pseudo-Dionysius urges us to unbuild all the truths, genuine though they are, which ultimately prevent us from acknowledging the utter Otherness of God, and the inability of our finite minds to comprehend him.

If one intention of this book has been to remind the Christian tradition of its transgressive core, another has been to offer a corrective to the cult of transgression that pervades contemporary culture. The overstepping of limits cannot be an end in itself, whether we are talking about the endless self-overcoming of human limitations that is called "progress" or have in mind the challenging of boundaries of artistic possibility and license that characterizes the contemporary art world. There is a place for art that challenges tradition, even for art that makes light of the most sacred realities—reminding us, perhaps, that all we have of God, ultimately, are representations in words, images, and actions, the reality remaining veiled and elusive. Such may well have been the impulse that animated the mocking images in the margins of Gothic manuscripts. As we discovered in these *drôleries*, transgressive art derives its meaning from the tradition it subverts; once nothing is left to subvert, transgression becomes an empty exercise, pathetically spinning out of control as it chases after ever new limits to conquer. Playing in the margins of cultural norms is fun—and has a real function—only as long as there is a center.

Excerpts from the Pseudo-Poitiers Gloss and from Denys the Carthusian's *Sentences* Commentary

The text of the prologue to the Pseudo-Peter of Poitiers gloss has been published a number of times, though only partially and transcribed from different manuscripts. The first modern scholar to note the interest of the text and to transcribe parts of it was Martin Grabmann, *Geschichte der scholastischen Methode*, vol. 2, *Die scholastische Methode im 12. und beginnenden 13. Jahrhundert* (Freiburg im Breisgau: Herder, 1911; reprint, Berlin: Akademie-Verlag, 1988), 504–6. Raymond-M. Martin, OP, edited the first half of the prologue from MS. London, British Library, Royal 7.F.XIII, in his "Notes sur l'œuvre litteraire de Pierre le Mangeur," *Recherches de théologie ancienne et medievale* 3 (1931): 54–66. Dom Odon Lottin then added the second half, transcribed from MS. Paris, Bibliothèque nationale de France, lat. 14423, in his article "Le prologue des Gloses sur les Sentences attribuées à Pierre de Poitiers," *Recherches de théologie ancienne et médiévale* 7 (1935): 70–73. The following transcription is my own; it is based on the earliest known manuscript of the Pseudo-Poitiers gloss, Naples, Biblioteca nazionale, VII C 14. The excerpt appears on fol. 2ra.

> composuit autem magister hunc librum propter tria genera hominum. scilicet propter timidos. siue fugitiuos. propter pigros. et propter blasphemos. qui omnes satis in ueteri testamento prefigurati sunt. positis enim a moyse terminis circa montem synai iuxta preceptum domini quos populo fas transire non erat ne uiderent dominum et perirent. [In the margin:] <Infra est ad timotheum omnis dictio diunitus inspirata utilis uel ad docendum ad arguendum etc.> cum moyses in montem domino uocante ascenderet secuti sunt eum. usque ad terminos ur et aaron et iosue. et lxx. qui de eius spiritu erant accepturi. Moyse autem in monte moram faciente cum domino. redierunt. Ur. et aaron. et lxx. di-

uine expectacionis tedio fagigati [*for* fatigati]. Solus iosue circa terminos remansit. sollicitus de reditu domini sui. potuit. et esse haec non legatur. quod plerique de populo transgressi terminos perierunt.

mons iste quem moyses ascendit mystice sacra scriptura intelligitur. immobili firmitate subsistens utriusque [testamenti]. munita est ut ei non sit fas obuiare. termini circa montem positi; sanctorum expositiones mystice intelliguntur. quorum tenemur sequi uestigia. ne transgrediamur terminos quos posuerunt patres nostri. per moysen. qui domino uocante ascendit montem mystice intelliguntur. qui in primitiua ecclesia per diuinam tantam inspirationem ad sacre pagine eminenciam ascenderunt. ut paulus et ceteri apostoli. qui spiritu sancto dictante. profunda et obscura. sacre scripture penetrauerunt. preter hos autem sunt qui usque ad terminos ascendunt. non tamen transcendunt. nec ex diffidentia redeunt. ut studiosi doctores. qui sacre doctrine perscrutande pertinaciter insistunt. et hii per Iosue designantur. sunt qui usque ad terminos procedunt. sed fatigati retro eunt. it pote qui librorum sacre pagine numerositatem attendentes de se ipsis diffidunt. ideoque ad ceteras facultates tanquam canes ad uomitum recurrunt. et hii timidi siue fugitiui dicuntur. qui per ur. et aaron. lxx. sunt figurati. sunt alii qui nec ad terminos accedunt. qui singularibus [*for* secularibus] negociis implicati nichil de sacra scriptura meditantur aut querunt. Hii sunt pigri. per eos qui nec castra exire sunt ausi. designati. sunt alii qui terminas [*for* terminos] transgrediuntur et pereunt. ut heretici. qui sanctorum expositiones suis adinuentionibus postponunt. Isti sunt blasphemi. per eos qui forte transgressi terminos perierunt designati.

Propter hec tria hominum genera magister hunc librum composuit. propter timidos siue fugitiuos. ut operis breuitate reuocaret. propter pigros ut operis facilitate excitaret. propter blasphemos. ut sanctorum auctoritatibus. confutaret.

The *Sentences* commentary by Denys the Carthusian is available only in a rare edition that few academic libraries own. I am therefore reproducing here the Latin text of the part of the proem that is discussed in Chapter 4. The text is from D. Dionysii Cartusiani, *Commentaria in primum librum Sententiarum*, Doctoris Ecstatici D. Dionysii Cartusiani *Opera Omnia* 19 (Tournai: Typis cartusiae S. M. de Pratis, 1902), prooemium, pp. 35–36.

Oportet ergo sapientiae operam dare, studioque salubri ordinate vacare, et ipsam notitiam ad sincerrimum Deitatis amorem referre: sicque per sapientiam amorosam ad plenam et aeternam beatudinem indesinenter adspirare, imo et accelerare: quoniam omnis sapientia vitae praesentis, omnis lux notitiae hujus viae, omnis profectus et splendor exercitationis viantium, respectu beatificae contemplationis ac luminis gloriae perfectionisque Beatorum, est velut ignorantia, tanquam umbra, et sicut defectuositas involuta in tantum, ut perfectissima cognitio quam de Deo altissimo habemus in mundo isto, sit per abnegationem et ablationem omnium prorsus ab ipso, quemadmodum et secundo Mysticae theologiae capitulo divinus Dionysius pandit, dicendo: Hoc est Deum vere cognoscere, ipsum supersubstantialem supersubstantialiter per omnium entium ablationem laudare. Sicut et super Joannem ait Chrysostomus, quod [p. 36] stanti in ripa Oceani, hoc est ipsum Oceanum intuenti, non possibile est totum perspicere, nec finem ejus visu attingere. Hoc et philosophi suo modo agnoverunt. Quorum unus in libro de Causis disseruit: Causa prima est superior omni narratione, et non narratur nisi per causas; itemque, Non est ei (inquit) diminutio nec complementum.

Ceterum, quamvis tanta sit defectuositas, parvitas ac paucitas sapientiae viae respectu sapientiae patriae; nihilo minus sapientia tempore legis evangelicae revelata in primis per Christum, deinde per missionem et inspirationem Spiritus Sancti, deinceps per gloriosos Apostolos et Evangelistas, ac demum per sanctos Patres, tandemque per doctores catholicos atque scholasticos, non solum in divinis Scripturis, sed in omni etiam philosophia nobiliter eruditos, praeclara et magna est valde: non solum philosophorum, sed et theologorum veteris Testamenti ac legis naturae, sapientiam atque scientiam vehementer transcendens. Nam ut, teste Gregorio, sapientia per temporum processum crevit ante Salvatoris adventum, ita et interim. Et maxime a tempore quo Magister Petrus Lombardus Parisiensis episcopus, librum comportavit Sententiarum, videtur sapientia multam et magnam elucidationem, excrescentiam exuberantiamque sortita. Quod olim Isaias praevidens: Repleta est (inquit) terra scientia Domini, quasi aquae maris operientis, id est valde abundanter. Et quae latebant, in lucem producta sunt; difficultasque Scripturarum sunt enodatae; et quae fidei christianae objici queunt, et a perfidis objecta sunt, egregie soluta. Imo non solum loca Scripturae difficiliora, sed insuper verba et scripta sanctorum Patrum in expositionibus Scripturarum aliisque tractatibus multa difficilia et obscura scribentium, per praefatum Magistrum et per viros illustres studiosos scholasticos, qui super librum Sententiarum inclyte scripserunt, subtiliter sunt discussa, magistraliter declarata, catholice pertractata.

APPENDIX

Quia vero jam quasi innumerabiles super ipsum Sententiarum librum scripsisse noscuntur, et aduc quotidie aliqui scribunt, etiam plus forsitan quam expedit, dum per scripta quaedam novorum minus praeclara, scripta antiquorum praeclariora minus curantur, leguntur et exquiruntur: hinc intentio mea est in opere isto, ex commentariis et scriptis doctorum magis authenticorum, famosiorum et excellentiorum, quamdam facere extractionem et collectionem, atque doctorum illorum mentem in unum volumen redigere: quatenus sicut ipse textus libri Sententiarum ex verbis et documentis sanctorum Patrum est collectus, ita et opus istud ex doctrinis et scriptis praetactorum super librum Sententiarum scribentium adunetur.

Bibliography

Abbt, Christine. *"Ich vergesse." Über Möglichkeiten und Grenzen des Denkens aus philosophischer Perspektive.* Frankfurt and New York: Campus, 2016.

Albertz, Rainer. "Das theologische Vermächtnis des Genesis-Kommentars von Claus Westermann." In *Claus Westermann: Leben—Werk—Wirkung*, edited by Manfred Oeming, 79–93. Beiträge zum Verstehen der Bibel 2. Münster: LIT-Verlag, 2003.

Allen, Joel S. "The Despoliation of Egypt: Origen and Augustine—from Stolen Treasures to Saved Texts." In *Israel's Exodus in Transdisciplinary Perspective: Text, Archaeology, Culture, and Geoscience*, edited by Thomas E. Levy, Thomas Schneider, and William H. C. Propp, 347–56. Quantitative Methods in the Humanities and Social Sciences. Cham, Switzerland: Springer, 2015.

———. *The Despoliation of Egypt in Pre-Rabbinic, Rabbinic, and Patristic Traditions.* Supplements to Vigiliae Christianae 92. Leiden: Brill, 2008.

Allison, Dale C., Jr. *The New Moses: A Matthean Typology.* Minneapolis: Fortress, 1993.

Ambrose of Milan. *Expositio Pslami CXVIII.* Edited by Michael Petschenig. Corpus Scriptorum Ecclesiasticorum Latinorum 62. Vienna: F. Tempsky; Leipzig: G. Freytag, 1913.

Appleyard, Bryan. "A One-Man Market." *Intelligent Life*, November/December 2011, 78–89.

Augustine. *Confessions.* Translated by Henry Chadwick. Oxford: Oxford University Press, 1991.

———. *Confessions.* Edited by James J. O'Donnell. 3 vols. Oxford: Clarendon, 1992.

————. *De doctrina christiana*. Edited and translated by R. P. H. Green. Oxford Early Christian Texts. Oxford: Clarendon, 1995.

Avicenna. *Liber de philosophia prima sive scientia divina V–X*. Edited by Simone Van Riet. Avicenna latinus. Louvain: Peeters; Leiden: Brill, 1980.

Bakhtin, Mikhail. *Rabelais and His World*. Translated by Hélène Iswolsky. Bloomington and Indianapolis: Indiana University Press, 1984.

Barclay, John M. G. "Crucifixion as Wisdom: Exploring the Ideology of a Disreputable Social Movement." In *The Wisdom and Foolishness of God: First Corinthians 1–2 in Theological Exploration*, edited by Christophe Chalamet and Hans-Christoph Askani, 1–20. Minneapolis: Fortress, 2015.

Barrett, C. K. *A Critical and Exegetical Commentary on the Acts of the Apostles*. Vol. 2. Edinburgh: T. & T. Clark, 1998.

Bartelink, G. J. M. *Hieronymus: Liber de optimo genere interpretandi (Epistula 57). Ein Kommentar*. Mnemosyne Supplementa 61. Leiden: Brill, 1980.

Bataille, Georges. *Erotism: Death and Sensuality*. Translated by Mary Dalwood. San Francisco: City Lights Press, 1986.

Batholeyns, Gil, Pierre-Olivier Dittmar, and Vincent Jolivet. *Image et transgression au moyen âge*. Lignes d'art. Paris: Presses universitaires de France, 2008.

Beatrice, Pier Franco. "The Treasures of the Egyptians: A Chapter in the History of Patristic Exegesis and Late Antique Culture." In *Studia Patristica*, vol. 43, *Papers Presented at the Fourteenth International Conference on Patristic Studies Held in Oxford 2003*, edited by Frances Young, Mark Edwards, and Paul Parvis, 150–83. Louvain: Peeters, 2006.

Bender, Claudia. *Die Sprache des Textilen. Untersuchungen zu Kleidung und Textilien im Alten Testament*. Beiträge zur Wissenschaft vom Alten und Neuen Testament 177. Stuttgart: Kohlhammer, 2008.

Benson, Bruce Ellis. *Pious Nietzsche: Decadence and Dionysian Faith*. Bloomington and Indianapolis: Indiana University Press, 2008.

Bernauer, James, SJ. "The Prisons of Man: An Introduction to Foucault's Negative Theology." *International Philosophical Quarterly* 27, no. 4 (December 1987): 365–80.

Biser, Eugen. *"Gott ist tot". Nietzsches Destruktion des christlichen Bewußtseins*. Munich: Kösel, 1962.

Bonaventure. *Liber IV Sententiarum*. Opera theologica selecta 4. Quaracchi: Collegium S. Bonaventurae, 1949.

Boring, M. Eugene. "The Gospel of Matthew." In *The New Interpreter's Bible*, 8:87–505. Nashville: Abingdon, 1995.

Bouyer, Louis. "'Mystique.' Essai sur l'histoire d'un mot." *La Vie spirituelle, Supplément* no. 9 (May 15, 1949): 3–23.

Brague, Rémi. *Eccentric Culture: A Theory of Western Civilization*. Translated by Samuel Lester. South Bend, IN: St. Augustine's Press, 2002.

Brock, Sebastian P. "Aspects of Translation Technique in Antiquity." *Greek, Roman, and Byzantine Studies* 20, no. 1 (1979): 69–87.

Brook, Timothy, Jerôme Bourgon, and Gregory Blue. *Death by a Thousand Cuts*. Cambridge, MA: Harvard University Press, 2008.

Brown, Rachel Fulton. *From Judgment to Passion: Devotion to Christ and the Virgin Mary, 800–1200*. New York: Columbia University Press, 2002.

Brown, Raymond E. *The Critical Meaning of the Bible*. Mahwah, NJ: Paulist Press, 1981.

Brueggemann, Walter. "The Book of Exodus." In *The New Interpreter's Bible*, 1:675–981. Nashville: Abingdon, 1994.

———. *Genesis*. Interpretation: A Bible Commentary for Teaching and Preaching. Atlanta: John Knox, 1982.

Bultmann, Christoph. *Die biblische Urgeschichte in der Aufklärung. Johann Gottfried Herders Interpretation der Genesis als Antwort auf die Religionskritik David Humes*. Beiträge zur historischen Theologie 110. Tübingen: Mohr Siebeck, 1999.

Bultmann, Rudolf. *Theology of the New Testament*. Vol. 2. Translated by Kendrick Grobel. New York: Scribner's Sons, 1955.

Buren, John van. "Aristotle Luther Heidegger: Travelling a Forgotten Path of Thought." *Existentia: An International Journal of Philosophy* 26 (2016): 257–74.

———. *The Young Heidegger: Rumors of the Hidden King*. Studies in Continental Thought. Bloomington and Indianapolis: Indiana University Press, 1994.

Burnett, Charles S. F. "Translating from Arabic into Latin in the Middle Ages: Theory, Practice, and Criticism." In *Éditer, traduire, interpréter. Essais de méthodologie philosophique*, edited by Steve G. Lofts and Philipp W. Rosemann, 55–78. Philosophes médiévaux 36. Louvain-la-Neuve: Éditions de l'Institut supérieur de philosophie; Louvain/Paris: Peeters, 1997.

Burton, Ernest De Witt. *A Critical and Exegetical Commentary on the Epistle to the Galatians*. Edinburgh: T. & T. Clark, 1977; first published in 1920.

Bynum, Carolyn Walker. *Fragmentation and Redemption: Essays on Gender and the Human Body in Medieval Religion.* New York: Zone Books, 1991.

Camille, Michael. "Dr. Witkowski's Anus: French Doctors, German Homosexuals and the Obscene in Medieval Church Art." In *Medieval Obscenities*, edited by Nicola McDonald, 17–38. York, UK: York Medieval Press, 2006.

———. *Image on the Edge: The Margins of Medieval Art.* Cambridge, MA: Harvard University Press, 1992.

Caputo, John D. *Radical Hermeneutics: Repetition, Deconstruction, and the Hermeneutic Project.* Studies in Phenomenology and Existential Philosophy. Bloomington and Indianapolis: Indiana University Press, 1987.

Chadwick, Owen. *From Bossuet to Newman: The Idea of Doctrinal Development.* Cambridge: Cambridge University Press, 1957.

Châtillon, Jean. "Le contenu, l'authenticité et la date du *Liber exceptionum* et des *Sermones centum* de Richard de Saint-Victor." *Revue du moyen âge latin* 4 (1948): 23–52 and 343–66.

Chevallier, Philippe. *Dionysiaca: Recueil donnant l'ensemble des traductions latines des ouvrages attribués au Denys l'Aréopagite.* 2 vols. Bruges: Desclée de Brouwer, 1937.

Chevallier, Philippe. *Foucault et le christianisme.* Lyons: ENS Éditions, 2011.

Childs, Brevard S. *The Book of Exodus: A Critical, Theological Commentary.* Philadelphia: Westminster, 1974.

Cohen, Jeremy. *Living Letters of the Law: Ideas of the Jew in Medieval Christianity.* Berkeley and Los Angeles: University of California Press, 1999.

Colish, Marcia L. "The Pseudo-Peter of Poitiers Gloss." In *Mediaeval Commentaries on the "Sentences" of Peter Lombard*, vol. 2, edited by Philipp W. Rosemann, 1–33. Leiden and Boston: Brill, 2010.

Congar, Yves, OP. *Tradition and Traditions: An Historical and a Theological Essay.* Translated by Michael Naseby and Thomas Rainborough. New York: Macmillan, 1966.

———. *True and False Reform in the Church.* Translated by Paul Philibert. Collegeville, MN: Liturgical Press, 2011.

Cook, John Granger. *Crucifixion in the Mediterranean World.* Wissenschaftliche Untersuchungen zum Neuen Testament 327. Tübingen: Mohr Siebeck, 2014.

Crowe, Benjamin D. *Heidegger's Religious Origins: Destruction and Authenticity.* Indiana Series in the Philosophy of Religion. Bloomington and Indianapolis: Indiana University Press, 2006.

Dagron, Gilbert. "Judaïser." *Travaux et Mémoires* 11 (1991): 359–80.

D'Alverny, Marie-Thérèse. "Anniyya—Anitas." In *Mélanges offerts à Étienne Gilson*, 59–90. Études de philosophie médiévale, hors série. Toronto: Pontifical Institute of Mediaeval Studies; Paris: Vrin, 1959.

Dán, Róbert. "'Judaizare'—the Career of a Term." In *Antitrinitarianism in the Second Half of the 16th Century*, edited by Róbert Dán and Antal Pirnát, 25–34. Studia humanitatis 5. Budapest: Akadémiai Kiadó; Leiden: Brill, 1982.

Danto, Arthur C. *After the End of Art: Contemporary Art and the Pale of History*. A. W. Mellon Lectures in the Fine Arts, 1995/Bollingen Series xxxv, 44. Princeton: Princeton University Press, 1997.

———. "The Artworld." *Journal of Philosophy* 61 (1964): 571–84.

Davies, W. D., and Dale C. Allison Jr. *A Critical and Exegetical Commentary on the Gospel according to Saint Matthew*. 3 vols. Edinburgh: T. & T. Clark, 1988–1997.

Defert, Daniel. "Chronologie." In Michel Foucault, *Dits et écrits, 1954–1988*, edited by Daniel Defert, François Ewald, and Jacques Lagrange, 1:13–90. 2 vols. Paris: Gallimard, 2001. English translation in *A Companion to Foucault*, edited by Christopher Falzon, Timothy O'Leary, and Jana Sawicki, 11–83. Chichester, UK: Wiley-Blackwell, 2013.

De Lubac, Henri. *Medieval Exegesis*. Vol. 1, *The Four Senses of Scripture*. Translated by Mark Sebanc. Ressourcement: Retrieval and Renewal in Catholic Thought. Grand Rapids: Eerdmans, 1998.

Denys the Carthusian. Doctoris ecstatici D. Dionysii Cartusiani *Opera omnia*. 42 vols. Montreuil, Tournai, and Parkminster: Typis Cartusiae S.M. de Pratis, 1896–1935.

Derrida, Jacques. *On Touching—Jean-Luc Nancy*. Translated by Christine Irizarry. Meridian: Crossing Aesthetics. Stanford: Stanford University Press, 2005.

De Waelhens, Alphonse. *La philosophie et les expériences naturelles*. Phaenomenologica 9. The Hague: Nijhoff, 1961.

Dilthey, Wilhelm. "Der Streit Kants mit der Zensur über das Recht freier Religionsforschung." In Dilthey, *Die Jugendgeschichte Hegels und andere Abhandlungen zur Geschichte des deutschen Idealismus*, 285–309. 2nd ed. Gesammelte Schriften 4. Stuttgart: Teubner; Göttingen: Vandenhoeck & Ruprecht, 1959.

Dollimore, Jonathan. *Sexual Dissidence: Augustine to Wilde, Freud to Foucault*. Oxford: Oxford University Press, 1991.

Dunn, James D. G. *Jesus, Paul, and the Law: Studies in Mark and Galatians*. Louisville, KY: Westminster John Knox Press, 1990.

Düsing, Wolfgang. "Die Interpretation des Sündenfalls bei Herder, Kant und Schiller." In *Bückeburger Gespräche über Johann Gottfried Herder 1988. Älteste Urkunde des Menschengeschlechts*, edited by Brigitte Poschmann, 227–44. Schaumburger Gespräche 49. Rinteln: Verlag C. Bösendahl, 1989.

Edgar, Andrew. "Kant's Two Interpretations of Genesis." *Journal of Literature & Theology* 6, no. 3 (1992): 280–90.

Edwards, Mark U., Jr. *Luther's Last Battles: Politics and Polemics, 1531–46.* Ithaca, NY: Cornell University Press, 1983.

Elsig, Frédéric. "La ridiculisation du système religieux." In Jean Wirth et al., *Les marges à drôleries des manuscrits gothiques (1250–1350)*, 276–326. Matériaux pour l'histoire publiés par l'École des chartes 7. Geneva: Droz, 2008.

Emery, Kent, Jr. *Monastic, Scholastic, and Mystical Theologies from the Later Middle Ages.* Variorum Collected Studies Series CS 561. Aldershot, UK, and Brookfield, VT: Variorum, 1996.

Evans, G. R., and Philipp W. Rosemann, eds. *Mediaeval Commentaries on the "Sentences" of Peter Lombard.* 3 vols. Leiden: Brill, 2002–2015.

Evans, J. Claude. "Phenomenological Deconstruction: Husserl's Method of *Abbau*." *Journal of the British Society for Phenomenology* 21, no. 1 (1990): 14–25.

Fiddes, Paul S., and Günter Bader, eds. *The Spirit and the Letter: A Tradition and a Reversal.* London: Bloomsbury, 2013.

Fischer, Norbert. "'Distentio animi'. Symbol der Entflüchtigung des Zeitlichen." In *Die Confessiones des Augustinus von Hippo. Einführung und Interpretationen zu den dreizehn Büchern*, edited by Norbert Fischer and Cornelius Mayer, 490–552. Forschungen zur europäischen Geistesgeschichte 1. Freiburg im Breisgau: Herder, 1998.

Florence, Maurice [Michel Foucault]. "Foucault." Translated by Robert Hurley. In *Essential Works of Foucault, 1954–1984*, edited by Paul Rabinow, vol. 2, *Aesthetics, Method, and Epistemology*, edited by James D. Faubion, 459–63. New York: New Press, 1998. Original French text in *Dictionnaire des philosophes*, edited by Denis Huisman, 1:942–44. Paris: Presses universitaires de France, 1984. Also in Michel Foucault, *Dits et écrits, 1954–1988*, edited by Daniel Defert, François Ewald, and Jacques Lagrange, #345, 2:1450–55. 2 vols. Paris: Gallimard, 2001.

Flynn, Thomas. "Foucault's Mapping of History." In *The Cambridge Companion to Foucault*, edited by Gary Gutting, 29–48. 2nd ed. Cambridge: Cambridge University Press, 2005.

Folliet, Georges. "La *spoliatio Aegyptiorum* (Exode 3:21–23; 11:2–3; 12:35–36). Les interprétations de cette image chez les Pères et autres écrivains écclésiastiques." *Traditio* 57 (2002): 1–48.

Foster, Hal. "Readings in Cultural Resistance." In Foster, *Recodings: Art, Spectacle, Cultural Politics*, 157–79. Seattle: Bay Press, 1985.

Foucault, Michel. *History of Madness*. Edited by Jean Khalfa. Translated by Jonathan Murphy and Jean Khalfa. London: Routledge, 2006.

———. *The History of Sexuality*. Vol. 1, *An Introduction*. Translated by Robert Hurley. New York: Vintage Books, 1990.

———. *Introduction to Kant's "Anthropology."* Translated by Roberto Nigro and Kate Briggs. Los Angeles: Semiotext(e), 2008. French edition: E. Kant, *Anthropologie d'un point de vue pragmatique*, précédé de Michel Foucault, *Introduction à l'"Anthropologie,"* edited by Daniel Defert, François Ewald, and Frédéric Gros. Bibliothèque des textes philosophiques. Paris: Vrin, 2008.

———. "Le retour de la morale." In *Dits et écrits, 1954–1988*, edited by Daniel Defert, François Ewald, and Jacques Lagrange, #354, 2:1515–26. 2 vols. Paris: Gallimard, 2001.

———. *The Order of Things: An Archaeology of the Human Sciences*. Translated by Alan Sheridan. New York: Vintage Books, 1994.

———. "Préface" [to the first edition of *Folie et déraison*]. In *Dits et écrits, 1954–1988*, edited by Daniel Defert, François Ewald, and Jacques Lagrange, #4, 1:187–95. 2 vols. Paris: Gallimard, 2001.

———. "A Preface to Transgression." Translated by Donald F. Bouchard and Sherry Simon. In *Essential Works of Foucault, 1954–1984*, edited by Paul Rabinow, vol. 2, *Aesthetics, Method, and Epistemology*, edited by James D. Faubion, 69–87. New York: New Press, 1998. Originally published in French as "Préface à la transgression." *Critique* 19, no. 195–96 (August/September 1963): 751–69, and reprinted in *Dits et écrits, 1954–1988*, edited by Daniel Defert, François Ewald, and Jacques Lagrange, #13, 1:261–78. 2 vols. Paris: Gallimard, 2001.

———. "Prisons et asiles dans le mécanisme du pouvoir." In *Dits et écrits, 1954–1988*, edited by Daniel Defert, François Ewald, and Jacques Lagrange, #136, 1:1389–93. 2 vols. Paris: Gallimard, 2001.

———. "The Thought of the Outside." Translated by Brian Massumi. In *Essential Works of Foucault, 1954–1984*, edited by Paul Rabinow, vol. 2, *Aesthetics, Method, and Epistemology*, edited by James D. Faubion, 147–69. New York: New Press, 1998. First published in English as "The Thought from Outside." In *Foucault/Blanchot*, translated by Brian Massumi, 7–58. New York: Zone Books, 1987. French text in "La pensée du dehors." In *Dits et écrits, 1954–1988*, edited by Daniel Defert, François Ewald, and Jacques Lagrange, #38, 1:546–67. 2 vols. Paris: Gallimard, 2001.

———. "What Is an Author?" Translated by Josué V. Harari. In *Essential Works of Foucault, 1954–1984*, edited by Paul Rabinow, vol. 2, *Aesthetics, Method, and Epistemology*, edited by James D. Faubion, 205–22. New York: New Press, 1998.

Frei, Hans W. *The Eclipse of Biblical Narrative: A Study in Eighteenth- and Nineteenth-Century Hermeneutics.* New Haven: Yale University Press, 1974.

Fretheim, Terence E. "The Book of Genesis." In *The New Interpreter's Bible*, 1:319–674. Nashville: Abingdon, 1994.

Gadamer, Hans-Georg. "*Destruktion* and Deconstruction (1985)." Translated by Jeff Waite and Richard Palmer. In *Dialogue and Deconstruction: The Gadamer-Derrida Encounter*, edited by Diane P. Michelfelder and Richard E. Palmer, 102–13. SUNY Series in Contemporary Continental Philosophy. Albany: State University of New York Press, 1989. The German text is available as "Destruktion und Dekonstruktion." In *Gesammelte Werke*, vol. 2, *Hermeneutik II*, 361–72. Tübingen: J. C. B. Mohr/Paul Siebeck, 1993.

Gaddi, Barbara Ellen. *Franz Rosenzweig and Jehuda Halevi: Translating, Translations, and Translators.* Montreal and Kingston, ON: McGill-Queen's University Press, 1995.

Glicksman, Andrew T. *Wisdom of Solomon 10: A Jewish Hellenistic Reinterpretation of Early Israelite History through Sapiential Lenses.* Deuterocanonical and Cognate Literature Studies 9. Berlin: de Gruyter, 2011.

Golitzin, Alexander. *Mystagogy: A Monastic Reading of Dionysius Areopagita.* Cistercian Studies Series 250. Collegeville, MN: Liturgical Press, 2013.

Gordon, Colin. "History of Madness." In *A Companion to Foucault*, edited by Christopher Falzon, Timothy O'Leary, and Jana Sawicki, 84–103. Chichester, UK: Wiley-Blackwell, 2013.

Grabmann, Martin. *Geschichte der scholastischen Methode.* Vol. 2, *Die scholastische Methode im 12. und beginnenden 13. Jahrhundert.* Freiburg im Breisgau: Herder, 1911; reprint, Berlin: Akademie-Verlag, 1988.

Gregory of Nyssa. *The Life of Moses.* Translated by Abraham J. Malherbe and Everett Ferguson. Classics of Western Spirituality. New York: Paulist Press, 1978.

Griffith, Paul. "Seeking Egyptian Gold: A Fundamental Metaphor for the Christian Intellectual Life in a Religiously Diverse Age." *Cresset* 63, no. 7 (2000): 5–16.

Gutting, Gary. "Review of Han, *Foucault's Critical Project.*" *Notre Dame Philosophical Reviews*, 2003.05.01 (http://ndpr.nd.edu/news/foucault-s-critical-project/, accessed December 27, 2017).

Haldane, John. "MacIntyre's Thomist Revival: What Next?" In *After MacIntyre: Critical Perspectives on the Work of Alasdair MacIntyre*, edited by John Horton and Susan Mendus, 91–107. Notre Dame: University of Notre Dame Press, 1994.

Hallamaa, Olli. "On the Limits of the Genre: Roger Roseth as a Reader of the *Sentences.*" In *Mediaeval Commentaries on the "Sentences" of Peter Lombard*, edited by Philipp W. Rosemann, 2:369–404. Leiden: Brill, 2010.

Han, Béatrice. *Foucault's Critical Project: Between the Transcendental and the Historical.* Translated by Edward Pile. Atopia: Philosophy, Political Theory, Aesthetics. Stanford: Stanford University Press, 2002.

Hanson, R. P. C. *Origen's Doctrine of Tradition.* London: SPCK, 1954.

Harnack, Adolf von. "Wie soll man Geschichte studieren, insbesondere Religionsgeschichte? Thesen und Nachschriften eines Vortrages vom 19. Oktober 1910 in Christiana/Oslo." Edited by Christoph Markschies. *Zeitschrift für neuere Theologiegeschichte* 2 (1995): 148–59.

Hays, Richard B. "The Letter to the Galatians." In *The New Interpreter's Bible*, 11:181–348. Nashville: Abingdon, 2000.

Hegel, Georg Wilhelm Friedrich. *Early Theological Writings.* Translated by T. M. Knox. Works in Continental Philosophy. Philadelphia: University of Pennsylvania Press, 1971.

Heidegger, Martin. *Being and Time.* Translated by John Macquarrie and Edward Robinson. San Francisco: Harper and Row, 1962.

———. *Being and Time.* Translated by Joan Stambaugh. Revised by Dennis J. Schmidt. SUNY Series in Contemporary Continental Philosophy. Albany: State University of New York Press, 2010.

———. *Die Grundprobleme der Phänomenologie.* Edited by Friedrich-Wilhelm von Hermann. Gesamtausgabe 24. Frankfurt am Main: Klostermann, 1975.

———. *Holzwege.* Frankfurt am Main: Klostermann, 1950.

———. "The Question concerning Technology." Translated by William Lovitt. In *Basic Writings*, edited by David Farrell Krell, 311–41. San Francisco: HarperSanFrancisco, 1993.

————. *Sein und Zeit*. Gesamtausgabe 2. Frankfurt am Main: Klostermann, 1977.

Hengel, Martin. *Crucifixion in the Ancient World and the Folly of the Cross*. Philadelphia: Fortress, 1977.

Holte, Ragnar. "Logos Spermatikos: Christianity and Ancient Philosophy according to St. Justin's Apologies." Translated by Tina Pierce. *Studia Theologica: Nordic Journal of Theology* 12 (1958): 109–68.

Horst, Pieter W. van der. "The Altar of the 'Unknown God' in Athens (Acts 17:23) and the Cults of 'Unknown Gods' in the Greco-Roman World." In Horst, *Hellenism—Judaism—Christianity: Essays on Their Interaction*, 187–220. 2nd ed. Contributions to Biblical Exegesis and Theology 8. Louvain: Peeters, 1998.

Houtman, Cornelis. *Exodus*. Historical Commentary on the Old Testament, vol. 2. Louvain: Peeters, 1996.

Hunter, Ian. "Kant's *Religion* and Prussian Religious Policy." *Modern Intellectual History* 2, no. 1 (2005): 1–27.

Husserl, Edmund. *The Crisis of European Sciences and Transcendental Phenomenology: An Introduction to Phenomenological Philosophy*. Translated by David Carr. Evanston, IL: Northwestern University Press, 1970. German text: *Die Krisis der europäischen Wissenschaften und die transzendentale Phänomenologie. Eine Einleitung in die phänomenologische Philosophie*. Edited by Walter Biemel. 2nd ed. Husserliana 6. The Hague: Martinus Nijhoff, 1962.

Inwood, Michael J. *A Hegel Dictionary*. Oxford and Malden, MA: Blackwell, 1992.

Isidore of Seville. *The Etymologies of Isidore of Seville*. Translated by Stephen A. Barney et al. Cambridge: Cambridge University Press, 2006.

Janson, H. W. *Apes and Ape Lore in the Middle Ages and the Renaissance*. Studies of the Warburg Institute 20. London: Warburg Institute, 1952.

Jerome. "Letter LVII: To Pammachius on the Best Method of Translating." Translated by W. H. Fremantle, G. Lewis, and W. G. Martley. In *Nicene and Post-Nicene Fathers*, edited by Philip Schaff and Henry Wace, 2nd ser., 6:112–19. Buffalo: Christian Literature Publishing Co., 1893. The Latin text is available in *Sancti Eusebii Hieronymi Epistulae*. Pars 1, *Epistulae I–LXX*, ed. Isidor Hilberg, 503–26. Corpus Scriptorum Ecclesiasticorum Latinorum 54.1. Vienna: F. Tempsky; Leipzig: G. Freytag, 1910.

Jirku, Anton. "Zur magischen Bedeutung der Kleidung in Israel." *Zeitschrift für die alttestamentliche Wissenschaft* 37, no. 1 (January 1918): 109–25.

Johnson, Luke T. "The New Testament's Anti-Jewish Slander and the Conventions of Ancient Polemic." *Journal of Biblical Literature* 108 (1989): 419–41.

Jordan, Mark D. *Convulsing Bodies: Religion and Resistance in Foucault.* Stanford: Stanford University Press, 2015.

Julius, Anthony. *Transgressions: The Offences of Art.* Chicago: University of Chicago Press, 2002.

Kant, Immanuel. "An Answer to the Question: What Is Enlightenment?" In Kant, *Practical Philosophy*, translated by Mary J. Gregor, 11–22. Cambridge Edition of the Works of Immanuel Kant. Cambridge: Cambridge University Press, 1996. For the German text: *Kant's gesammelte Schriften*. Edited by Preußische Akademie der Wissenschaften. Erste Abtheilung, vol. 8, *Abhandlungen nach 1781*, 33–42. Berlin and Leipzig: de Gruyter, 1923.

———. "Conjectural Beginning of Human History." Translated by Allen W. Wood. In Kant, *Anthropology, History, and Education*, edited by Günter Zöller and Robert B. Louden, 160–75. Cambridge Edition of the Works of Immanuel Kant. Cambridge: Cambridge University Press, 2007. For the German text: *Kant's gesammelte Schriften*. Edited by Preußische Akademie der Wissenschaften. Erste Abtheilung, vol. 8, *Abhandlungen nach 1781*, 107–23. Berlin and Leipzig: de Gruyter, 1923.

———. "Idea for a Universal History with a Cosmopolitan Aim." Translated by Allen W. Wood. In Kant, *Anthropology, History, and Education*, edited by Günter Zöller and Robert B. Louden, 107–20. Cambridge Edition of the Works of Immanuel Kant. Cambridge: Cambridge University Press, 2007. For the German text: *Kant's gesammelte Schriften*. Edited by Preußische Akademie der Wissenschaften. Erste Abtheilung, vol. 8, *Abhandlungen nach 1781*, 15–32. Berlin and Leipzig: de Gruyter, 1923.

Kaufmann, Thomas. *A Short Life of Martin Luther*. Translated by Peter D. S. Krey and James D. Bratt. Reformation Resources, 1571–2017. Grand Rapids: Eerdmans, 2016.

Kedar-Kopfstein, Benjamin. "The Vulgate as a Translation: Some Semantic and Syntactical Aspects of Jerome's Version of the Hebrew Bible." PhD diss., Hebrew University of Jerusalem, 1968.

Kittel, Gerhard, and Gerhard Friedrich. *Theological Dictionary of the New Testament*. Translated by Geoffrey W. Bromiley. 10 vols. Grand Rapids: Eerdmans, 1964–1976.

Koch, Hugo. *Pseudo-Dionysius Areopagita in seinen Beziehungen zum Neu-*

platonismus und Mysterienwesen. Forschungen zur Christlichen Litte-
ratur- und Dogmengeschichte 1. Mainz: Franz Kirchheim, 1900.

Kreuzer, Johann. "Der Abgrund des Bewußtseins. Erinnerung und Selbsterkenntnis im zehnten Buch." In *Die Confessiones des Augustinus von
Hippo. Einführung und Interpretationen zu den dreizehn Büchern*, edited by Norbert Fischer and Cornelius Mayer, 445–87. Forschungen zur
europäischen Geistesgeschichte 1. Freiburg im Breisgau: Herder, 1998.

Kristeva, Julia. *Powers of Horror: An Essay on Abjection*. Translated by
Leon S. Roudiez. New York: Columbia University Press, 1982.

Kühnel, Harry. "Fastnacht." In *Lexikon des Mittelalters*, vol. 4, cols. 313–
14. 9 vols. Munich and Zurich: Artemis & Winkler/LexMA-Verlag,
1980–1999.

Kumler, Aden. "Manufacturing the Sacred in the Middle Ages: The Eucharist and Other Medieval Works of *Ars*." *English Language Notes* 53, no. 2
(Fall/Winter 2015): 9–43.

———. "The Multiplication of the Species: Eucharistic Morphology in the
Middle Ages." *RES: Anthropology and Aesthetics* 59/60 (Spring/Autumn
2011): 179–91.

Kyle, Donald G. *Spectacles of Death in Ancient Rome*. London: Routledge,
1998.

Lachièze-Rey, Pierre. "Saint Augustin précurseur de Kant dans la théorie
de la perception." In *Augustinus Magister. Congrès international augustinien, Paris 21–24 septembre 1954*, 1:425–28. 3 vols. Paris: Études
augustiniennes, 1954.

Lämmerzahl, Elfriede. *Der Sündenfall in der Philosophie des deutschen
Idealismus*. Neue Deutsche Forschungen, Abteilung Philosophie 3.
Berlin: Junker und Dünnhaupt, 1934.

Landgraf, Artur Michael. *Dogmengeschichte der Frühscholastik*. Vol. III/2,
Die Lehre von den Sakramenten. Regensburg: Pustet, 1955.

Lanza, Lidia, and Marco Toste. "The *Sentences* in Sixteenth-Century Iberian Scholasticism." In *Mediaeval Commentaries on the "Sentences" of
Peter Lombard*, vol. 3, edited by Philipp W. Rosemann, 416–503. Leiden
and Boston: Brill, 2015.

Lehmann, Karl. "'Sagen, was Sache ist': Der Blick auf die Wahrheit der Existenz. Heideggers Beziehung zu Luther." In *Heidegger und die christliche Tradition*, edited by Norbert Fischer and Friedrich-Wilhelm von
Herrmann, 149–66. Hamburg: Meiner, 2007.

Lehner, Ulrich L. *Kants Vorsehungskonzept auf dem Hintergrund der deutschen Schulphilosophie und theologie.* Brill's Studies in Intellectual History 149. Leiden and Boston: Brill, 2007.

Lemert, Charles G., and Garth Gillan. *Foucault: Social Theory as Transgression.* New York: Columbia University Press, 1982.

Ljungman, Henrik. *Das Gesetz erfüllen. Matth. 5,17ff. and 3,15 untersucht.* Lunds Universitets Årsskrift, N.F., Avd. 1, Bd. 50, Nr. 6. Lund: Gleerup, 1954.

Lottin, Odon, OSB. "Le prologue des Gloses sur les Sentences attribuées à Pierre de Poitiers." *Recherches de théologie ancienne et médiévale* 7 (1935): 70–73.

Louth, Andrew. "Maximus the Confessor on the Foolishness of God and the Play of the Word." In *The Wisdom and Foolishness of God: First Corinthians 1–2 in Theological Exploration,* edited by Christophe Chalamet and Hans-Christoph Askani, 89–99. Minneapolis: Fortress, 2015.

Luther, Martin. "Heidelberg Disputation." In *Luther's Works,* vol. 31, *Career of the Reformer I,* edited by Harold T. Grimm, 35–70. Philadelphia: Fortress, 1957. German text: *D. Martin Luthers Werke. Kritische Gesammtausgabe.* Vol. 1, pp. 353–74. Weimar: Hermann Böhlau, 1883.

———. *Lectures on Galatians (1535).* Translated by Jaroslav Pelikan. *Luther's Works* 26–27. Saint Louis: Concordia, 1963–1964.

MacIntyre, Alasdair. *Whose Justice? Which Rationality?* Notre Dame: University of Notre Dame Press, 1988.

Macy, Gary. "Of Mice and Manna: Quid Mus Sumit as a Pastoral Question." *Recherches de théologie ancienne et médiévale* 58 (1991): 157–66.

Marion, Jean-Luc. *God without Being.* Translated by Thomas A. Carlson. Religion and Postmodernism. Chicago: University of Chicago Press, 1995.

Marquard, Odo. "Felix culpa?—Bemerkungen zu einem Applikationschicksal von Genesis 3." In *Text und Applikation. Theologie, Jurisprudenz und Literaturwissenschaft im hermeneutischen Gespräch,* edited by Manfred Fuhrmann, Hans Robert Jauß, and Wolfhart Pannenberg, 53–71. Poetik und Hermeneutik 9. Munich: Fink, 1981.

Marshall, Bruce. "Christ and Israel: An Unsolved Problem in Catholic Theology." In *The Call of Abraham: Essays on the Election of Israel in Honor of Jon D. Levenson,* edited by Gary A. Anderson and Joel S. Kaminsky, 330–50. Notre Dame: University of Notre Dame Press, 2013.

Martin, Raymond-M., OP. "Notes sur l'œuvre littéraire de Pierre le Mangeur." *Recherches de théologie ancienne et médiévale* 3 (1931): 54–66.

McGrath, S. J. *The Early Heidegger and Medieval Philosophy: Phenomenology for the Godforsaken*. Washington, DC: Catholic University of America Press, 2006.

Mellinkoff, Ruth. *The Horned Moses in Medieval Art and Thought*. Berkeley: University of California Press, 1970.

Mezger, Werner. "Narr, V. Brauchtum." In *Lexikon des Mittelalters*, vol. 6, cols. 1026–27. 9 vols. Munich and Zurich: Artemis & Winkler/LexMA-Verlag, 1980–1999.

Milman, Henry Hart. *The History of Christianity, from the Birth of Christ to the Abolition of Paganism in the Roman Empire*. Vol. 2. London: John Murray, 1840.

Mitscherling, Jeff. "Deconstruction, *Destruktion*, and Dialogue." *Analecta Hermeneutica* 6 (2014): 1–8.

Mueller, Joseph G. "Forgetting as a Principle of Continuity in Tradition." *Theological Studies* 70 (2009): 751–81.

Murray, Michele. *Playing a Jewish Game: Gentile Christian Judaizing in the First and Second Centuries CE*. Studies in Christianity and Judaism 13. Waterloo, ON: Wilfrid Laurier University Press, 2004.

Mussies, Gerhard. "The Use of Hebrew and Aramaic in the Greek New Testament." *New Testament Studies* 30 (1984): 416–32.

Newman, John Henry. *An Essay on the Development of Christian Doctrine*. Notre Dame Series in the Great Books. Notre Dame: University of Notre Dame Press, 1989.

Nielsen, Lauge Olaf. *Theology and Philosophy in the Twelfth Century: A Study of Gilbert Porreta's Thinking and the Theological Expositions of the Doctrine of the Incarnation during the Period 1130–1180*. Acta theologica danica 15. Leiden: Brill, 1982.

Nietzsche, Friedrich. *The Birth of Tragedy and Other Writings*. Edited by Raymond Geuss and Ronald Speirs. Translated by Ronald Speirs. Cambridge: Cambridge University Press, 1999. German in *Werke. Kritische Gesamtausgabe*. Edited by Giorgio Colli and Mazzino Montinari. Dritte Abteilung, vol. 1. Berlin: de Gruyter, 1972.

Nirenberg, David. *Anti-Judaism: The Western Tradition*. New York: Norton, 2013.

Norden, Eduard. *Agnostos Theos. Untersuchungen zur Formengeschichte religiöser Rede*. 5th ed. Stuttgart: Teubner, 1971.

Novero, Cecilia. "Painful Painting and Brutal Ecstasy: The Material Actions of Günter Brus and Otto Muehl." *Seminar: A Journal of Germanic Studies* 43, no. 4 (November 2007): 453–68.

Oberman, Heiko. *Forerunners of the Reformation: The Shape of Late Me-*

dieval Thought, Illustrated by Key Documents. New York: Holt, Rinehart and Winston, 1966.

―――. *The Harvest of Medieval Theology: Gabriel Biel and Late Medieval Nominalism.* Cambridge, MA: Harvard University Press, 1963.

―――. *The Roots of Anti-Semitism in the Age of Renaissance and Reformation.* Translated by James I. Porter. Philadelphia: Fortress, 1984.

O'Connor, Mary Catherine. *The Art of Dying Well: The Development of the Ars Moriendi.* Columbia University Studies in English and Comparative Literature 156. New York: Columbia University Press, 1942.

Origen. "Letter of Origen to Gregory." Translated by Allan Menzies. In *The Ante-Nicene Fathers: Translations of the Writings of the Fathers down to A.D. 325, Original Supplement to the American Edition,* edited by Allan Menzies, 10:295–96. Grand Rapids: Eerdmans, n.d. Greek text: Grégoire le Thaumaturge. *Remerciement à Origène, suivi de la lettre d'Origène à Grégoire.* Edited and translated by Henri Crouzel, 185–95. Sources chrétiennes 148. Paris: Cerf, 1969.

Otto, Rudolf. *The Idea of the Holy: An Inquiry into the Non-Rational Factor in the Idea of the Divine and Its Relation to the Rational.* Translated by John W. Harvey. 2nd ed. Oxford: Oxford University Press; London: Humphrey Milford, 1950.

Overbeck, Franz. *Ueber die Auffassung des Streits des Paulus mit Petrus in Antiochien (Gal. 2, 11ff.) bei den Kirchenvätern.* In *Werke und Nachlaß,* vol. 2, *Schriften bis 1880,* edited by Ekkehard W. Stegemann and Rudolf Brändle, 221–334. Stuttgart and Weimar: J. B. Metzler, 1994.

Ozment, Steven. *The Age of Reform, 1250–1550: An Intellectual and Religious History of Late Medieval and Reformation Europe.* New Haven: Yale University Press, 1980.

Pereira, Matthew J. "From the Spoils of Egypt: An Analysis of Origen's *Letter to Gregory.*" In *Origeniana Decima: Origen as Writer,* edited by Sylwia Kaczmarek, Henryk Pietras, and Andrzej Dziadowiec, 221–48. Bibliotheca Ephemeridum Theologicarum Lovaniensium 244. Louvain: Peeters, 2011.

Peter Lombard. *The Sentences.* Translated by Giulio Silano. 4 vols. Mediaeval Sources in Translation 42, 43, 45, and 48. Toronto: Pontifical Institute of Mediaeval Studies, 2007–2010. Latin text: *Sententiae in IV libris distinctae.* Edited by Ignatius Brady, OFM. 2 vols. Spicilegium Bonaventurianum 4–5. Grottaferrata: Editiones Collegii S. Bonaventurae Ad Claras Aquas, 1971–1981.

Pieper, Josef. *Tradition: Concept and Claim*. Translated by E. Christian Kopff. South Bend, IN: St. Augustine's Press, 2010.

Plotinus. *Enneads V*. Translated by A. H. Armstrong. Loeb Classical Library 444. Cambridge, MA: Harvard University Press, 1984.

Pontifical Biblical Commission. *The Jewish People and Their Sacred Scriptures in the Christian Bible*. Boston: Pauline Books and Media, 2003.

Pope, Hugh, OP. *English Versions of the Bible*. Revised by Sebastian Bullough, OP. Saint Louis and London: Herder, 1952.

Porphyry. "On the Life of Plotinus and the Order of His Books." In *Plotinus I*, translated by A. H. Armstrong, 1–85. Loeb Classical Library 440. Cambridge, MA: Harvard University Press; London: Heinemann, 1966.

Preus, James Samuel. *From Shadow to Promise: Old Testament Interpretation from Augustine to the Young Luther*. Cambridge, MA: Belknap Press of Harvard University Press, 1969.

Prümmer, Dominicus M., OP, and Marie-Hyacinthe Laurent, OP, eds. *Fontes vitae S. Thomae Aquinatis*. Toulouse: Privat, 1912–1937.

Pseudo-Dionysius the Areopagite. *The Complete Works*. Translated by Colm Luibheid. Classics of Western Spirituality. Mahwah, NJ: Paulist Press, 1987.

———. *The Divine Names*. In *The Complete Works*, translated by Colm Luibheid, 47–131. Classics of Western Spirituality. Mahwah, NJ: Paulist Press, 1987.

———. *The Ecclesiastical Hierarchy*. In *The Complete Works*, translated by Colm Luibheid, 193–259. Classics of Western Spirituality. Mahwah, NJ: Paulist Press, 1987.

———. *The Mystical Theology*. In *The Complete Works*, translated by Colm Luibheid, 131–41. Classics of Western Spirituality. Mahwah, NJ: Paulist Press, 1987. Greek text: *Corpus Dionysiacum II*. Edited by Günter Heil and Adolf Martin Ritter. 2nd ed. Patristische Texte und Studien 67. Berlin: de Gruyter, 2012.

———. *Über die Mystische Theologie und Briefe*. Translated by Adolf Martin Ritter. Bibliothek der griechischen Literatur 40. Stuttgart: Hiersemann, 1994.

Quain, Edwin A., SJ. *The Medieval Accessus ad Auctores*. New York: Fordham University Press, 1986.

Rad, Gerhard von. *Genesis: A Commentary*. Translated by John H. Marks. Old Testament Library. Philadelphia: Westminster, 1961.

Ratzinger, Joseph [Pope Benedict XVI]. *"In the Beginning...": A Catholic Understanding of the Story of Creation and the Fall*. Translated by Boniface

Ramsey. Ressourcement: Retrieval and Renewal in Catholic Thought. Grand Rapids: Eerdmans, 1995.

———. *The Theology of History in St. Bonaventure*. Translated by Zachary Hayes, OFM. Chicago: Franciscan Herald Press, 1989. Now published unabridged in the original German version: *Offenbarungsverständnis und Geschichtstheologie Bonaventuras. Habilitationsschrift und Bonaventura-Studien*. Gesammelte Schriften 2. Freiburg im Breisgau: Herder, 2009.

Reichert, Klaus. "'It Is Time': The Buber-Rosenzweig Bible Translation in Context." In *The Translatability of Cultures: Figurations of the Space Between*, edited by Sanford Budick and Wolfgang Iser, 169–85. Irvine Studies in the Humanities. Stanford: Stanford University Press, 1996.

Richardson, William J., SJ. *Heidegger: Through Phenomenology to Thought*. 4th ed. New York: Fordham University Press, 2003.

Rico, Christophe. "L'art de la traduction chez saint Jérôme. La Vulgate à l'aune de la Néovulgate: l'exemple du quatrième évangile." *Revue des études latines* 83 (2005): 194–218.

Römer, Thomas. *Les cornes de Moïse. Faire entrer la Bible dans l'histoire*. Leçons inaugurales du Collège de France. Paris: Collège de France/Fayard, 2009.

Roques, René. "Note sur la notion de *theologia* selon le Pseudo-Denys l'Aréopagite." *Revue d'ascétique et de mystique* 25 (1949): 200–212. Reprinted in the author's *Structures théologiques. De la gnose à Richard de Saint-Victor*, 135–45. Bibliothèque de l'École des hautes études. Section des sciences religieuses 72. Paris: Presses universitaires de France, 1962.

Rorem, Paul. *Biblical and Liturgical Symbols within the Pseudo-Dionysian Synthesis*. Studies and Texts 71. Toronto: Pontifical Institute of Mediaeval Studies, 1984.

———. *Pseudo-Dionysius: A Commentary on the Texts and an Introduction to Their Influence*. Oxford: Oxford University Press, 1993.

Rosemann, Philipp W. "The Historicization of the Transcendental in Postmodern Philosophy." In *Die Logik des Transzendentalen. Festschrift für Jan A. Aertsen zum 65. Geburtstag*, edited by Martin Pickavé, 701–13. Miscellanea Mediaevalia 30. Berlin: de Gruyter, 2003.

———. "The Lutheran Heidegger: Reflections on S. J. McGrath, *The Early Heidegger and Medieval Philosophy*." *Philotheos: International Journal for Philosophy and Theology* 7 (2007): 327–32. Reprinted in *Analecta Hermeneutica* 1 (2009): 343–50.

————. *Omne agens agit sibi simile: A "Repetition" of Scholastic Metaphysics.* Louvain Philosophical Studies 12. Louvain: Leuven University Press, 1996.

————. *Peter Lombard.* Great Medieval Thinkers. New York: Oxford University Press, 2004.

————. "Postmodern Philosophy and J.-L. Marion's Eucharistic Realism." In *The Mystery of Faith: Reflections on the Encyclical Ecclesia de Eucharistia,* edited by Maurice Hogan, SSC, and James McEvoy, 224–44. Blackrock, Co. Dublin: Columba Press, 2005. Republished with corrections in *Transcendence and Phenomenology.* Edited by Peter M. Candler Jr. and Conor Cunningham, 84–110. London: SCM, 2007.

————. "Robert Grosseteste." In *The Oxford History of Literary Translation in English,* edited by Roger Ellis, 1:126–36. Oxford: Oxford University Press, 2008.

————. *The Story of a Great Medieval Book: Peter Lombard's "Sentences."* Rethinking the Middle Ages 2. Toronto: University of Toronto Press, 2007.

————. "Wandering in the Path of the Averroean System: Is Kant's Doctrine on the *Bewußtsein überhaupt* Averroistic?" *American Catholic Philosophical Quarterly* 73 (1999): 187–230.

Rosenzweig, Franz. "Scripture and Luther." In Martin Buber and Franz Rosenzweig, *Scripture and Translation,* translated by Lawrence Rosenwald with Everett Fox, 47–69. Indiana Studies in Biblical Literature. Bloomington and Indianapolis: Indiana University Press, 1994.

Ross, J. M. "Amen." *Expository Times* 102 (1991): 166–71.

Sampley, J. Paul. "The First Letter to the Corinthians." In *The New Interpreter's Bible,* 10:771–1003. Nashville: Abingdon, 2002.

Sardinha, Diogo. "L'éthique et les limites de la transgression." *Lignes,* no. 17 (2005): 125–36.

Schaap, Sybe. *Die Unfähigkeit zu vergessen. Nietzsches Umwertung der Wahrheitsfrage.* Translated [from Dutch] by Monique J. and Gershom M. H. Ratheiser-van der Velde. Würzburg: Königshausen & Neumann, 2002.

Schäublin, Christoph. "*De doctrina christiana*: A Classic of Western Culture?" In *De doctrina christiana: A Classic of Western Culture,* edited by Duane W. H. Arnold and Pamela Bright, 47–67. Christianity and Judaism in Antiquity 9. Notre Dame: University of Notre Dame Press, 1995.

Schildenberger, Johannes. "Kleidung. I. Biblisch." In *Lexikon für Theologie und Kirche*, vol. 6, cols. 324–25. 2nd ed. Freiburg im Breisgau: Herder, 1961.

Seybold, Klaus. "Zur Vorgeschichte der liturgischen Formel 'Amen.'" *Theologische Zeitschrift* 48 (1992): 109–17.

Sgarbi, Marco. "Immanuel Kant, Universal Understanding, and the Meaning of Averroism in the German Enlightenment." In *Renaissance Averroism and Its Aftermath: Arabic Philosophy in Early Modern Europe*, edited by Anna Akasoy and Guido Giglioni, 255–69. International Archives of the History of Ideas 211. Dordrecht: Springer, 2013.

Simmel, Georg. *The Philosophy of Money*. Translated by Tom Bottomore and David Frisby. 3rd ed. London: Routledge, 2004.

Simonsohn, Shlomo. *The Apostolic See and the Jews: Documents, 492–1404*. Studies and Texts 94. Toronto: Pontifical Institute of Mediaeval Studies, 1988.

———. *The Apostolic See and the Jews: History*. Studies and Texts 109. Toronto: Pontifical Institute of Mediaeval Studies, 1991.

Sommer, Christian. *Heidegger, Aristote, Luther. Les sources aristotéliciennes et néo-testamentaires d'Être et temps*. Épiméthée. Paris: Presses universitaires de France, 2006.

Stang, Charles M. *Apophasis and Pseudonymity in Dionysius the Areopagite: "No Longer I."* Oxford: Oxford University Press, 2012.

———. "Dionysius, Paul and the Significance of the Synonym." In *Rethinking Dionysius the Areopagite*, edited by Sarah Coakley, 11–25. Chichester, UK: Wiley-Blackwell, 2009.

Stavans, Ilan, and Jorge J. E. Gracia. "On Desecration: Andres Serrano, *Piss Christ*." In Stavans and Gracia, *Thirteen Ways of Looking at Latino Art*, 49–60. Durham, NC: Duke University Press, 2014.

Steiner, Reinhard. "'Deposuit potentes de sede': Das 'Narrenfest' in der Plastik des Hoch- und Spätmittelalters." In *Aufsätze zur Kunstgeschichte. Festschrift für Hermann Bauer zum 60. Geburtstag*, edited by Karl Mösender and Andreas Prater, 92–108. Hildesheim: Olms, 1991.

Stoelen, Anselm, OCart. "Denys the Carthusian." In *Spirituality through the Centuries: Ascetics and Mystics of the Western Church*, edited by James Walsh, 220–32. New York: P. J. Kenedy, 1965.

Sullivan, Nikki. *Tattooed Bodies: Subjectivity, Textuality, Ethics, and Pleasure*. Westport, CT: Praeger, 2001.

Surya, Michel. *Georges Bataille: An Intellectual Biography*. Translated by Krzysztof Fijalkowski and Michael Richardson. London: Verso, 2002.

Teichtweier, Georg. "Kleidung. IV. Mode/V. Fehlhaltungen." In *Lexikon für*

Theologie und Kirche, vol. 6, cols. 325–26. 2nd ed. Freiburg im Breisgau: Herder, 1961.

Thijssen, J. M. M. H. *Censure and Heresy at the University of Paris, 1200–1400*. Middle Ages Series. Philadelphia: University of Pennsylvania Press, 1998.

Thurnher, Rainer. "Heideggers Distanzierung von der metaphysisch geprägten Theologie und Gottesvorstellung." In *Die Gottesfrage im Denken Martin Heideggers*, edited by Norbert Fischer and Friedrich-Wilhelm von Herrmann, 175–94. Blaue Reihe. Hamburg: Meiner, 2011.

Towner, W. Sibley. "Interpretations and Reinterpretations of the Fall." In *Modern Biblical Scholarship: Its Impact on Theology and Proclamation*, edited by Francis A. Eigo, 53–85. Villanova, PA: Villanova University Press, 1984.

Trawny, Peter. *Heidegger and the Myth of a Jewish World Conspiracy*. Translated by Andrew J. Mitchell. Chicago: University of Chicago Press, 2016.

Vaihinger, Hans. *The Philosophy of "As If": A System of the Theoretical, Practical, and Religious Fictions of Mankind*. Translated by C. K. Ogden. 2nd ed. International Library of Psychology, Philosophy, and Scientific Method. London: Routledge and Kegan Paul, 1935.

Van Fleteren, Frederick. "St. Augustine, Neoplatonism, and the Liberal Arts: The Background to *De doctrina christiana*." In *De doctrina christiana: A Classic of Western Culture*, edited by Duane W. H. Arnold and Pamela Bright, 14–24. Christianity and Judaism in Antiquity 9. Notre Dame: University of Notre Dame Press, 1995.

Vanneste, Jan, SJ. "Is the Mysticism of Pseudo-Dionysius Genuine?" *International Philosophical Quarterly* 3 (1963): 286–306.

———. *Le mystère de Dieu. Essai sur la structure rationnelle de la doctrine mystique du pseudo-Denys l'Aréopagite*. Museum Lessianum, Section philosophique 45. Bruges and Paris: Desclée de Brouwer, 1959.

Wall, Robert W. "The Acts of the Apostles." In *The New Interpreter's Bible*, 10:1–368. Nashville: Abingdon, 2002.

Wassermann, Dirk. *Dionysius der Kartäuser. Einführung in Werk und Gedankenwelt*. Analecta cartusiana 133. Salzburg: Institut für Anglistik und Amerikanistik, 1996.

Weir, Anthony, and James Jerman. *Images of Lust: Sexual Carvings on Medieval Churches*. London: B. T. Batsford, 1993.

Wentersdorf, Karl P. "The Symbolic Significance of *Figurae Scatologicae* in Gothic Manuscripts." In *Word, Picture, and Spectacle*, edited by Clifford

Davidson, 1–19. Early Drama, Art, and Music Monograph Series 5. Kalamazoo, MI: Medieval Institute Publications, 1984.

Westermann, Claus. *Genesis*. Vol. 1, *Genesis 1–11*. 3rd ed. Biblischer Kommentar, Altes Testament I/1. Neukirchen-Vluyn: Neukirchener Verlag, 1983.

———. *Genesis 1–11: A Commentary*. Translated by John J. Scullion. Minneapolis: Augsburg, 1984.

———. *Welt und Mensch im Urgeschehen. Die biblische Urgeschichte Genesis (1. Mose) 1–11*. Stuttgart: Deutsche Bibelgesellschaft, 1999.

Williams, Thomas. "Biblical Interpretation." In *The Cambridge Companion to Augustine*, edited by Norman Kretzmann and Eleonore Stump, 59–70. Cambridge: Cambridge University Press, 2001.

Wilson, Jeffrey Dirk. "Foucault as Inverted Neo-Platonist in 'A Preface to Transgression.'" Paper delivered at the Sixty-Second Annual Conference of the Metaphysical Society of America in 2011 (http://www.meta physicalsociety.org/2011/Session%20V.Wilson.pdf, accessed December 28, 2017).

Winter, Thomas Arne. *Traditionstheorie*. Philosophische Untersuchungen 42. Tübingen: Mohr Siebeck, 2017.

Wirth, Jean. "Les singes dans les marges à drôleries des manuscrits gothiques." *Micrologus* 8 (2000): 429–44.

Zenger, Erich. *Israel am Sinai. Analysen und Interpretationen zu Exodus 17–34*. Altenberge: CIS-Verlag, 1982.

Index of Subjects and Names

Abbt, Christine, 140n14
abject, abjection, 55, 106, 190–91; and crucifixion, xii, 51, 53–58, 77–78, 101–2, 147, 186, 198; and the Eucharist, 56–57, 190
Albertz, Rainer, 167n5
Allen, Joel S., 89n28, 90n31, 91nn34–35, 92, 92n37, 95n42
Allison, Dale C., Jr., 52, 54n7, 57, 59, 61, 63
Alverny, Marie-Thérèse d', 130n50
Ambrose, 94
"amen," 127–29
anathema, 67–68, 88
anitas, 130
Antioch, incident at, 66–76, 78, 103, 116, 144, 150
Apollonian vs. Dionysian. *See* Nietzsche: and Apollonian vs. Dionysian
Appleyard, Bryan, 197n83
Aristotle, 130, 132
ars moriendi, 137
"as if," 82–83, 85, 192
Auerbach, Erich, 176
Augustine, 53n2, 109, 136–37; *Confessions*, 136–42; *De doctrina christiana*, 95–99, 104, 123, 128, 142; on despoliation narrative, 95–99; on forgetting, 139–40, 143; on memory, 136–40, 143; and Neoplatonism, 3, 119; on time, 141–43
Averroës, 181–82n41
Avicenna, 130, 132

Bakhtin, Mikhail, 195n75
Barclay, John M. G., 78n2
Barrett, C. K., 84–85
Bartelink, G. J. M., 122n26
Bataille, Georges, 16n31, 18, 55n11
Batholeyns, Gil, 188n58, 194n72
Bayer, John, OCist, 75n55
Bender, Claudia, 28n8, 55n9, 172n19
Benson, Bruce Ellis, 22n55
Bernauer, James, SJ, 17n35
Biel, Gabriel, 146
big bang, 141
Biser, Eugen, 166n2
Blue, Gregory, 55n11
Bonaventure, 47n41, 57n14, 107, 132
Boring, M. Eugene, 58n18, 59–61, 64n30, 65n32
Bouchard, Donald F., 5n7
Bourgon, Jerôme, 55n11
Bouyer, Louis, 36, 39n33
Brague, Rémi, 100
Brock, Sebastian P., 123–24
Brook, Timothy, 55n11
Brown, Rachel Fulton, 16n32
Brown, Raymond E., SS, 66n33
Brueggemann, Walter, 25, 90, 100, 101n5, 166–67, 170
Brus, Günter, 195
Buber, Martin, 132
Bultmann, Christoph, 175n24
Bultmann, Rudolf, 86n22, 88, 152–53

Buren, John van, 147nn28–29, 153n45
Burgundio of Pisa, 130–31
Burnett, Charles S. F., 130
Burton, Ernest De Witt, 67n35
Bynum, Carolyn Walker, 16n32

Callixtus II (pope), 151
Camille, Michael, 191, 194n72
Capreolus, John, 146
Caputo, John D., 160n63, 162n67, 163
Chadwick, Henry, 139n12
Chadwick, Owen, 114n18
Châtillon, Jean, 193n69
Chevallier, Philippe (Foucault scholar), 12n23, 14n27, 15n29, 16n31
Chevallier, Philippe (editor of *Diony-siaca*), 129n47
Childs, Brevard S., 25n2, 26, 30
Christ. *See* Jesus Christ
Christianity: and despoliation/"pil-laging," 6, 114, 117–19, 131 (*see also* despoliation narrative); and Gre-co-Roman culture, 3, 77–78, 80–81, 83–90, 92–99, 102–3, 117–21, 144, 146; and identity formation, 66–76, 79–83, 87–88, 97–98, 100, 102–4, 113–19, 121, 144, 150; and reform, 146 (*see also* Reformation); and scholasticism (*see* scholasticism)
Chrysostom, John, 81, 130
Cicero, 122, 131
Clement of Alexandria, 76
clothes, ritual and social significance, 28, 171–72, 179–80. *See also habitus* theory (of the incarnation)
Cohen, Jeremy, 71
Colish, Marcia L., 43n37
Congar, Yves, OP, xii, 109–10n10, 150
Constance, Council of, 146
Cook, John Granger, 54nn5–6, 8
Corinth, 78, 80
Crowe, Benjamin D., 146, 153n45

Dagron, Gilbert, 67n34, 74
Dán, Róbert, 67n34
Danto, Arthur C., 195–96

Davies, W. D., 54n7, 59, 61, 63
"death of God," 6, 17–18, 24, 165–66, 166n2
Defert, Daniel, 16n34
Denys the Carthusian (Dionysius Cartusianus), 105–13, 129, 133–34, 146, 202–4; on hierarchy of revelation, 109–13; and negative theology, 108–9; and Peter Lombard, 110–13; and Pseu-do-Dionysius, 107–8, 112; on tradition, 106–13, 133–35, 143–45
Derrida, Jacques: and deconstruction, xii–xiii, 155–56, 163
despoliation narrative (Exod. 3:21–22), 3, 6, 89–92, 114, 120, 131–32; Chris-tian use *contra* Judaism, 90, 94, 103, 131–32; Christian use of Greco-Roman culture, 3, 92–99, 103, 117–19, 131–32, 198–99. *See also* Christianity: and despoliation/"pillaging"
destruction, xii; vs. *Abbau*, 154–55; vs. deconstruction, xii, 155, 163; in Heidegger, 156–61; in Luther, 146–50
dialectic, 4–8, 15, 21, 36, 84, 116; of Apol-lonian/Dionysian, 11–13; and culture, 11–13, 72; and Hegel, 3, 6, 8–9; of mem-ory/forgetting, 138, 140, 140n14
Dilthey, Wilhelm, 184n48
Dittmar, Olivier, 188n58, 194n72
Dollimore, Jonathan, 88n26
Douay-Rheims translation of Scripture. *See* translation
Dunn, James D. G., 67n35, 68, 68n38
Düsing, Wolfgang, 175n24

Edgar, Andrew, 184n48
Edwards, Mark U., Jr., 151, 151nn41, 43
Elsig, Frédéric, 187n56
Emery, Kent, Jr., 106n4
Enlightenment, 113, 115, 117, 195; and Kant, 157, 166, 175–77, 183–84
Epicureanism, 84, 87
Erasmus, Desiderius, 146
Eriugena, John Scottus, 119, 143
Euripides, 8, 10
Ewald, François, 14

fall narrative (Gen. 2:4–3:24): and civilization, 172, 179–80; compositional aspects of, 167, 170–71, 173–74; as fable, 167, 173–74; Kant on, 174–84, 184n8, 185; and limits, 166, 169–71, 177–79, 184–85; and tradition, 166; and transgression, 167–74, 178–81, 185

festa stultorum, 191–94

Ficino, Marsilio, 120

Fischer, Norbert, 142n20, 143n22

Flynn, Thomas, 10n19

Folliet, Georges, 91n34

fomen peccatis, 16

foolishness of the cross, 78–88, 101, 192

forgetting, 1–2, 111–13, 133–35. *See also* Augustine: on forgetting; dialectic: of memory/forgetting; tradition (Christian): and forgetting.

Foster, Hal, 185

Foucault, Michel, 6n9; and Apollonian vs. Dionysian, 10–14, 22, 194; on Christian mysticism, 6, 15–19; on empirico-transcendental doublet, 20–21; and the *episteme* / historical *a priori*, 7, 7n11, 14, 19–21, 161; on "founder of discursivity," 110–11, 111n14; and Hegel, 8–9; and Heidegger, 14, 21; *The History of Sexuality*, 10, 171n16; and Kant, 14–22, 166; on the limit, 5, 10–12, 16–20, 22–24, 29, 72–73, 103, 165–66, 171n16, 197; on madness, 10–11, 22, 24, 194; and Nietzsche, 7–14, 21–22, 166n2; on Occident vs. Orient, 10–12, 12n23; *The Order of Things*, 7n11, 15, 20–21, 142n18; on the Other/Outside, 10–14, 17–19, 22–24, 29, 72–76, 101, 103, 150, 165; "Préface" (to 1st ed. *Folie et déraison*), 7, 9–11, 13, 15, 18, 21–22; "A Preface to Transgression," 5–6, 15–17, 17nn37–38, 18–19, 21–23; on sexuality, premodern vs. modern, 15–18; "The Thought of the Outside," 16–17; on transgression, 5–7, 14–19, 23–24, 100–101, 165, 171n16, 197

Frei, Hans W., 176

Frend, W. H. C., 135n6

Fretheim, Terence, 169, 170n12

Freud, Sigmund, 12, 17, 111nn12,14, 140n14, 178, 191

Gadamer, Hans-Georg, 156n53, 163

Gaddi, Barbara Ellen, 132n54

Galen, 130

Galileo, 154

Gillan, Garth, 23n56

Glicksman, Andrew T., 91n32, 126n37

Golitzin, Alexander, 36n25

Gordon, Colin, 11n22

Gracia, Jorge J. E., 186–87

Gregory of Nyssa, 42

Gregory Thaumaturgus (Gregory of Neocaesarea), 92–95

Grosseteste, Robert, 129–30

Gutting, Gary, 15n29

habitus theory (of the incarnation), 52–53

Haldane, John, 121n24

Hallamaa, Olli, 145

Han, Béatrice, 15n29

Hanson, R. P. C., 92n37

Harnack, Adolf von, 3n4

Hays, Richard B., 68n38, 74

Hegel, Georg Wilhelm Friedrich, 13–14, 195; and dialectic, 3, 6, 8–9; on Jews, 74; and sublation, 3, 70, 70n43

Heidegger, Martin: *Being and Time*, 154–63; and *Destruktion*, xii–xiii, 154–56, 158–64; and Foucault, 14, 21; and *Holzweg*, 164; on Jews, 74; and Kant, 157, 160; and limits, 159–61, 164; and Luther, 153–55, 158; "The Question concerning Technology," 21, 182; on tradition, 156–61, 163–64; on *Wiederholung*, 161–64

Heine, Heinrich, 74

Hengel, Martin, 54, 54n6, 55

Herder, Johann Gottfried, 175–76, 181n41

Hilary of Poitiers, 53n2, 96

Hilduin, 119

Holte, Ragnar, 98n47

Honorius of Autun, 189–90

Horst, Pieter W. van der, 86n21
Houtman, Cornelis, 27n6, 28n8, 32n17
human sciences, 20–21
Hunter, Ian, 184n48
Husserl, Edmund, 154–55, 157

Inwood, Michael J., 70n43
Isidore of Seville, 188n59

Janson, H. W., 188n57
Jerome, 30–31, 86, 121–26, 199
Jesus Christ: and Aramaic, 60–61, 63,
    127; crucifixion of, 2–3, 51–59, 61–62,
    66, 77–83, 87–88, 101–2, 127, 198 (see
    also Luther: and theology of the
    cross; Serrano: Piss Christ); incarna-
    tion of, 2, 51–53, 56–57, 77, 101, 141, 143,
    198; and the law, 57, 59–66, 70–71, 86,
    88, 102, 109–10, 128, 198; as new Moses
    (Gospel of Matthew), 42, 51–52, 57–59,
    66; Sermon on the Mount, 59–62; and
    transgression/radicalization, 62–66,
    83, 102, 198
Jews/Judaism and Christianity, 2–4,
    66–69, 71–76, 80, 87–88, 94, 100, 103,
    118–19, 121, 150–53 (see also law: Chris-
    tian sublation of); "hermeneutic
    Jews," 71; and Holocaust, 74–75, 132,
    152; and "Judaizing," 66–67, 69, 71, 75;
    in Luther, 150–52
Jirku, Anton, 28n8
Johnson, Luke T., 73
Jolivet, Vincent, 188n58, 194n72
Jordan, Mark D., 16n31
Josephus, Titus Flavius, 91
Julius, Anthony, 186, 195
Justin Martyr, 98

Kant, Immanuel: "An Answer to the
    Question: What Is Enlightenment?,"
    157, 183–84; Anthropology from a
    Pragmatic Point of View, 15; and the a
    priori, 14, 19–21; "Conjectural Begin-
    ning of Human History," 174, 183–84,
    184n8; on the fall, 174–84, 184n8, 185;
    and Herder, 175–76, 181n41; on Jews,

74; and limits, 19–20, 160–61, 166, 177,
    184–85. See also Foucault: and Kant
Kaufmann, Thomas, 150n36, 151n39
Kedar-Kopstein, Benjamin, 124n33
Kittel, Gerhard, 53n4, 66n34, 68n36
Koch, Hugo, 33n18
Kreuzer, Johann, 140
Kristeva, Julia, 55n10
Kühnel, Harry, 194n74
Kumler, Aden, 190n60
Kyle, Donald G., 77

Lachièze-Rey, Pierre, 142n20
Lämmerzahl, Elfriede, 178n32
Landgraf, Artur Michael, 56n13
Lanza, Lidia, 110n11
Lateran, Fifth Council of the, 146
law: Christian sublation of, 2–3, 25,
    70–76, 86–87, 94, 103, 105, 109, 116, 118;
    as covenant, 2–3, 25, 41, 49–50, 87–88,
    100–101, 115, 118–19, 143; and Jesus, 57,
    59–66, 70–71, 86, 88, 102, 109–10, 128;
    and Luther, 149–50; and Moses, 2, 26,
    29, 32–33, 41, 49–50, 57, 59–60, 143;
    and Paul, 4, 65n32, 67–76, 88, 116, 149;
    and purification/cleanliness, 28–29,
    32, 34, 36, 64–66, 68, 172
Lefèvre-d'Étaples, Jacques, 146
Lehmann, Karl, 153n45
Lehner, Ulrich L., 183n47
Lemert, Charles G., 23n56
Lille, MS. Bibliothèque municipale, 116
limit, limits, 4–5, 11–12; premodern vs.
    modern, 17–19, 165, 185, 196–97, 200.
    See also fall narrative: and limits;
    Foucault: on the limit; Heidegger:
    and limits; Kant: and limits; Mount
    Sinai narrative: and physical limits/
    boundaries; Mount Sinai narrative:
    and spiritual limits/boundaries;
    Pseudo-Peter of Poitiers gloss: on
    limits
lingchi, 55n11
Livy (Titus Livius Patavinus), 134–35
Ljungman, Henrik, 63n28
logocentrism, 8

logos spermatikos, 98
Louis de Nevers, 187–91, 195
Lubac, Henri de, SJ, 74n50, 97n45
Luibheid, Colm, 39n32
Luria, Aleksandr, 134
Luther, Martin: anti-Judaism of, 150–53; and "destruction," xii–xiii, 146–50, 155, 164; and Heidegger (*see under* Heidegger); *Heidelberg Disputation*, 147–49, 153; *On the Jews and Their Lies*, 151–52; and theology of the cross, xii, 147–49, 199; and translation, 119, 124, 127, 199

MacIntyre, Alasdair, 27, 43, 113–19, 143
Macquarrie, John, 156n54, 158–59, 162n67, 163–64
Macy, Gary, 56n13
madness, 10–12. *See also* foolishness of the cross
Maimonides, 132
Mapplethorpe, Robert, 196–97
Marion, Jean-Luc, 56n12, 82n11
Marius Victorinus, 119
Marquard, Odo, 180–82
Marshall, Bruce, 150n37
Martin, Raymond-M., OP, 44–45n39
Massumi, Brian, 17n35
McGrath, S. J., 153n45
Mellinkoff, Ruth, 31
memory. *See* Augustine: on memory; dialectic: of memory/"forgetting"; "tradition" (Christian): and memory. *Cf.* forgetting
Mezger, Werner, 194n74
Michael Scot, 119
Milman, Henry Hart, 135
Mitscherling, Jeff, 156n53
Morrison, Jim, 21n49
Moses: ascent on Mount Sinai, 25–34, 36–38, 40–41, 101, 140, 198; "horned," 30–32, 38, 42, 48, 50, 53, 101, 199; in *The Mystical Theology*, 34, 36–37, 40–41
Mount Sinai narrative (Exod. 19, parts of Exod. 24, 34), 2, 25–27, 51, 77; compositional aspects of, 30, 40, 115, 167; in Exodus, 25–33, 40–42, 100–101,

115, 167, 169; in Galatians, 71–72; in *The Mystical Theology*, 25, 34–42; and physical limits/boundaries, 28–31, 33, 37–39, 42–43, 47–50, 57–58, 101, 126–27, 140; in the Pseudo-Peter of Poitiers gloss, 26, 42–50; and spiritual limits/boundaries, 38–39, 42–51, 53, 101, 165; and transgression, 26, 29–31, 33, 37–40, 42, 45–50, 101, 165–66, 198
Mueller, Joseph, 133–34
Murray, Michele, 68–69n38
Mussies, Gerhard, 60n23

negative/apophatic theology, 6, 70, 81, 109; and Denys the Carthusian, 108–9; and Foucault, 15, 17; and Pseudo-Dionysius, 17, 36, 38–40, 81, 108, 165, 199–200
Neoplatonism, 3, 12, 35, 37, 112, 119, 143
Newman, John Henry, 114, 117
Nicholas of Cusa, 33n18
Nielsen, Lauge Olaf, 53n2
Nietzsche, Friedrich, 76n57, 82n12; *Advantages and Disadvantages of History for Life*, 133; and Apollonian vs. Dionysian, 7–12, 170, 193–94; *The Birth of Tragedy*, 7–11; and death of God, 6, 17–18, 166n2; and Foucault, 7–14, 21–22, 166n2; and madness, 22; and transgression, 14–15, 22n55; transvaluation of values, 3–4; and the *Übermensch*, 21–22, 195
Nirenberg, David, 73, 74n52, 150–51
Norden, Eduard, 84n15, 85–86
Novero, Cecilia, 195n77

Oberman, Heiko, 106n3, 146n27, 151n40
Ockham, William of, 146
O'Connor, Mary Catherine, 137n8
Origen, 76, 96–97, 118, 131; *Letter to Gregory*, 92–96, 103
Other/Outside. *See* Foucault: on the Other/Outside; Jews/Judaism; limit/limits
Otto, Rudolf, 55
Overbeck, Franz, 76n57

Oxford, MS. Bodleian Library, Douce 5, 187–91, 194–95
Ozment, Steven, 146n26

Paul: Areopagus narrative, 83–88, 102; and believers in Antioch, 66–73, 78, 103, 115–16, 150; and believers in Corinth, 78–82; and eschatology, 82–83, 102; and sublation, 3, 69–76, 86–88, 116, 166–67. *See also* specific epistles (Scripture index)
Pereira, Matthew J., 92–93n37
Peter Comestor, 45n39
Peter Lombard, 110–11; *The Book of Sentences,* 26, 43–45, 53n2, 56, 105–7, 110, 113, 145, 146n25, 184–85n49. *See also* Denys the Carthusian; Pseudo-Peter of Poitiers gloss
Philo of Alexandria, 91–92
Pieper, Josef, 98–99n48
Plotinus, 1, 12, 16, 117; and Foucault, 16n34; and *tolma,* 1, 142–43
Pontifical Biblical Commission, 74–75, 118–19
Pope, Hugh, OP, 125n35
Porphyry, 12
Preus, James Samuel, 74n50
Proclus, 33, 35–36
Pseudo-Dionysius the Areopagite, 17, 33–35, 83, 119, 165, 199–200; and Denys the Carthusian, 107–8, 112; Dionysius the Areopagite (Acts 17:34), 33, 42, 87; *The Divine Names,* 35–37, 81, 83; *The Ecclesiastical Hierarchy,* 35–37; on Mount Sinai narrative, 25, 34–42; on mystical ascent, 34, 36–42, 50; *The Mystical Theology,* 25, 34–42, 104, 108; and negative theology, 17, 36, 38–40, 81, 108, 165, 199–200; and transgression, 37–40, 42, 50, 165; and translation, 41–42, 129
Pseudo-Peter of Poitiers gloss (on *The Book of Sentences*), 26, 43, 49, 104–5, 201–2; on hierarchy of revelation/mediation, 49–50, 104–5; on limits, 47–50, 105; and Mount Sinai narra-

tive, 26, 43–50, 104–5; and *revelatio,* 46–48, 105; and tradition, 104–5; and transgression, 47–50, 105

Quain, Edwin A., SJ, 43n38
Quintus Curtius Rufus, 134

Rad, Gerhard von, 172–74
Ratzinger, Joseph (Pope Benedict XVI), 46–48, 114n18, 170
Reformation, 6, 199; and Luther, 146–53
Reichert, Klaus, 132
repetition/retrieval (*Wiederholung*), 161–64
revelation (*revelatio*), 46–47
Richard of St. Victor, 192–94
Richardson, William J., SJ, 163
Rico, Christophe, 124
Ritter, Adolf Martin, 33n19
Robinson, Edward, 156n54, 158–59, 162n67, 163–64
Römer, Thomas, 31n15
Rorem, Paul, 35–36
Rosenzweig, Franz, 119n21, 123n28, 127n39, 132
Roseth, Roger, 145
Rousseau, Jean-Jacques, 181

Sade, Donatien-Alphonse-François, Marquis de, 17
Sampley, J. Paul, 78–79
Sardinha, Diogo, 23n57
satyr, 8–9, 31
Schaap, Sybe, 133–34n2
Schäublin, Christoph, 95n44
Schildenberger, Johannes, 172n19
scholasticism; and Heidegger, 153n45, 158; history of, 26, 45, 56–57, 106, 110, 112, 119, 144–47, 190; and the Reformation, 199; and *revelatio,* 46–48. *See also* Denys the Carthusian; Peter Lombard; Pseudo-Peter of Poitiers gloss; Thomas Aquinas
Schopenhauer, Arthur, 74
Serrano, Andres: *Piss Christ,* 186–87, 194–95

Serres, Michel, 93n37
Seybold, Klaus, 129n45
Sgarbi, Marco, 182n41
Simmel, Georg, 196n81
Simmons, Lance, 121n24
Simon, Sherry, 5n7
Simonsohn, Shlomo, 151n42
Socrates, 8, 10, 83–88
Sommer, Christian, 149nn32–33,
    153nn45, 47
Speirs, Ronald, 8n15
Stambaugh, Joan, 156n54, 158–59,
    162n67
Stang, Charles M., 34n20
Steiner, Reinhard, 193–94n70
Stoelen, Anselm, OCart, 106n5
Stoicism, 84, 87
sublation: Christian, of Greco-Roman
    culture, 87, 93–94; Christian, of Juda-
    ism, 3, 70–76, 86–87, 94, 103, 105, 109,
    116, 118–19, 132, 166; fulfillment (Matt.
    5:17), 3, 51, 59–66, 70; and Hegel (*Auf-
    hebung*), 3, 70; two models of, 131–32
Sullivan, Nikki, 185n50
Surya, Michel, 55n11

Teichtweier, Georg, 172n19
Thijssen, J. M. M. H., 113n16
Thomas Aquinas, 3, 4, 107, 111–12, 120,
    146, 160
Thurnher, Rainer, 166n2
Toste, Marco, 110n11
Towner, W. Sibley, 167n4
tradition (Christian), 2–4, 33, 45–46,
    53–54, 58, 75, 85, 87–88, 93, 99, 143–50,
    166–67, 175–77; constitution through
    difference, 51, 73, 77, 100–103; and
    destruction, xii–xiii, 146–50, 155, 199;
    and forgetting, 43, 62, 102–3, 133–35,
    144–45, 149–50, 199; in Matt. 15:2–3,
    65; and memory, 134–35, 143–45; and
    Mount Sinai narrative, 25, 31n14,
    41–43, 46–50, 57, 115; and transgres-
    sion, 4, 26, 48–50, 64–65, 100, 149–50,
    198–200; and translation, 41–42, 119–
    21, 131. *See also* Denys the Carthusian;

despoliation narrative; Pseudo-Peter
    of Poitiers gloss; sublation
tradition (general concept), 2, 8, 11–12,
    26–27, 110n10, 134–35, 157–58; as
    betrayal/forgetting, 134–35; and
    constitution through difference,
    2; and destruction, xi–xii, 154–55,
    158–64; and "epistemological crisis,"
    116–18; structure of, 113–19. *See also*
    Heidegger: on tradition; tradition
    (Christian)
transgression, 4–5, 23–24; in avant-
    garde art, 186–87, 194–97; and
    destruction (*see under* tradition
    [Christian]; tradition [general con-
    cept]); etymology, 4–5; and irruption
    of the divine (*see* Jesus Christ: incar-
    nation of; Mount Sinai narrative); in
    Matt. 15:1–4, 64–65; in medieval art
    and culture, 187–95, 200. *See also* fall
    narrative: and transgression; Fou-
    cault: on transgression; Jesus Christ:
    and transgression/radicalization;
    limit, limits; Mount Sinai narrative:
    and transgression; Nietzsche: and
    transgression; Pseudo-Dionysius
    the Areopagite: and transgression;
    Pseudo-Peter of Poitiers gloss: and
    transgression; tradition (Christian):
    and transgression; translation: as
    transgression.
translation, 55, 60–61, 63, 70, 85, 119–32;
    and Douay-Rheims translators, xiv,
    53, 63, 69, 80n6, 82, 85, 125–28, 199;
    and Luther, 124; and Jerome, 30–31,
    121–26; *sensus de sensu*, 122–27; and
    the Septuagint, 31, 58n17, 121, 123–26,
    130; as transgression, 199; *verbum e
    verbo*, 121–26, 129–31

Vaihinger, Hans, 82n12
Valla, Lorenzo, 146
Van Fleteren, Frederick, 95n44, 104n1
Vanneste, Jan, SJ, 37, 37n29
Vielhauer, Philipp, 86n22

Wall, Robert W., 84n14, 86n23

Warhol, Andy, 196–97

Wassermann, Dirk, 106n4

Wentersdorf, Karl P., 191n63

Westermann, Claus, 167–68, 171–73

William of Moerbeke, 119

Williams, Thomas, 123n29

Wilson, Jeffrey Dirk, 16n34

Winter, Thomas Arne, 161n66, 162n67

Wirth, Jean, 188n57

Wood, Allan W., 176n25, 177n28, 181n38

Zenger, Erich, 27

Index of Scripture

OLD TESTAMENT

Genesis

1	87, 141
1:3	140–41
1:26	169, 180
1:28	89, 169, 180
1:28–31	180
1:31	149
2	177
2:4–3:24	166–67
2:8	168
2:16–17	168, 175
2:17	126–27
2:25	171
3:1	170
3:1–6	168
3:5	169
3:6	170
3:7	172
3:7–8	171
3:7–19	168
3:8	169
3:10	172
3:11	173
3:13–19	179
3:21	172, 179
3:22	169, 173
3:22–24	168, 179–80
3:23	173

15:14	91
16	72

Exodus

1:22	89
3:21–22	3, 89
11:2–3	90
12:29	89
12:35–36	89
19	25–33, 40
19:9	27, 29
19:10	28
19:11	29
19:12	28, 126
19:13	28
19:15	28
19:16	28
19:18	28–29
19:19	28, 32n17
19:20	29
19:21	28
19:23	28
19:24	28, 30n12, 40
20:15	90
20:17	90
20:26	172
24	26, 30, 33, 40, 48
24:1	30
24:2	30
24:9	40

24:10	40
24:13	45
24:14	30, 45
24:15–18	27
33:20	27, 140
33:23	27
34	26, 30–31
34:29	58n17
34:30	31
34:33	31
34:35	31

Leviticus

27:28	68

Numbers

21	170

Deuteronomy

21:10–14	97n45
21:14	97n45

2 Samuel

14:17	169

1 Kings

1:36	129
3:9	169
11:14–25	95
11:26–14:20	95
19:19	172

2 Kings

2:8–14	172
18:4	170

Job

5:17	60

Psalms

1:1	60
9:24	193
17:36	138
30:20	136–37
41:2	187
62:4	138
62:9	138
119:162	94

Proverbs

26:11	44

Isaiah

11:9	107
21:14	79
33:18	79
44:9	193

Jeremiah

4:4	192
23:13	193
28:6	129

Ezekiel

13:6	193
25:6	193

Daniel

4:33	188

Malachi

4:5	58

DEUTEROCANONICAL BOOKS

Wisdom of Solomon

10:16–18	91, 125

10:17	125–26

NEW TESTAMENT

Matthew

5	59
5–7	59
5:1	59
5:2–3	59
5:17	3, 51, 63–65, 70n43, 121
5:17–18	59–60, 62–63, 127–28
5:18	63, 88
5:20–22	60
5:22	62, 102, 127
5:27–30	61
5:32	61
5:33–37	61
5:38–42	61
5:43–48	61
5:48	62
6	62
7	62
7:6	39–40
7:29	60
10:34–37	65, 83
10:42	129
11:14	58
11:25	57
11:27	57
11:30	57
12	65
12:1–14	64
12:5	64
12:8	64
12:11	64
13:11	39
15:1–4	64
15:1–20	64
15:2	65
15:3	65
15:11	64–65
15:17–20	64
17	57
17:1	57

17:1–8	57n16
17:2	57
17:5	58
17:6	58
17:7	58
19:16–24	82
20:1–16	190
22:19–21	190
26:15	190
27:3	190
27:31–35	54
27:35	54
27:46	127

Mark

4:11	39
7:1–23	65n32
7:9–13	64n30

Luke

1:46–55	192
1:52	192
8:10	39
14:26	4, 65

John

3:7	149n32
10:14–15	124

Acts

7:22	96
11:26	67
17:16	84
17:17	84
17:18	84–85
17:19	84–85
17:21	84
17:22–23	85
17:23	3, 85
17:24	87
17:26	87
17:32	87
17:34	33, 87

Romans

4:17	82, 82n11, 192

5:12–21	166–67	6:7	79	**Philippians**	
6:6	66	7:29–31	82	2:6–8	52–53
7	4	7:32	82	2:7	53, 56, 149n32
7:12	149	7:32–33	4	3:12–14	138, 138–39n11
7:14	94			3:18	148
10:4	88	**2 Corinthians**			
14:14–23	65n32	3:6	73	**Colossians**	
				1:17	94
1 Corinthians		**Galatians**		1:26	39
1	147	1:1–3	67		
1:18	83	1:6–9	67	**1 Timothy**	
1:18–25	2	2:11–14	69	4:4	149
1:18–29	79–80	2:12	68		
1:21	148	2:14	66	**2 Timothy**	
1:22	83	2:16	70	2:4	44
1:23	78	2:19	66		
1:24	80	4:21–30	71	**Hebrews**	
1:25	147	5:19–21	192	8:6	2–3
1:26	80			12:18	25
1:28	82, 82n11, 147	**Ephesians**		12:22	25
5	79	3:9	39		
5:2	79	4:23	192	**2 Peter**	
6	79	6:19	39	2:22	44
6:5–6	79				

COMPLETE LIST OF SERIES TITLES

Conor Cunningham, *Darwin's Pious Idea:*
Why the Ultra-Darwinists and Creationists Both Get It Wrong (2010)

Stewart Goetz and Charles Taliaferro, *Naturalism* (2008)

Nicholas M. Healy, *Hauerwas: A (Very) Critical Introduction* (2014)

Michel Henry, *Words of Christ* (2012)

Johannes Hoff, *The Analogical Turn:*
Rethinking Modernity with Nicholas of Cusa (2013)

Karen Kilby, *Balthasar: A (Very) Critical Introduction* (2012)

S. J. McGrath, *Heidegger: A (Very) Critical Introduction* (2010)

Edward T. Oakes, SJ, *A Theology of Grace in Six Controversies* (2016)

Adrian Pabst, *Metaphysics: The Creation of Hierarchy* (2012)

Marcus Pound, *Žižek: A (Very) Critical Introduction* (2008)

Aaron Riches, *Ecce Homo: On the Divinity of Christ* (2016)

Philipp W. Rosemann, *Charred Root of Meaning:*
Continuity, Transgression, and the Other in Christian Tradition (2018)

CENTRE OF THEOLOGY AND PHILOSOPHY

(www.theologyphilosophycentre.co.uk)

Every doctrine which does not reach the one thing necessary, every separated philosophy, will remain deceived by false appearances. It will be a doctrine, it will not be Philosophy.

Maurice Blondel, 1861–1949

This book series is the product of the work carried out at the Centre of Theology and Philosophy (COTP), at the University of Nottingham.

The COTP is a research-led institution organized at the interstices of theology and philosophy. It is founded on the conviction that these two disciplines cannot be adequately understood or further developed, save with reference to each other. This is true in historical terms, since we cannot comprehend our Western cultural legacy unless we acknowledge the interaction of the Hebraic and Hellenic traditions. It is also true conceptually, since reasoning is not fully separable from faith and hope, or conceptual reflection from revelatory disclosure. The reverse also holds, in either case.

The Centre is concerned with:

- the historical interaction between theology and philosophy.
- the current relation between the two disciplines.
- attempts to overcome the analytic/continental divide in philosophy.
- the question of the status of "metaphysics": Is the term used equivocally? Is it now at an end? Or have twentieth-century attempts to have a postmetaphysical philosophy themselves come to an end?
- the construction of a rich Catholic humanism.

I am very glad to be associated with the endeavours of this extremely important Centre that helps to further work of enormous importance. Among its concerns is the question whether modernity is more an interim than a completion—an interim between a pre-

modernity in which the porosity between theology and philosophy was granted, perhaps taken for granted, and a postmodernity where their porosity must be unclogged and enacted anew. Through the work of leading theologians of international stature and philosophers whose writings bear on this porosity, the Centre offers an exciting forum to advance in diverse ways this challenging and entirely needful, and cutting-edge work.

Professor William Desmond, Leuven